Answers to Real Problems

Answers to Real Problems

Harry Emerson Fosdick Speaks to Our Time

Selected Sermons of
HARRY EMERSON FOSDICK

Compiled and Introduced by
MARK E. YURS

WIPF *&* STOCK · Eugene, Oregon

ANSWERS TO REAL PROBLEMS
Harry Emerson Fosdick Speaks to Our Time

www.wipfandstock.com

ISBN 13: 978-1-55635-948-4

Contents

Introduction

HARRY EMERSON FOSDICK (1878-1969) was an influential and controversial preacher whose career spanned the first half, and continued to impact the second half, of the twentieth century.[1] He is well-known for what he called the project method of preaching.[2] He thought of preaching as an engineering operation bridging the chasm between the spiritual and material worlds, transporting to the hearer something of the unsearchable riches of Christ.[3] He wrote in his famous article "What Is the Matter with Preaching?" that he believed the main business of the sermon is to solve "some problem—a vital, important problem, puzzling minds, burdening consciences, distracting lives."[4]

He came to this understanding of preaching early in his career, which began at First Baptist Church, Montclair, New Jersey, and continued for twenty years at what came became known as Riverside Church, New York City. For several years, he also preached weekly on the "National Vespers" radio program. Sermon by sermon, week by week, with great effectiveness and wide popularity, he engaged in this engineering enterprise that seeks to address human need and deliver spiritual help.

Fosdick's sermons, brilliant and highly acclaimed in his day, are worth reconsidering, for the issues he faced, boldly and with clarity, are

1. The full, standard and scholarly biography of Fosdick is Robert Moats Miller, *Harry Emerson Fosdick: Preacher, Pastor, Prophet* (New York: Oxford University Press, 1984). Fosdick's autobiography is *The Living of These Days* (New York: Harper and Brothers, 1956).

2. For complete treatments of Fosdick's theory and practice of preaching, see Edmund Holt Linn, *Preaching As Counseling: The Unique Method of Harry Emerson Fosdick* (Valley Forge: Judson Press, 1966); and *Harry Emerson Fosdick's Art of Preaching*, compiled and edited by Lionel Crocker (Springfield, IL: Charles C. Thomas, 1971).

3. Fosdick, *The Living of These Days*, p. 99.

4. This article first appeared in *Harper's Magazine*, Vol. CLVII, July 1928, p. 133–141. It has been reprinted many times, most recently in O. C. Edwards, *A History of Preaching*, Vol 2 (Nashville: Abingdon, 2004), p. 535ff; and *What's the Matter with Preaching Today?*, edited by Mike Graves (Louisville: John Knox Press, 2004), p. 7ff.

alive now and require his kind of insight. The nature of his contribution to the contemporary discussion of religious and political issues can be found in these lines of his from the 1920s:

> Half our fiery controversies would die out for lack of fuel if it were not for . . . partisanship. In the present juncture of religious affairs . . . few things are more needed than fundamentalists with some honest doubts about fundamentalism and modernists with some searching misgivings about modernism.[5]

Certainly with the way church and society alike are divided now, we need someone with the engineering know-how to bridge this gap, help liberals and conservatives learn from one another and thus make for real progress.

Fosdick himself was just such a thinker and preacher. He is best described as an evangelical liberal.[6] He openly and unashamedly referred to himself as a liberal, but he had evangelical sympathies and tendencies. Though open to higher criticism of the Bible and unwilling to take scripture literally, he knew the Bible well, loved it immensely and took it seriously. He was not about to repudiate scriptural truth, though he was ready to discount some biblical claims. His aim was to help people think through the old truth in new language. He repeatedly referred to Copernicus who did not abandon the stars even though he devised a new astronomy. Just so, in theology, Fosdick believed there to be abiding truths that ought never to be surrendered and, at the same time, categories of expression and understanding that ought always be open to reformulation.[7]

Since Fosdick's evangelical liberalism can be so helpful today, it is a shame to let his sermons remain hidden in the past. But the person who sets out to choose which Fosdick sermons to re-issue is at a heavy disadvantage. All are worthy. All are breath-taking. All are stellar examples of clear thinking and models of the homiletician's art. So the selection

5. Harry Emerson Fosdick, *Adventurous Religion and Other Essays* (New York: Harper and Brothers, 1926), p. 258–259.

6. For a treatment of evangelical liberalism, see Donald K. McKim, *What Christians Believe About the Bible* (Nashville: Thomas Nelson Publishers, 1985), p. 43ff.

7. Fosdick worked much of this out in *The Modern Use of the Bible* (New York: The Macmillan Company, 1924), his Beecher Lectures at Yale. Early expression of these ideas can also be found in his *Adventurous Religion and Other Essays*. He reviewed the course of his thinking, particularly on the relationship between liberalism and conservatism, in *The Living of These Days*, especially chapter IX.

offered here is personal. Many of the sermons that follow are ones that spoke to me when I was a young pastor. I turned to them often, particularly "Making the Best of a Bad Mess" and "Handling Life's Second-Bests," and found hope and encouragement every time.

The selection is also rooted in current needs. This volume is not to be thought of as a treasury of Fosdick's finest sermons so much as it is a collection which presents Fosdick asking and answering questions which still weigh—or ought to weigh—on the minds of people today. The sermons that follow give Fosdick's thoughts on issues that press in upon our day with the same force with which they pressed in upon his: worship, war, nationalism, inequality, the relationship between liberals and conservatives, the plight of the church, public ethics, private morality, and more.

Some of the language in these sermons is most assuredly dated. Aspects of his style may have been out of fashion even in his own day. None of it, however, has been altered here. Fosdick himself might be appalled at that. He would have been among the first to advocate and use gender-inclusive language, had the need occurred to him. He would readily repent, I believe, of the paternalistic and condescending nature of some of his illustrations, especially the missionary ones. Nevertheless, no effort is made here to modernize the language and style. Rather, Fosdick is allowed to speak as he spoke, and I am most grateful to HarperCollins for allowing these sermons to be reproduced.

Fosdick testified that his prayer before preaching went like this: "O God, some one person here needs what I am going to say. Help me to reach him!"[8] Now, may the same Lord answer that prayer afresh and use this collection of sermons to bring practical help where it is needed. So may God be glorified, the church enhanced, and lives strengthened.

—Mark E. Yurs

---

8. Fosdick, *The Living of These Days*, p. 100.

The Hope of the World in Its Minorities[1]

ONE OF THE MOST arresting statements recently made by a public man was made by Mr. Einstein when he said that if two per cent of our population should take a personal, resolute stand against the sanction and support of another war, that would end war. Whether or not this estimate of Mr. Einstein's is as accurate as his cosmic mathematics, I presume no one of us can say, but there is no doubt about the historical evidence on which the principle of his judgment rests.

The creative ideas destined to remake society have always been the possession of the minority. History has depended, not on the ninety-eight per cent, but on the two per cent. Far from being a matter of sociological and political interest alone, this principle gave Christianity its start. When the Master in Palestine began calling out his first disciples from the mass of their countrymen, he was interested not in quantity but in quality—in seed, though but a few kernels, which, if carefully sown, might multiply itself. He was thinking not primarily of the ninety-eight per cent but of a germinal two per cent. To use his own figure in the thirteenth chapter of Matthew's Gospel: "The kingdom of heaven is like unto leaven, which a woman took, and hid in three measures of meal, till it was all leavened." Quantitatively small, vitally active leaven—that is a true simile of the method of Christianity's transformation of the world.

But is Christianity working like that now? Take the measure of our American churches. Are we the germinal two per cent on which the future of mankind depends? Are we the little group of forward-looking men and women on whom, as on the first disciples of our Lord, has fallen the vision of a new world-order so that we are custodians of prophetic principles

---

1. From *The Hope of the World* by Harry Emerson Fosdick, Copyright 1933 by Harper & Brothers. Copyright renewed © 1961 by Harry Emerson Fosdick. Reprinted by permission of HarperCollins Publishers.

that shall remake society? Are we the minority ready to sacrifice fame or fortune or life itself for those ideas which shall some day permeate mankind with their healing and their truth?

You see, we do not answer to that description. Too frequently forgetting the mission that the Master left us and the way of working he committed to us, we have become a majority movement standing for the status quo, so that many are even startled when they hear a man like Mr. Einstein say that if two per cent should take a personal, resolute stand against war it would mean the end of war. What if, however, something like that is true? What if the future of mankind is in the hands of a minority? What if a little leaven hid in three measures of meal can leaven the whole?

There is no need of elaborating the historical evidence regarding this matter. In every realm the pathfinders have been few and the truths that at last triumphed were at first the possession of a minority. We all know that, but in our thought and life are certain factors which frequently prevent the full force of it from reaching us.

For one thing, we live in a democracy, where the only way of carrying on public business is to accept the voice of the majority. In consequence, the notion naturally prevails that the majority in the end probably is right and that, anyway, the majority rules. But neither of those ideas is true. The majority is almost certain to be wrong on any matter of fine taste or sound judgment, and, whether or not the majority is right, it certainly does not rule. The dominant influence in every situation is a militant minority. The decision of public policy in this country now is largely determined by resolute, militant, compact, closely organized minorities that want something and get it.

Look at this city. Is Tammany Hall a majority? Upon the contrary, it is a self-seeking, highly organized minority and it runs the metropolis. The majority are apathetic, careless, attending to their own business, not the city's, with no very strong convictions one way or the other, and that gives a resolute minority its chance. There is no use fooling ourselves that the majority rules. The United States today is ruled by organized minorities.

If, therefore, at first some were inclined to think that the doctrine of the two per cent is impractical idealism, let us disabuse our minds of that supposition. The serious truth is that the controlling power of the minority, so far from being impractical idealism, is most practical politics. Even in a democracy the minority rules.

The full force of this truth which Jesus puts into his figure of the meal and the leaven is deflected from many modern minds also by our inveterate habit of romanticizing history. When we start in to glorify our ancestors for some outstanding achievement, such as, for example, the winning of the American Revolution, we make a thorough job of it and glorify all our ancestors. What a splendid outpouring of cooperative and unanimous zeal it was, we think, that all those colonists put their lives, their fortunes, their sacred honor at the disposal of the cause! That sounds splendid but there is not a word of truth in it. There were probably more Tories than Revolutionists among the colonists and more than either were the men who see-sawed back and forth, who stood first on one side, then on the other, who had no strong convictions either way, and only hoped they were betting right on who was going to win. I venture that more than one family is represented here this morning who wanted to join the Sons or Daughters of the Revolution and so looked up their ancestors—and have kept still about it ever since.

The Revolutionary War was won, the government established, and the Constitution put in force by a compact, highly intelligent, loyal minority. Do you remember John Adams' apostrophe to his posterity? "Posterity! you will never know how much it cost the present generation to preserve your freedom! I hope you will make a good use of it. If you do not, I shall repent it in heaven that I ever took half the pains to preserve it."

Such is the situation with every gain humanity ever made. It was the two per cent who fought for popular education, for religious liberty, for freedom of scientific research, against the majority. Always the majority has been dough, the few have been leaven; so that out of history there rises an admonition—in any cause that concerns the progress of mankind, put your faith in the creative minorities!

Again, this truth of Jesus is deflected from many modern minds because of our worship of bigness. One of my friends calls it "Jumboism." Especially in this country many people are impressed by nothing that is not big—big cities, big buildings, big corporations. We all are tempted to worship size. But size is an utterly fallacious standard when we are trying to estimate power. Could any one, at the height of Rome's colossal power, have thought of anything much smaller than Paul in a Roman prison writing his few letters? But the result! Whoever would have dreamed that that little man with his brief epistles would dig down so deeply, take hold so strongly, penetrate so powerfully the thoughts and motives of men?

3

The things that are big are utterly misleading as to the location of the ideas that are powerful.

We have in our modern time a vivid illustration of this truth. Whatever else we may think about it, there are few more dramatic incidents in mankind's history than Gandhi confronting the British Empire. The greatest empire in history stands over against one man trying to make terms with him, while he will not fight with outward weapons, is ready to die if his followers use violence, and employs nothing but the ideas of a minority and a certain quality of soul to set them aflame. There are few things that we American Christians need much more to learn than the lesson of that. Bigness is not power. Power is in the ideas to which the future belongs, and they always have been the possession, not of the ninety-eight per cent, but of the two per cent.

Looked at from one angle, this truth is encouraging. When one thinks of the causes that are on our hearts today,—peace rather than war, industrial welfare rather than this desperate situation we are in, better education for the nation's children, or whatever it may be,—we should welcome the good news that we do not have to wait for the majority. Whenever a true idea is born and a creative minority rallies around it, there is the beginning of victory. That is encouraging and it is true. It is not, however, a truth to go to sleep on. We Christians were intended to be that minority. We were to be the salt of the earth, said Jesus. We were to be the light of the world. We were to be the leaven in the lump of the race. There is no possibility of misunderstanding his meaning, my friends. When a man becomes a real Christian he is supposed to move over into that small, creative, sacrificial minority seized upon by visions of a better world and standing for them until they shall permeate mankind with their truth. That does make being Christian serious business! That is more than believing in a creed. That is more than partaking of the sacraments. That is more than the comfort of worship or the use of beauty as a road to God. That is joining the real church in the original Greek meaning of the word "church," *ecclesia*—called out—a minority selected from the majority to be leaven.

Only as we succeed in getting more Christians like that will power return to the Christian movement. When was Christianity the most powerful? Shall we select some scene like that at Canossa, when the Pope bestrode Europe with his rule and even an emperor waited three days in the snow at his doorsill begging for audience and pardon? That seems powerful, yet even a scene like that, when time has worn its meaning off, loses its glamour. There was a time, however, when Christianity was very powerful. Little groups of men and women were scattered through the Roman Empire—"not many mighty," said Paul, "not many noble." They were far less than two per cent and the heel of persecution was often on them, but they flamed with a conviction that they represented truths to which the future belonged.

Do you remember what Paul called them in his letter to the Philippians? "We are a colony of heaven," he said. The Philippian Christians would understand that figure, for their city of Philippi was a Roman colony. When Rome wanted to Romanize a new province, it took Roman people and planted them as a colony in the midst of it. There, as a powerful minority, they stood for Roman law, Roman justice, Roman faith, and Roman custom, leaven in the lump of the province, until the whole province was leavened. Rome understood the art of government. When, therefore, Paul said to that little group of Philippian Christians, "We are a colony of heaven," they understood. They were a minority thrown out, as pioneers, in the midst of an unchristian world to represent the ideals, faiths, and way of living of a nobler realm until the earth should be the Lord's and the fulness thereof.

In those days Christianity was very powerful. It stopped ancient curses like infanticide. It put an end to the bloody shambles of the gladiatorial shows. It laid hold on an old polytheism that had been glorified in literature, extolled in art, established in custom, and supported by government, and ended it in the interests of one God revealed in Christ. Then Christianity was very powerful. It was a minority movement with nothing to lose, with everything to gain, joining which a man pledged his very life as a forfeit. At last it became so powerful that it captured the Empire, entrenched itself in wealth and worldly prestige, stopped challenging the world, began compromising with the world, and never again, I fear, on so vast a scale has exhibited such creative, superhuman power.

Let us, therefore, for our own sakes and for the sake of our generation, see if we can recover even a little the meaning of that saying of Jesus, "The kingdom of heaven is like unto leaven, which a woman took, and hid in three measures of meal, till it was all leavened."

In the first place, this clearly applies to our churches themselves. Not infrequently one is asked in these days whether or not one believes in the church. Just what is meant by the "church" in that question? These sectarian organizations that carry over from old political quarrels and theological debates denominational divisions that have no pertinency to modern life—are they the church? These sects so often splitting and over-lapping their labor in our American communities, absorbed in their self-maintenance until they hardly think of the real issues on which the future of mankind depends, so that the best citizens often feel that they must pull up the church rather than be pulled up by it—are they the church? And by having faith in the church does one mean that he stakes his hope of the future of the race upon this inherited network of denominational organizations? Then let an honest answer be given: How can a man be-lieve in the church?

My own faith is not in these formal organizations. Personally, I think most of them will have to die. Their lines of division and their points of emphasis have no just claim upon contemporaneous interest even, much less on permanency. My faith is in the church within the churches, the two per cent, the spiritual leaven, the inner group of men and women who have been genuinely kindled by Christ's spirit and are today living and thinking above the average and ahead of the time. Always the real church has been not the dough of the mass but the leaven of the few.

As for these formal organizations, let not the lesson of Russia be forgotten. The Greek Church in Russia allied itself with the status quo. It surrendered its prophetic mission and became the religious right arm of the most despotic government on earth and, becoming thus the defender and ally of a political and social régime that could not last, it went out with the system it was tied to. Religion is not dead in Russia. It will not die. Though it seems to die, it will have its resurrection day. But the church as a whole could not save it. Once more in Russia history will have to repeat itself—a little leaven beginning again to work in three measures of meal. My friends, whether by violence or by slow starvation, that is the fate of every ecclesiastical organization that allies itself with a dying order. Church of Christ in America, with all your wealth and our prestige, beware! Could Paul say of you, "Ye are a colony of heaven"?

If someone protests that the real church, then, must forever be stand-ing for new ideas only and never for old ones, so that in consequence the real church becomes merely a radical, iconoclastic group, I am glad to answer that protest as a constructive contribution to our thought. Being a saving minority is a much deeper matter than that protest understands.

Vital experience of God, for example, as a living force in daily life, has always been the possession of a minority. The faith of most men in God has been inherited, picked up from superficial education, assumed as a plausible explanation of the universe. But that inner flame of spiritual life which burns upon the high altar of a man's soul because of himself he can say, "O God, thou art my God," always has belonged to the few. The many have occasionally borrowed it.

So, too, a living faith in Christ, which enables one in some deep sense to say, "I live; yet not I, but Christ liveth in me," has always belonged to a minority. The majority have worshiped Christ, indeed, have recited resounding creeds about him and made obeisance at his altars, but to live Christ in private quality, in social life, in sacrificial devotion, has that belonged even to the two per cent?

This matter, therefore, of being a saving minority is not cheap and superficial; it goes deep. Indeed, in the Bible there are two kinds of religious minorities: first, Paul's "colony" thrown out as pioneers in an unchristian world, and, second, Isaiah's "remnant," the little group of the true Israel which, in a time that is surrendering old sanctities, clings to them and despite the pressure of an alien generation preserves them for children yet unborn. How much we do need both—minorities that pioneer and minorities that keep the high values of the faith amid a time that popularly surrenders them!

My friends, I am jealous for the church. So much of our Christianity is dough; I want the church to be leaven.

Our truth applies also to social problems. Men today, making their characteristic reactions to the social, economic, international difficulties which beset us, fall into three classes: first, those below the average—lawless, criminal, anti-social; second, those on the average, who play the game according to the rules with a fine sense of honor for observing them; and, third, those above the average, who question the rules. Are the rules themselves fair? Is the game itself equitable? Does it not minister to the advantage of the few against the many, and cannot the rules be altered so that the game itself will be more just? The hope of the world depends upon that third class.

The truth of this classification can be clearly seen when it is applied to a social problem of the past like slavery. In the days when slavery was in power there were: first, the dishonorable slaveholders, the Simon Legrees, below the average; second, the honorable slaveholders who accepted slavery and the rules of slavery's game and played it like gentlemen, caring for their slaves, ministering solicitously to their physical and spiritual welfare; but, third, both north and south, the people who questioned the whole game of slavery. The rules themselves were not right. The game itself was wrong. High-minded and honorable as the second class was, the future depended upon that third two per cent.

Often in these trying days, as your preacher, I think of you business men. You face heavy burdens, practically complicated and ethically difficult. The more I know of you the better I appreciate the fine code of honor with which you handle your responsibilities. Yet, after all, with you as with me, the final test of a social attitude is at this point to which our thought has brought us. Not for all the world would you run your business in lawless disregard of the rules. You have a careful sense of honor about observing them. But are you dedicating your brains—and the best brains of American are in the business world—to this third matter: Cannot the rules be improved? Cannot the whole game be made more just?

Only the other day I was talking with my friend, a representative of a great corporation. This spring that corporation is casting off into unemployment, absolutely unprovided for, thousands of its men. My friend told me that the corporation had built up a surplus of many millions of dollars to protect the stockholders against emergency. The stockholders are safe against crisis for years to come but not one cent of financial responsibility has that corporation taken for its employees, now cast off into unemployment. The only hope I found in that situation was that my friend himself belonged to the two per cent. He saw that that policy would never do, that it did not fit this new industrial order into which the machine has introduced us, that business must take financial responsibility against emergency, not simply for investors of money but for investors of life and labor.

This test of social attitude is the same in my realm as it is in yours. Suppose I should accept the present situation in the churches, settle down in my churchmanship to make myself as comfortable as I could, get what I might for myself out of it, and be undisturbed by it; you know that for me that would be a betrayal of trust. The least that a minister of Christ, if he is in earnest, can do today is to stand above the alliance of the church with this dying order and try to help bring forth that new church in which the spiritual life of the future can find its home.

That same test applies to all of us. Wanted in church, business, states-manship, and international relationships men and women who are not simply playing the game according to the rules but who are trying to better the rules and make the game more just!

Of course, the fact that a man happens to be a member of a minority is no guarantee that he is right. There are all sorts of minorities, good, bad, and indifferent, and not simply every saving idea but every foolish fad can be a minority. That fact, however, argues not against but for our plea. Just because today there are so many uninformed, irresponsible, even violent minorities, let the forward-looking and responsible citizens the more assume their obligations!

As for being Christian, I suppose that, reduced to simplest terms, it means answering Christ's two-worded appeal, "Follow me." Where do we think it takes a man when he does follow him? Never into a majority. I wonder where you and I are this morning—three measures of meal or leaven?

2

Christianity at Home in Chaos[1]

M ANY PEOPLE FEEL THAT this is an exceedingly difficult time for Christianity. Even under fortunate circumstances, they say, it is not easy to hold Christian ideas about the love of God, the value of the human soul, and a new society of goodwill among men, but in distracted days like these how can such unworldly faiths seem true?

That mood comes to all of us. The unpromising qualities of human nature, dismay at wide-spread destitution, collapse of confidence, and the confusion of world affairs frown down upon the fragile, unearthly, idealistic faiths of Christianity. Nevertheless, if we look at history we shall find that the eras when Christianity was most certainly believed and sacrificially supported, when it made its great advances and won its resounding victories, were not prosperous times but chaotic days like these.

So, in the familiar story, Brer Rabbit persuades his enemy, Brer Fox, to throw him into a brier-patch on the supposition that that would be the worst thing which could befall him, but now, thrown into it, Brer Rabbit runs happily away, saying, "Bred en bawn in a brier-patch, Brer Fox—bred en bawn in a brier-patch!"

Similarly Christianity, far from feeling strange in a troubled time, was born and bred in a brier-patch like this. It started with a cross. The first Christian from Nazareth lived through difficult days. The early Christian community won its amazing victory against the opposition of a pagan world and the first church established itself amid the ruins of a collapsed empire and a wrecked civilization. We children of the Reformation would better not forget the travail out of which we were born, with Calvin crying about the people of his time: "Their wickedness has, however, reached

1. From *The Hope of the World* by Harry Emerson Fosdick, Copyright 1933 by Harper & Brothers. Copyright renewed © 1961 by Harry Emerson Fosdick. Reprinted by permission of HarperCollins Publishers.

such a pitch, that I hardly hope to be able any longer to retain any kind of position for the Church, especially under my ministry. My influence is gone, believe me, unless God stretch forth His hand." Especially we American Christians display a strange forgetfulness of our history with its struggle to plant the gospel in the wilderness of this new continent, if we accept a weak picture of a fragile, unearthly, idealistic Christian faith unfitted to deal with trouble. It ought to be wholesome to say to ourselves today that Christianity was born and bred in a brier-patch.

Indeed, it would be strange if I were not now speaking to some one who is persuaded that Christian faith is only an idealistic dream. It is beautiful and comforting, you think, if one can believe it, but it fails to take account of the tragic nature of the world. It turns its eyes away from the dark, cruel aspects of life, you say, to center its regard on what is cheering and comfortable, and so constructs theories of God and man and the possibilities of a new society incredible to one who honestly grapples with the terrific facts of human life. When you see a disbeliever like Bertrand Russell saying that there is no God, no unity or purpose in the universe, no human hope except temporary ameliorations of our earthly fate, and that at last on man "and all his race the slow, sure doom falls pitiless and dark," there, you say, is one who candidly faces the ruthless processes of nature and the essential tragedy of life.

My friend, we are not debating the whole question between theism and atheism, but this surely is certain: whatever else one may say about the historic Christian faith, one may not thus claim that it has failed to grapple with tragedy. The symbol of Christianity is the cross. Christianity started with tragedy, took tragedy for its very password and countersign. Open the New Testament anywhere and you will find, I think, not so much idealistic dreamers as men and women who, as the Epistle to the Hebrews says, were stoned, sawn asunder, tempted, slain with the sword, going about in sheepskins and goatskins, destitute, afflicted, illtreated, of whom the world was not worthy. Look at Christian history anywhere and you find Christianity grappling with tragedy, sometimes causing tragedy, often suffering tragedy, and, at its best, learning lessons from tragedy, changing the situations which produced it, and getting a new grasp on the meaning of faith because of it.

"In the world ye have tribulation," said Jesus to his disciples that last night before he died. That does not sound as though he were blinking difficulty. "In the world ye have tribulation: but be of good cheer, I have overcome the world."

Consider, then, some of the ways in which the historic Christian faith has faced difficult eras—ways that in these times we might well emulate and reproduce.

For one thing, repeatedly in desperate, dangerous times Christians have caught a new vision of the value and indispensableness of Christ's moral principles. Why does moral character in individuals and society find the test of long-continued material prosperity so difficult? We all know what poverty does to people, how it can shut doors of opportunity, wreck families, and leave bedraggled and distressed countless lives that might have been radiant and happy. Poverty is one of the major curses of mankind and we must wage tireless war against it. Nevertheless, it is also true that one of the severest tests which moral character in individuals and societies ever faces is the long continuance of material prosperity. Said Andrew Carnegie, "As a rule the 'almighty dollar' bequeathed to sons or daughters by millions proves an almighty curse."

This is not simply true about individuals but about generations. In Jewish history, out of which our Christian faith emerged, where shall we look for the outstanding eras of moral and religious insight? In Solomon's time? Judah was prosperous then but we seek in vain for great spiritual truths discovered or moral ventures undertaken. The outstanding eras of moral and religious insight were times like the Exile. Torn from their native land, impinged upon by the brilliant paganism of Babylonia, stabbed every day by antagonistic faiths and morals, shaken by an international earthquake which made the slumberous soul impossible, those Jews saw new things and spoke new words which Judaism had never seen or heard before. Strange,—is it not?—out of what places the notable advances of the race's faith and character have come! Born and bred in a brier-patch!

What, then, do we think about our situation? Do we still believe that those post-war years which led up to 1929 were, as we called them, good times? Upon the contrary, history will write them down as bad times— bad for everything that makes for moral stamina as a nation. It will be many a year before we shall altogether escape from the wild gambling, the loose living, the decay of citizenship, the collapse of personal integrity, the growth of selfish cynicism, the desertion of religious faith, that marked those post-war years. And did some one come here this morning complaining that *these* days are bad for Christianity? Rather, this is the kind of weather in which Christianity habitually has achieved its strongest growth.

Let me say personally that in trying to present to you the principles of Jesus I find a clear contrast between the atmosphere of 1929 and today. Then, when we rode high, when our acquisitive society seemed all success, when, no matter what we did, the wealth of the world poured in to us, the moral principles of Jesus did seem idealistic. In Thackeray's Vanity Fair, Becky Sharp says that she thinks she might be a good woman on five thousand pounds a year. Such was our mood, and that mood always makes the moral principles of Jesus seem idealistic. Do they seem so to you now?

"Inasmuch as ye did it unto one of these my brethren, even these least, ye did it unto me"—that is not idealistic; that is basic. Any man must see that the crux of our problem today is what is happening to the common man. Look at him even with the economist's eye only—he is the ultimate consumer. Only if he can buy will business thrive. Only if he have confidence can the economic life go on. If he is poor, everybody will be poor. If he is panicky, the wheels of business must stop. We cannot see into the heart of our present catastrophe and the way out unless we see deeply the meaning of those ancient words, "Inasmuch as ye did it unto one of these my brethren, even these least."

"Whosoever would be first among you, shall be servant of all"—that is not idealistic; that is basic. When, in his inaugural address, President Roosevelt spoke with indignation about the unscrupulous misuse of economic power regardless of the welfare of all the people, he was voicing—was he not?—a wide-spread, deep-seated, dangerous indignation in the American people. Half blind though we the people are and ourselves involved in all the mistakes our scapegoats have made, nevertheless we do see, as we never in prosperous days saw half so well, that business cannot be merely an acquisitive game, every man for himself; business must be the loyal servant of the common interests of all the people, and, no matter how radical the changes required to incarnate that and make it real in our economic system, we must be prepared to face them. For a bank to sell bonds to the people and make millions out of them when the bank knows that those bonds are worse than dubious is not good business—not for the people; as it turns out, not for the bank; as we all see now, not for the nation. Whosoever would be first among you, shall be servant of all.

So one could run the gamut of the ethical teachings of Jesus. "Blessed are the peacemakers"—that is absolutely basic. And as for what he said about integrity of personal character, "Let your speech be, Yea, yea; Nay, nay,"—that is to say, Let your word be as good as your bond,—we are lost without that.

This is not a bad time for Christian morals. Christian morals were born and bred in a brier-patch like this. This is a bad time for anything except Christian morals, bad for selfishness and cynicism, bad for lapses of integrity and poor citizenship. These are even times when I, for one, a modernist, look on a shaken generation and out of the New Testament hear with fresh meaning and authority those words about Christ, "There is none other name under heaven given among men whereby we must be saved."

Again, more than once in Christian history, in difficult and shaken times Christians have caught a fresh vision of the meaning and indispensableness of their faith in God and the eternal values of personality.

Why is it that religious faith never reaches its depth until it is faced with tragedy? Suppose a man who had met only the musical-comedy aspect of life, and we know at once, however correct the forms of his faith, his religion would be shallow and superficial. Some modern doubters persist in saying that religious faith is an idealistic dream because it never has grappled with tragedy. I say, upon the contrary, that no great religious faith in all history has ever even come into existence without grappling with tragedy. Did not Gautama the Buddha's faith begin that day when he issued from the soft protection of his father's palace and for the first time looked on human misery demanding explanation and cure? Did not the Hebrew religion begin with a man concerning whom the Scripture says, "When Moses was grown up, . . . he went out unto his brethren, and looked on their burdens"? Did not the Hebrew religion take its decisive turn upward in the character and ministry of Jeremiah, whose very name is a symbol of tragedy? The great faiths that have gone ahead of the race like pillars of cloud by day and fire by night have been born out of tribulation. As for *our* faith, no cross, no Christianity.

Nor is it difficult to see why this should be so. When a man faces tragedy, he discovers the utter unlivableness of irreligion. When we are comfortable, stimulated and sustained by favoring circumstance, we can get on without thinking deeply about the human problem and often without conscious need of God. But when tragedy befalls and we are stripped of the cushioning of circumstance and in a dark hour the soul stands lonely and quivering before the eternal mystery, then there appears the utter unlivableness of irreligion—no spiritual source behind life, no eternal purpose running through it, no goal ahead of it, so sense in it. In dark hours like that the human soul at its best has risen up with an authentic surety that there is more to be said about human life than that. Out of such hours have come the creative faiths of the human race. Without some such hour no man has ever yet plumbed the depths of an invincible faith in God. A man must sometimes have faced an experience of deep and difficult need where he looked into what Carlyle called the "Everlasting Nay" of irreligion, if he is to understand the full meaning of the "Everlasting Yea" of religious faith.

What can we mean, then, by supposing that these days are an alien time for Christian faith? The only basis for so shallow a judgment is the identification, commonly made, of Christian faith with easy-going optimism. Now, Christian faith is optimistic but only in the sense of Jesus' saying, "In the world ye have tribulation: but be of good cheer; I have overcome the world." That is to say, Christian faith is an optimism that comes from facing pessimism. As one of our wise contemporaries has put it, "Religion is the hope that grows out of despair. It is the ultimate optimism which follows in the wake of a thorough pessimism. One reason why our generation is not religious is that it has been too sentimental to be thoroughly pessimistic." Walk around that for a moment and you will find truth in it. The greatest Christian faith in history is always like a Rembrandt portrait—an illuminated face shining out of a dark background.

The other day I ran upon some sentences from a once-famous portrait painter, William Morris Hunt. He says: "I tell you it's no joke to paint a portrait! . . . Into the painting of every picture that is worth anything, there comes, sometime, this period of despair!" That is true to experience, is it not? The greatest musical compositions were never written, no worth-while sermon, I think, was ever preached, no supreme monument of architecture ever was built, without the creative artist's facing at one point despair about his work. No more has religious faith been easily won, as so many people think.

How many of you would say today what I say, that there have been hours when I thought I saw into the profound depths of a triumphant Christian faith and they were not hours in the lecture room of a theological seminary but when I went down into the valley to keep a rendezvous with tragedy, and when against the Everlasting Nay I saw the Everlasting Yea victoriously rise up?

That experience has sometimes been entered into on a large scale by a whole generation. The eighteenth century, for example, with its French Revolution, its collapse of an old social order, its appalling economic maladjustment and poverty, its rampant immorality and atheism, such that men said they were taking the "not" from the Commandments and putting it into the creed, was more like our generation than any other period in history. Christians were in despair. Did not their enemies say that Christianity already had one foot in the grave and needed only decent obsequies to complete its history?

My friends, when any generation backs Christian faith into a corner like that, a recoil is imminent. Then came the Wesleys to light a fire that broke into such a conflagration of triumphant faith and humanitarian endeavor as the English-speaking world never had known before. Once more came an authentic outburst of spiritual life, hope born out of despair, the Everlasting Yea rising as though in desperation to overcome the Everlasting Nay.

If we Christians were worth our salt we could reproduce that now. Did some one come here today saying, This is no time for Christian faith! I tell you this is no time for atheism. This is no time to tell men there is no God, no eternal purpose through life, no goal ahead of it, no sense in it. This is no time for cynicism and skepticism and materialism. Such things we can stand a little of in prosperity. I ask you, What are you going to do with them now? This is a time to see again the deep meanings of the Christian faith.

Once more in many a generation like this, Christians have laid fresh hold upon their social hopes.

It is a strange thing—is it not?—that we should so commonly say that a discouraging time is the time when people really are discouraged. The fact is that if we wish to see outstanding examples of courage we must always look in a discouraging time to find them. In consequence, out of discouraging times have come the main forward movements of the race's social hope.

It is not difficult to see why this is true. Hope is not, as we commonly think, merely the denial of despair. Hope springs out of despair. Again and again in history, personal and social, despair has been the womb out of which hope has been born. Out of the despair of the Egyptian bondage came the hope of a free Hebrew people. Out of the despair of the Exile came the hope of a reconstituted Jewish state. Out of the despair of a falling Roman Empire came the hope of a universal church. Out of the despair of tyrannical monarchy was born the hope of democracy. And today out of the disheartening tragedy of war has risen the hope of peace, and out of the sickness of an acquisitive society springs strong the hope of a more humane, cooperative, economic life. Some of you are ready, as you never have been before, to agree to wide-spread, deep-seated, radical changes in economic life on behalf of the welfare of all the people. It is precisely out of days like these that the great social hopes of the race have sprung.

Some of you may be tempted to discouragement about Christianity even more than about the economic crisis. Christian principles, faiths, and institutions face, you think, a disheartening day. I wish I could change your tune. I think you are playing Brer Fox over again. You see Christianity thrown into a brier-patch and you think that is likely to finish it. "Bred en bawn in a brier-patch, Brer Fox."

That is true even of the church itself. The Jewish synagogue was born out of the need for spiritual fellowship in the Exile. The church was born out of the difficult situation of the early Christian brotherhood in the Roman Empire. The Protestant churches were born out of the terrific collapse of old Europe, and if we have in us anything like the spirit of our sires we will build in these days a better kind of church, freer in mind, more inclusive in hospitality, more communal in service, in a generation when men and women need spiritual sustenance and fellowship as seldom before.

As for our own interior, spiritual life, we know well that we never tap the deepest levels of power until we face something hard, where we crucially need it. No man ever gets his second wind save in a long race. It is only when we have something for which we need power that power can come. We say that Jesus had inner power with which to face the cross. Turn it around. It was facing of the cross that called out the power. O my soul, grasp that philosophy! Make your hardships develop your resources. Make your tasks call out your reserves. Face the tragedies of life like a veritable pessimist: "In the world—tribulation." Never blink that fact. But make tribulation release the deeper levels of divine resource, so that you too may say, "Good cheer; I have overcome the world."

3

Handling Life's Second-Bests[1]

W E ARE CONCERNED TODAY about a factual personal problem so nearly universal in its application that we need not be bothered by its exceptions: namely, that very few persons have a chance to live their lives on the basis of their first choice. We all have to live upon the basis of our second and third choices. To one who reads biography this comes to be so much a matter of course that he takes it for granted.

Whistler, the artist, for example, started out to be a soldier and failed at West Point because he could not pass chemistry. "If silicon had been a gas," he used to say, "I should have been a major-general." Instead, he failed in soldiering, half-heartedly tried engineering, and then tried painting—with such remarkable results as one sees in the portraits of his own mother, Miss Alexander, and Carlyle.

Let us approach this unescapable human problem of handling life's second-bests by way of one of the most impressive exhibitions of it in history. In the sixteenth chapter of the book of The Acts, in the record of Paul's journeys, we read this: "When they were come over against Mysia, they assayed to go into Bithynia; and the Spirit of Jesus suffered them not; and passing by Mysia, they came down to Troas. And a vision appeared to Paul in the night: There was a man of Macedonia standing, beseeching him, and saying, Come over to Macedonia, and help us. And when he had seen the vision, straightway we sought to go forth into Macedonia, concluding that God had called us to preach the gospel unto them."

So simple and succinct is this narrative that one would little suspect that we are dealing with one of the most significant events in human history. Here Christianity passed over from Asia into Europe. It was a momentous

1. From *The Hope of the World* by Harry Emerson Fosdick, Copyright 1933 by Harper & Brothers. Copyright renewed © 1961 by Harry Emerson Fosdick. Reprinted by permission of HarperCollins Publishers.

day when Columbus set sail from the shores of Spain or Vasco da Gama discovered the sea route to the Indies, but could even such events be more pregnant with consequence than the day when Paul carried Christianity out of Asia, in a few centuries to be overrun by Mohammedanism, through Troas into Macedonia and into Europe, where Christianity was going to have its chance? But Paul had not planned to go to Europe. That was a second choice. Paul had planned to go to Bithynia. "They assayed," it reads, "to go into Bithynia." And no wonder, for Bithynia was one of the riches provinces of Asia Minor, and to have carried Christianity there would have been a triumph indeed.

Morever, we may be sure that if Paul wanted to go into Bithynia he wanted to go very much and tried to go very hard, for Paul was never a half-way man. And he could not go; the way was blocked; his plan was broken. We read, "The Spirit of Jesus suffered them not," but that is only another way of saying that some circumstance blocked their course. It must have seemed to Paul lamentable at first. I picture him arriving on the shores of the Ægean, saying, I wanted to go to Bithynia and here I am in Troas! And lo! through Troas a way opened to the preëminent ministry of his career. Paul rendered his most significant service with the left-overs of a broken plan.

Wanting Bithynia and getting Troas, how familiar an experience is that! But to take Troas, the second-best, the broken plan, the left-over of a disappointed expectation, and make of it the greatest opportunity we ever had, how much less familiar that is! Yet, as one reads the story of human life, one sees that powerful living has always involved such a victory as Paul won in Troas over his own soul and his situation.

When a career has at last been finished and the halo of well-deserved reputation now hangs over it so that one cannot think the name without thinking of some high enterprise with which the name is indissolubly associated, then in the glamour of that retrospect we are tempted to forget that almost always the turning point of the career is the experience that Paul had—getting Troas when he wanted Bithynia.

When, for example, we think of Phillips Brooks, we think of spiritual ministry, a great personality pouring his soul out with abundant power upon the people. Of all the letters that Phillips Brooks received, it is said that he cherished most this one from a small tailor shop near Copley Square in Boston: "Dear Mr. Brooks: I am a tailor in a little shop near your Church. Whenever I have the opportunity I always go to hear you preach.

Each time I hear you preach I seem to forget all about you, for you make me think of God." Nevertheless, remember that Phillips Brooks did not plan to be a preacher. He planned to be a teacher. That was his Bithynia. As soon as he graduated from college he plunged into his chosen profession of teaching and he failed. He failed completely. Listen to young Brooks writing about his scholars as he is failing: "They are the most disagreeable set of creatures without exception that I have ever met with. . . . I really am ashamed of it but I am tired, cross, and almost dead, so good night." Listen to Phillips Brooks after he had failed and been dropped from his position: "I don't know what will become of me and I don't care much"; "I shall not study a profession"; "I wish I were fifteen years old again. I believe I might make a stunning man: but somehow or other I don't seem in the way to come to much now." Listen to Phillips Brooks' father, concerned about his son, so humiliated that he will not talk even with his friends: "Phillips will not see anyone now, but after he is over the feeling of mortification, he will come and see you."

There is a sense in which Brooks never recovered from the disappointment. At the flower of his career he came down once from the office of President Eliot of Harvard white as a sheet and fairly trembling because he had declined what he knew to be his last opportunity to become a teacher. He wanted Bithynia and he got Troas but through Troas he found the door into a service that if he had lived a hundred lives he might never have found again.

Or consider Sir Walter Scott. We think of him as the novel-writer whose stories charmed our youth, so that for many years some of us would have voted Ivanhoe the best tale ever told. Sir Walter, however, did not want to be a novelist; he planned to be a poet, but Byron's sun rose and dimmed his lesser light. "Byron hits the mark," he said, "where I don't ever pretend to fledge my arrow." Then he turned to writing novels, so ashamed that, as you know, he published the first of them anonymously. He did not want any one to know that he was writing novels. He wanted Bithynia; he got Troas and through Troas an open door to the best work he ever did.

Is there anybody here who has not wanted Bithynia and gotten Troas? We older people watch the youths come up, as we did, with their ambitions and plans for Bithynia and we wonder what they will do when they face the unescapable experience. When they are shut out from some Bithynia and land in Troas, will they know how to handle that? Will they have the spirit and attitude and the technique to make of it their finest chance? And since it is so unescapable a problem, we well may ask what it was in Paul that enabled him to turn his defeat into victory.

For one thing, his religion entered in. Whatever else was shaken when he got to Troas, his conviction still was there that God had a purpose for his life, that if God had led him to Troas there must be something in Troas worth discovering, that God's purposes included Troas just as much as Bithynia, that God never leads any man into any place where all the doors are shut. Paul's religion entered in.

It is in just such situations as this that one can tell how much real religion a man has. We hear a man reciting a familiar creed: "I believe in God the Father Almighty, Maker of heaven and earth," but no matter how serious he may seem about it you cannot tell from that alone how real it is to him. You hear a man singing,

> He leadeth me: O blessed thought!
> O words with heavenly comfort fraught!
> Whate'er I do, where'er I be,
> Still 'tis God's hand that leadeth me.

But however much in earnest he may seem you cannot tell from that alone how deep it goes with him. When, however, you see a man who, wanting Bithynia, gets Troas and, still certain that there is a purpose for his life, takes a positive attitude toward Troas as if to say, If God has led me here there is something worth while here to do, you know that that man's religion is practically operative. If, therefore, Paul had merely said what he did say, "To them that love God all things work together for good," we might have cocked suspicious eyebrows at him, thinking that that proposition is extraordinarily difficult to prove. What is impressive about Paul is that whenever he did land in a disappointing Troas, and he landed in a good many of them, he did so effectively love God that he *made* all things work together for good. Paul's religion meant to him a positive faith about life and a positive attitude toward life so effective that watching his career is again and again like watching the Battle of Marengo—in the morning an obvious defeat, in the afternoon a resounding victory.

Consider a modern counterpart to Paul, Adoniram Judson. When Judson was a young man he gave himself to missionary service and his ambition centered on India. That was his Bithynia. When at last he reached India they would not let him in. The East India Company would not allow him to stay and the governor told him to take the first ship back to America. For a year he labored to open the doors of India and they were bolted shut. So he turned to Burma. That was his Troas, unknown, untouched Burma. Can one suppose that through all that humiliation and disappointment Judson could always see the leadership of God? Of course he could not; he was human. Can one suppose during those months that he lay in the prison of the Emperor at Ava and Oung-Pen-La he could always see evidences of the divine purpose? Of course he could not; he was human. But he did so handle the affair in Burma that the doors began to open until no well-instructed man today can think of Burma without thinking of Adoniram Judson, or think of Adoniram Judson without thinking of Burma; and when the consequence began to appear he could look upon his life in retrospect as though it had been planned of God. To live your life through—not argue it through; that is never sufficient—to *live* your life through into the conviction that there is an eternal Purpose with which a man can ally himself is one of the finest achievements of the human spirit.

Altogether the most thrilling story in the Old Testament is on this theme. One day in Palestine we stopped our automobile by the roadside and ate our lunch at Dothan where long ago Joseph had been sold by his brethren. Still the camel trail goes up from across Jordan, and then runs down to the coast cities and so to Egypt. Now Joseph, stolen from his home, betrayed by his brethren, dropped into a pit, sold to Midianite slave-dealers, made a man-servant in a household in Egypt, lied about by his master's wife and put in prison—can one suppose that during all that humiliation and disgrace he could see where God was taking him? Of course he could not. But he so kept his faith and handled his life that the doors opened into the biggest business of his career, and when at last those penitent and frightened brethren stood before him, you remember what he said: "I am Joseph your brother, whom ye sold into Egypt. And now be not grieved, nor angry with yourselves, that ye sold me hither: for God did send me before you to preserve life.... So now it was not you that sent me hither, but God."

Such was Paul's feeling as he looked back on the day he missed Bithynia and found Troas, and such will be ours if in Troas we let our religion enter in.

In the second place it was not simply Paul's religion that enabled him to win this victory but the fine fruit of his religion, his care about people.

The trouble with so many of us when we land in Troas is that we begin to pity ourselves. Paul could have done that. He could have started the process we indulge in-"ifing."

> If I had not missed Bithynia; if my plans had not been broken, if, if! I have given up everything for Jesus Christ. I could today be one of the great rabbis of Jerusalem saluted in the market place. I have given it all up for Christ. I spent a long time in Arabia thinking through the gospel. I have been fourteen years in a trying, difficult, unrecognized ministry in Cilicia, at odds even with my Christian brethren because once I persecuted them. And now, when I am beginning to get on a good footing with my fellow Christians, with Barnabas and a few others trusting me, I have come up through Asia Minor on a preaching mission. See what they have done to me. They stoned me and left me for dead in Lystra. Even after that, all I asked was that I might have a chance to get into Bithynia and do some good work, and now I cannot; I am foiled; my plan is broken.

How easy it would have been for Paul in Troas to feel sorry for himself!

Upon the contrary, he at once began thinking about other people. He wondered if there was not some one who might be better off because he landed in Troas. He had not been there a night before he saw a man from Macedonia saying, Come over and help us. It was Paul's unselfishness, his generosity, his magnanimity that opened the doors for him in Troas.

Once there was a man named William Duncan who gave himself to the missionary cause and in time was sent by his board to a little Indian island off Alaska called Metlakatla. It was an unlikely Troas for a young man to land in who had doubtless dreamed of some Bithynia, for those Indians were a poor, ignorant, miserable tribe, and their morals were vile beyond description. Dean Brown of Yale, however, who visited Metlakatla after William Duncan had been there about forty years, makes this report, that you will find every Indian family in a separate house with all the decent appointments of home life, that you will find a bank, a cooperative store, a saw-mill, a box factory, and a salmon cannery run by Indians in profitable industry, that you will find a school where Indian boys and girls learn to read and write and think and live, and a church where an Indian minister preaches the gospel of eternal life and an Indian musician, who once was a medicine man playing a tom-tom, now plays a pipe organ, and a congregation of Indians sing the great hymns of the church to the praise of Almighty God—and all because a man named William Duncan, landing in Troas, cared enough about people to find there the chance of his life!

My friends, there is nothing in that spirit or consequence that cannot be transferred to our lives. We are all in Troas. Just as at Sebastopol each heart thought a different name while they all sang Annie Laurie, so when today we say "Troas" each one of us thinks of some situation we would not have planned to be in. There is only one way—love. Was it not George Macdonald who said: "Nothing makes a man strong like a cry for help"? You walk down the street utterly fatigued, so tired that you would like to lie down on the curb to go to sleep, and suddenly there is a cry; there has been an accident; a child is hurt; and you never will remember how tired you are until it is all over. Nothing makes a man so strong as a call for help.

A mother is completely fatigued. She has been telling her friends for weeks that there is nothing left of her, and then a child falls ill and needs her. Week after week, by night and day, she stands by and never thinks of being tired. Nothing makes a man strong like a call for help.

It would be strange indeed if there were not some young men and women here not altogether dull to the dangers of our civilization, not altogether blind to the possibility of losing it, thinking that perhaps there is something in them that might help build a more decent world for human children to be born in. That is their strength. Nothing makes a man so strong as a call for help. And the trouble is that when we get into Troas we pity ourselves; we miss that man from Macedonia, saying, Come over and help us.

Indeed, so true is this principle of life that it holds good of even small excursions into Troas. When annoyances and irritations come, when one is lied about and hated and denounced, there is only one way out—goodwill. You remember Edwin Markham's lines:

> He drew a circle that shut me out—
> Heretic, rebel, a thing to flout.
> But Love and I had the wit to win:
> We drew a circle that took him in!

If in the midst of life's harassments and irritations one has grace enough to do that, he sometimes will find in that very difficulty his choicest opportunity for usefulness.

This, then, is the conclusion of the matter: that because Paul had these two elements in his life, as soon as he landed in Troas his imagination was filled, not with defeat but with victory. Coué was right that it is the imagination which makes or unmakes us. If you put a thirty-foot plank as high as a cathedral tower hardly anybody can walk it, and it is not because the physical difficulties are greater than they would be on the ground but because one's imagination keeps picturing him falling off. So when we get into Troas we think we are defeated. I wanted Bithynia, we say; I have got Troas. So we think defeat, we say defeat, we imagine defeat, and we are defeated. But as soon as Paul landed in Troas he saw an open door, a beckoning man, a new chance, and a successful issue.

What helped him most, I suspect, was that his thought went back, as it so habitually did, to the cross of his Master. That was a Troas to land on! What a Bithynia it would have been if his people had accepted Jesus as Messiah! And now, shut out from that Bithynia, he came to his Troas, his Calvary, and he so clothed it with the purpose of God and the love of man that

> All the light of sacred story
> Gathers round its head sublime.

He took a very hard thing and he made of it a triumph.

4

The Peril of Worshiping Jesus[1]

THE WORLD HAS TRIED in two ways to get rid of Jesus; first, by crucifying him, and second, by worshiping him. The first did not succeed. It required more than a cross to stop the influence of that transcendent character. Like an airman taking off against the wind and using the very force of the opposing air to rise by, so Jesus took off on his amazing flight. The cross did not crush—it lifted him.

The world, therefore, foiled in its first attempt to be rid of Jesus by crucifying him, turned to the second, far more subtle and fatal way of disposing of great spiritual leadership—it worshiped him. Throughout history it has been true that when a spiritual leader has been too powerful to be crushed by opposition there has been still another way to escape his moral insights and his ethical demands, and that is to worship him. To dress him up in elaborate, metaphysical creeds, hide his too-piercing eyes in the smoke of sacramental adoration, build beautiful sanctuaries where his challenging social ideals may fade out in vague mysticism, get him off somewhere on a high altar, pray to him, sing to him, do anything for him rather than let him get back again where he started, walking the common ways of men and talking about how to live—that always has been the most successful way of getting rid of Jesus.

If at first this seems a dangerous thing to say, remember that Jesus himself said it. He did not fear being opposed. He knew that the blood of the martyrs is the seed of the church, and concerning his own cross John reports his saying: "I, if I be lifted up from the earth, will draw all men unto myself." He did not fear being opposed; he feared being worshiped.

1. From *The Hope of the World* by Harry Emerson Fosdick, Copyright 1933 by Harper & Brothers. Copyright renewed © 1961 by Harry Emerson Fosdick. Reprinted by permission of HarperCollins Publishers.

For one thing, he saw his own contemporaries by this method getting rid of their prophets. First, their fathers had hated the prophets, opposed them, stoned them, sawn them asunder. Then, when the prophets proved too powerful in personality and influential in message to be disposed of in that way, the ever-available, second method had been tried. Listen to Jesus, himself, as he describes it—"Woe unto you, scribes and Pharisees, hypocrites! for ye build the sepulchres of the prophets, and garnish the tombs of the righteous, and say, If we had been in the days of our fathers, we should not have been partakers with them in the blood of the prophets. Wherefore ye witness to yourselves, that ye are sons of them that slew the prophets."

Jesus saw that stoning the prophets on one side and garnishing their sepulchres on the other, different as the two things appear, come practically to the same end: they are two ways of getting rid of the prophets, escaping what the prophets really stood for, dodging their moral message. The fathers who killed the prophets and the children who garnish their sepulchres belong to the same race, says Jesus, and are up to the same thing—they are evading the spirit of the prophets.

Even in his lifetime, Jesus feared this way of being evaded. How else will you explain his stern rebuke to the sentimental woman who cried, "Blessed is the womb that bare thee, and the breasts which thou didst suck"? Jesus came back at her like thunder, saying, "Yea rather, blessed are they that hear the word of God, and keep it." It is as though you could hear him saying to himself, See, they are beginning to worship me; they are evading what I am driving at by adoring emotions about me; they will get rid of me yet, as they have gotten rid of the prophets, by idolizing me. Or how else will you explain his swift retort to the man who came bowing to him, saying, "Good Teacher"? Said Jesus, "Why callest thou me good? none is good save one, even God." One can fairly read his thoughts as though he said to the man, Beware of worshipful deference to me—I fear it; come, stop this bowing and this "Good Master"; what about your attitude to the kind of living I am standing for, whose springs are in God? And once, as though to leave no doubt that this fear of being worshiped was ever before him, he cried, "Not every one that saith unto me, Lord, Lord, shall enter into the kingdom of heaven; but he that doeth the will of my Father who is in heaven." O, wise Master, with what prophetic eye you saw the way men would successfully evade you! For all these centuries since, cherishing evils that your spirit would have spurned, all Christendom has been saying from countless temples, "Lord, Lord!"

It is an amazing thing that the historic church has so unanimously worshiped Jesus and has so seldom stopped to ask what Jesus himself would think of it. Is it not true that most Christians have taken it for granted that Jesus would enjoy it—enjoy being prayed to, sung to, talked about in exalted, theological terms, and enshrined on the high altars of the church? Do not many Christians still suspect that he would feel grieved, hurt, rejected, and jealous if he were not thus adored? All this, however, obviously is the reflection of our own littleness. Little people like extravagant praise, adoration, flattery. Little people push their egos to the front, claiming attention and wanting to be idolized; but great personalities are never like that. When a capacious soul comes, standing for something that he cares so much about he will die for it on Calvary, you cannot flatter him. He has identified himself with something greater than himself, of which he regards himself as the incarnation and instrument. He thinks of himself as the vehicle and agent of an eternal matter. He does not want his ego idolized; he wants his cause supported.

Take the truth into a realm quite different from religion and consider Abraham Lincoln, who, if you use the word "worship" as we are using it this morning, in its general and human sense, comes as near being worshiped as any American. That began when he died. While he lived men tried to crush him by opposition, but he was too strong to be overcome. When he died, however, they began using the other method to dispose of him. They adored him. They garnished his sepulchre. Nothing too marvelous could be said of him. But in the ten years after he died Congress put into effect a policy towards the South that denied everything Lincoln had stood for and wanted. They praised his name and they scuttled his policies. They flattered his memory and denied his magnanimity. They alike adored Lincoln and refused to follow him, so that they made the reconstruction era in the South one of the horrors of our history.

What would Lincoln have said? We know. Stop this evading of my spirit by praising me! What do I care about the idolizing of my ego? I want my cause supported. Of course Lincoln would have said that because he was a large soul, and not a little one.

Can one doubt, then, what Jesus' attitude would be? We all sing, for example, that great hymn,

In the cross of Christ I glory,
Towering o'er the wrecks of time.

Who wrote that? Sir John Bowring. Who was he? He was the British Governor at Hong Kong at a time when the British Empire was forcing the opium traffic on China, and he was the agent of the imperial policies. Everybody acknowledges, our British brethren first of all, that the forcing of opium on China was one of the most outrageous things in Western history. Well, the man who was Governor of Hong Kong while that policy was in force had written, years before, "In the Cross of Christ I glory."

You will recall the man who said that he could take care of his enemies himself, but prayed to be delivered from his friends. Jesus Christ might have said that. The most disastrous events in the history of his movement have not come from his opposers, but from his worshipers who said, "Lord, Lord!"

When today I plead against the peril of worshiping Jesus, you see it is not because I, myself, do not exalt him. You know I do exalt him. He is supremely great. That constitutes the seriousness of the situation. He is really great—not to be flattered, not to be pleased by creedal praise or sacramental worship, wanting just one thing so much that he died for it—the Divine Will done in personal lives and social relationships. And the tragedy is that it has proved too deceptively easy to join in forcing opium on China while at the same time singing "In the cross of Christ I glory." I am not specially blaming Sir John Bowring; we cannot do that. He was like the rest of us. He was not consciously hypocritical, but a sincere, honest, and in many ways eminently admirable man. He simply fell victim, as many of us have fallen, to this most popular of all ways of getting rid of Christ. We would not crucify him, not one of us, but, alas, we worship him—we dispose of him that way. We say, "Lord, Lord!"

Consider, for one thing, how easy it is to get rid of Christ by worshiping him, because thereby we can substitute emotions for morals. There are two sets of faculties in us, the esthetic and the ethical—the sense of beauty and the sense of duty—and Christ appeals to both. Especially as the tradition of history has woven its alluring spell about him, setting him in stories that begin with singing angels over Bethlehem and end with worshiping women in a garden, he is beautiful. He has been set to music, glorified in poetry, enshrined in architecture, until the approach to Christ is clothed in beauty. But when we approach Christ esthetically, through beauty, it may end in emotional adoration only, saying, "Lord, Lord!"

So you, a youth here in New York City, may adore your mother. How do you adore her, emotionally or morally? That is, do you simply love her with tender sentiment, or are you living the kind of life which does honor to her and developing the sort of character which, if she knew about it, would make her glad? The difference is deep. Mothers at their finest are beautiful and most men adore them; but it is one thing to have the emotional sentiments of the heart go out to a mother and it is another thing to be morally true to her. It would be strange, indeed, if some youth here did not at this moment acutely feel the difference. Well, Christ must acutely feel the difference in his disciples. Indeed, he never said, "Worship me!" He said, "Follow me!"

To put the matter in a figure that combines both beauty and morals, Christ played his life like music meant to be played over again. When Beethoven wrote a symphony, he did not write it merely to be admired but to be reproduced. When once a Beethoven has created harmony, one does not have to be Beethoven to reproduce it. It can be played again and again. So Christ, in his unselfishness, his faith in God, his reverence for personality, his practice of brotherhood, his devotion to a nobler social order, was not creating a piece of music for the world to stand before and cry, "How lovely!" He wanted it reproduced—played again and again by boys and girls, men and women, on all the human instruments that God had given them, until the whole earth should be full of his music.

He wanted that, but he has not seen that—only here and there has that come to pass. What he has seen is something different—countless millions of people worshiping him emotionally but not morally. Emperors like Constantine, drenched in blood, who murdered his own wife, his son, and other more remote and less significant relatives, worshiped Christ. Ecclesiastics who sold their influence for private gain and stained the garments of the church with fornication and simony have worshiped Christ. Men who believed that little babies were damned to eternal hell have worshiped Christ. Men who persecuted their fellows for conscience' sake and made the torture chambers of Christendom the horror of the world have worshiped Christ. Churches that have shut off their fellow Christians from the kingdom of God because of diversities in theology that Jesus never heard of and would have scorned as mint, anise, and cummin, have worshiped Christ.

John Newton ran a slave-ship between Africa and the slave-markets of his time in the days when the horrors between decks were enough to make even the reading of them turn one white. He wrote in his diary that he had never known sweeter or more frequent hours of divine communion than on his slave journeys, and every Sunday he read the church liturgy twice with his crew. How incredible, in retrospect, such a combination of worshiping Christ with ruthless inhumanity appears? Yet how many have been and are guilty of it and how few, like John Newton, see new light, repent of their blindness, and change, as he did, both opinion and life!

You see what we have done with Christ—we have kept his name on the label, but we have changed the contents of the bottle. That is a summary of much of Christendom's history—the name kept on the label, "Christ," but the contents not of his moral quality.

We cannot suppose—can we?—that that suddenly has stopped in our time? Upon the contrary, the churches of this country are full of people who worship Christ, who have no more idea what Christ means about war, race relationships, the color line, about the money standards of the day, the profit motive in industry, than Constantine had about Christ's attitude toward his bloody imperialism, or the Duke of Avla about Christ's care for the victims of his persecution. This seems to me the very nub of the Christian problem today. The crucial matter is not theological controversy. Real problems are involved there, but they are not the crux. The crux is moral. A Christianity that worships Christ emotionally but does not follow him morally is a conventional sham, and too much of our ecclesiastical Christianity today is precisely that. Let us say it to ourselves in our beautiful churches, amid the loveliness of our architecture, lest we should ever be tempted to substitute esthetics for ethics or formal worship for downright righteousness. Jesus would care more about our attitude towards the color line or war than he would care about all our processionals, however stately, and all our architecture, however fine. For obviously, Jesus, above all else, intended to be taken in earnest morally.

We cannot, then, leave our text in history. It comes down the centuries, accumulating significance with every year, and walks up to our own doors and knocks. "Not every one that saith unto me, Lord, Lord."

Consider how easy it is to dispose of Christ by worshiping him, because we can thereby substitute theological opinion for spiritual experience. In this regard, much of Christianity has gotten rid of Christ just as

Buddhism has gotten rid of Buddha. Think what you will about the basic presuppositions of Buddha's philosophy—and I heartily disagree with them—he, nevertheless, was a tremendous character, and his noble eight-fold path of moral living *is* noble. At first men fought against him, but that did not succeed; he was too great to be overthrown by opposition. Now, however, conventional Buddhism has gotten rid of him by worshiping him. It is one of the strangest ironies in the history of religion. For Buddha himself did not believe in a personal God at all, and now Buddhism has made a personal God out of him. That disposes of him! Now they can build up rituals, construct theologies, worship him in sacramental regularities, and his noble eightfold path of moral living can be obscured in the smoke of incense. The Christians, however, are no better than the Buddhists in that regard. That is what we have done with Jesus.

I can imagine some one saying, But, then, do you not believe in the divinity of Jesus? To which I answer that I believe in the divinity of Jesus with all my faculties if we can come to an understanding about what we mean by *divinity*. Are you willing to start with John's idea of *divinity* in the New Testament: "God is love"? That is divinity—love. Divinity is not something supernatural that ever and again invades the natural order in a crashing miracle. Divinity is not in some remote heaven, seated on a throne. Divinity is love. Here and now it shines through the highest spiritual experiences we know. Wherever goodness, beauty, truth, love are—there is the Divine. And the divinity of Jesus is the divinity of his spiritual life.

If some one says, Well, we all have some of that divine spark in us; we all have some goodness, truth, love, and therefore on that basis the divinity of Jesus differs from ours in degree, indeed, but not in kind, I answer, Are you afraid of that conclusion? Of course the divinity of Jesus differs from ours in degree but not in kind. You cannot imagine there be-ing one God and two kinds of godlikeness. Paul prayed that his disciples might be filled unto all the fullness of God. John said, "He that abideth in love abideth in God, and God abideth in him." Was the God that Paul and John prayed might be in them a different kind of God than was in Jesus? To be sure not. There is only one God. To say therefore that God was in Christ seems to me no theological puzzle at all. I think God was in my mother, the source of all the loveliness that blessed us there! And I rise up from that with a profound sense of the reality of what I am doing when I profess my faith that God was in Christ.

If, now, some one says, Very well, but that reduces Jesus to our level, I answer, How do you make that out? I feel in relationship to Christ like a land-locked pool beside the sea. The water in the land-locked pool is the same kind of water that is in the sea. You cannot have one sea and two kinds of sea-water. But look at the land-locked pool, little, imprisoned, soiled it may be in quality, and then look at the sea, with deeps and distances and tides and relationships with the world's life the pool can never know. So is my life beside his. So is my soul beside his soul. The same God, to be sure, but what a contrast the difference in capacity can make!

If, then, we mean by Jesus' divinity the quality of his spiritual life, of course I believe in it and glory in it. But the historic church too often has meant something else, has pushed him far off to a supra-mundane world, throned him in a distant heaven, garbed him beyond all recognition in heavily brocaded garments of theology, until the real Jesus has been gotten rid of altogether. Listen to this about Jesus of Nazareth: "The second person in the Trinity, being very and eternal God, of one substance, and equal with the Father, did . . . take upon him man's nature," so that "two whole, perfect, and distinct natures, the Godhead and the manhood, were inseparably joined together in one person, without conversion, composition, or confusion." They have done that to the divine teacher of Galilee, and they have gloried in it when all the time they were getting rid of him,—at last successfully crucifying him,—laying him in a theological tomb and rolling a great stone before the door.

I read recently a passage from a sermon that seemed to me to cry out for an answer—the preacher was glorying in the fact that Jesus had conquered Europe. Very conceivable, said the preacher, that Jesus might appeal to Asia, but what a marvel that he should appeal to Europe, to hard-headed, practical, militant Europe! What does the preacher mean—Jesus conquering Europe? What Jesus conquered Europe? A conventionalized Jesus as unlike the real one as the floral patterns on wall paper are unlike the flowers of the field. A Jesus who was called by the most resplendent, metaphysical titles in history, but who supported bloody imperialism, blessed bloody persecutions, gave his benediction to economic exploitation, put his cross on the banners of the most sanguinary crusades in history, insisted on the damnation of infants to hell, and said that slavery was ordained of God. That caricature of Jesus has, as a matter of plain history, too largely conquered the Western world. But the Jesus of the Good Samaritan, the Prodigal Son, the Beatitudes, the Jesus who used a little child as his symbol of the kingdom's spirit, the Jesus who said, "Ye cannot serve God and mammon," and "A man's life consisteth not in the abundance of the things which he possesseth," the Jesus who reverenced every human personality and died that there might come a kingdom of God and human brotherhood on earth—that Jesus has not yet conquered either Europe or America.

To be sure, I know that this is not all there is to religion. Christianity is more than ethical effort. If you take the word "worship" in its original meaning, "worthship"—the recognition of worth—then there are few things more important that we ever do. And especially we moderns need ever to grow quiet, like pools at evening, in the presence of the highest that we know in Christ, that his beauty may be reflected in us. If that is what one means by "worship" then we should worship him with all our hearts. We need, however, to imagine what would happen if somehow he could be released from all the brocaded velvets and golden crowns of our too-conventional and formal adoration and could speak to us in his own voice. How little he would care for anything that did not involve personal character and social righteousness! How little he would care whether a man idolized his ego, if only he possessed his spirit! What a company he would claim as his own—men and women of all races, colors, creeds, religions, some who had worshiped him and some who had not, in whom he found his spirit! For he supremely would care that what he stood for should permeate the world. Not every one, not *any one*, who merely says, "Lord, Lord!" but he that doeth the Father's will!

5

Making the Best of a Bad Mess[1]

L ET US GET AT our subject through a letter which Paul once wrote to a young disciple of his named Titus. I shall take it for granted that Paul wrote this letter, although some scholars think that he did not. Paul, so the record runs, had left Titus upon the great island of Crete in the eastern Mediterranean, and the island of Crete was not at all a desirable place for a Christian to be left. The situation is summarized in one blistering verse of this letter: "One of themselves," says Paul, "a prophet of their own, said, Cretans are always liars, evil beasts, idle gluttons. This testimony is true." Such is Paul's summary of the situation in Crete and of the character of its inhabitants. But listen to him as he writes to Titus: "For this cause left I thee in Crete, that thou shouldest set in order the things that were wanting."

That is a queer reason for leaving a man in Crete, that the Cretans are always liars, evil beasts, and idle gluttons. It sounds like a good reason for getting out of Crete. But Paul was a man of stern fiber. He himself never shrank, and he never wanted his followers to shrink, from the challenge of a difficult situation. He felt the stimulus of a hostile environment. There is something profoundly characteristic of the man himself and of Christianity at its best in that attitude. Crete—a hard place; the Cretans—a bad lot: "For this cause left I thee in Crete."

Put yourself in Titus' place as he received this letter. I surmise that it must have been a letter that Paul wrote to Titus in answer to one which he had received from him, and it ought not to be difficult to reconstruct the spirit in which Titus wrote. "Dear Paul," I suspect he had said, "this is an awful place. The inhabitants are hopeless, and the poor, struggling

1. From *The Hope of the World* by Harry Emerson Fosdick, Copyright 1933 by Harper & Brothers. Copyright renewed © 1961 by Harry Emerson Fosdick. Reprinted by permission of HarperCollins Publishers.

Christian movement is only rags and tatters. I am remaining here until you say 'Go' but I can't get away fast enough. For pity's sake, don't make me stay here all winter. There isn't a decent chance. Obediently but unhappily yours, Titus." And then he got this letter. "Titus," said Paul in effect, "you are right about the Cretans. They are liars, evil beasts, idle gluttons. There isn't anything too bad that you can say about them. Crete is in deep need. For this cause left I thee in Crete."

Let us put ourselves in Titus' place. It ought not to be difficult. One way or another we are always getting into Crete. There are many differences that separate us here this morning, but any preacher could be sure of one thing which unites us: we all have been in Crete, we are all going to be in Crete, probably most of us are in Crete now. Moreover, we are human and complaining, and we want to get out of Crete. I wonder what Titus said to himself when he faced this ringing message, "For this cause left I thee in Crete."

In the first place, he must have reminded himself of some simple but profound common sense about life which he ought never to have forgotten. I think he said to himself, "Paul is right. After all, happiness is not something that you find. It is something that you create. And if you start with that attitude you might just as well create happiness in Crete as anywhere else."

When a man lands in Crete, you see, as probably Titus did, hoping to find it a pleasant place, he is foredoomed to disappointment. He walks up and down Crete looking for happiness, but it isn't to be found. The Cretans are a bad lot. Then he gets this message that changes his inner attitude. He walks up and down Crete now, not looking for ready-made happiness, but looking for an opportunity. He has been left in Crete to use it as so much raw material out of which to make something. He is saying to himself over and over again, "Life is not something that you find; life is something you create." And, lo! approached in that way, Crete becomes an El Dorado. That is not poetry; that is history. Crete did turn out to be one of the greatest opportunities that Christianity had in that ancient world. Today in Crete they are excavating the foundations of stately churches from which, in those early days when the gospel went out in the crusade against the paganism of the Roman Empire, came teachers, preachers, and missionaries of the cross. Whose name is on those churches? Titus'! Saint Titus'! Think of it! In the very place from which once he could not soon enough get away! Paul was right. "For this cause left I thee in Crete, that thou shouldest set in order the things that were wanting."

Surely, this principle runs through all of life. Life is not what you find; it is what you create. Many people wander into the world and pick up everything they can get their hands upon looking for life. They never get it. What they get is existence. Existence is what you *find*; life is what you *create*.

Biography is a running commentary on that. Who, for example, is this Scotch boy who landed in Boston a half century and more ago? He came over in the steerage when the steerage was a beastly place. His old Scotch father had told him that his abilities were below average. He began his life in America as a foundryman and he roomed over a liquor saloon in the north end of Boston. Such was his existence to start with. What he made of it, however, was a great life. For he was George A. Gordon, one of the best scholars Harvard ever graduated, who in Old South Church, Boston, a few years ago celebrated the fortieth anniversary of his pastorate—one of the most notable for intellectual quality and spiritual influence in the annals of American churches—and who now has fallen on sleep, full of years and honor. His existence was what he found; his life was what he created.

One wonders if this ability to tackle life as Titus tackled Crete, without which America would lose nine-tenths of her glory, is going to be distinctive of the new generation. Many of our children are going to schools where, as Dean Hawkes of Columbia says, they are asked in the morning what, if anything, they wish to study that day. We are surrounding them in our families with luxuries that we never knew, that our fathers never dreamed. They are told on every side that personality is a creature of environment and that the great thing is for everybody to be surrounded by commodious and comfortable circumstances. I do not think that that is going to make them morally wild, but I am sure that it is deceiving many of them as to the real secret of living. They are expecting to find life, pick it up, get it out of circumstances, and that is a fallacy. You never find life; you create it. Often the best friend a man ever has is not comfort but the stimulus and challenge of antagonistic environment to awaken the resistance of his slumbering soul.

This principle, that all life has to be tackled as Titus tackled Crete, applies not simply to an elemental matter like character, but also to some of our dearest relationships. What is the matter with our sadly shaken married life in the United States? Many people say that the laws are wrong. The laws about divorce are very chaotic and should be greatly improved, but all the tinkering that we do with the laws will not solve the problem of our family life. The deeper trouble is that young people approaching marriage think of it merely as a road to happiness. They expect magically to alight on happiness in marriage. They expect some day to fall in love and float into bliss. The fact is, there is little about marriage in itself to make happiness, while there are plenty of things about marriage to make perdition. Two personalities wanting to be happy come into a relationship the most intimate that earth knows, where all the peculiarities of one are thrust at the sensitiveness of the other. That situation by itself is much more likely to make agony than bliss.

There is, however, one glorious thing about marriage. It is an opportunity, the most beautiful opportunity that life knows. It is an opportunity to create a friendship stronger than death. It is an opportunity for children, the loveliness of their companionship, and the social service rendered to the world by their fine upbringing. It is an opportunity to build a school for character which shall make it easier for all who see it to believe in the fatherhood of God and the brotherhood of man. Take marriage as a spiritual opportunity, the raw material, with many hostile and difficult elements in it, out of which strong souls can build a great result, and you will have a real home. But you will never find one. Real homes are never found; they are spiritually created.

All life must be tackled as Titus tackled Crete. What existence hands us is raw material out of which something must be spiritually made. A man who faces life like that needs a soul undergirded by great faiths, overarched by high convictions, and blessed with inward power. As a man thinks of life in this way, he hears the echo of an old word, "What shall a man give in exchange for his soul?"

A second thing Titus must have said when he received Paul's letter. "Paul is right," I think he said. "This principle which he recommends is not only common sense; it is good Christianity." There is no use pretending to be a disciple of Jesus if we are unwilling to stay in Crete because it is difficult. He belongs to Crete. Jesus particularly belongs in Crete. He belongs in Crete, not in spite of the fact that the Cretans are liars, beasts, gluttons, but because they are. "This man receiveth sinners, and eateth with them," said his enemies. He was always trying to discover Crete. "The publicans and sinners were drawing near unto him to hear him." He always attracted

Crete to himself. There is no use pretending to be his disciples if we are dodging Crete!

Imagine the Master, if you can, in some discouraged hour when things were going badly with his ministry, saying, "O God, human beings are a cruel lot. They are selfish, sensual, hateful, brutish. Already I can see that what their fathers did to the prophets they are going to do to me. A crooked and perverse generation!" What voice would he have heard out of the unseen? "For this cause sent I thee into the world." You cannot imagine the Master going into any situation without making it his first business to look up Crete. "They that are whole have no need of a physician, but they that are sick . . . I came not to call the righteous, but sinners."

Ah, we respectable Christians! We have gone on building churches, elaborating complicated creeds, worshiping through splendid rituals, but how often the real spirit of Jesus has been somewhere else! Whenever in this modern world there is a Crete, where the situation is difficult and people needy, where for love's sake some soul puts itself alongside the need and lifts, there is the real spirit of Jesus, who "though he was rich, yet for your sakes he became poor, that ye through his poverty might become rich."

One cannot speak of this without thinking of some of our modern Tituses, whom one knows personally, who have really gone to Crete. I baptized one years ago. She has graduated from college since. She has had all that American culture and education can give her. She has married a young physician. This morning they are up the Congo in Central Africa. I suppose still the Cretans are liars, beasts, gluttons, but in that spot, where under the magic of unselfish service a better day is dawning, there is a challenge in the very degradation: For this cause sent I thee to Crete.

When a man does live in this spirit of Jesus, it is more satisfying than anything beside. Consider: the deepest joy in life is creativeness. To find an undeveloped situation, to see the possibilities, to brood over it, pray about it, think concerning it, work for it, to get something done there that would not have been done except for your creative soul—that is a satisfaction in comparison with which superficial joys are trivial.

This is true even when creativeness is turned toward things physical, like the conquest of the air. Some time ago one of our aviators, who carried mail from New York to Cleveland, fell in the mountains of Pennsylvania and was killed. They found upon his body a letter addressed "To My

Beloved Brother Pilots and Pals" and marked "To be opened only after my death." Listen to what he said: "I go west, but with a cheerful heart. I hope what small sacrifice I have made may be of use to the cause. When we fly we are fools, they say. . . . But every one in this wonderful aviation service is doing the world far more good than the public can appreciate. We risk our necks, we give our lives, we perfect a service for the benefit of the world at large. . . . But stick to it, boys. I'm still very much with you all. See you all again."

You pity that boy? I don't. He had more fun in his short life than all the satiated pleasure-seekers who habitually try to feed their souls on superficial foam. For the elemental joy is creativeness and when that spirit of creativeness is turned to spiritual ends and helps to transform personalities and societies it is so satisfying that I do not know whether it is selfish or unselfish. After Titus got started in Crete you could not have dragged him away.

The joy of every true preacher is not that he preaches to this number of people or that, but that once in a while he comes within reach of an individual soul upon whom he can exercise a creative influence. I am thinking today of a Christian home, one of the most promising Christian homes I know. Who is the wife? She was a chorus girl on Broadway. The current was too strong for her. She went under. She touched the bottom of the pit in this perilous city. You never would guess it now. Christ did in her a thing so beautiful that not only have the wounds been healed, but I do not know how you ever would find the scars. Columbus must have gotten deep satisfaction out of discovering America, but no more thrilling, I think, than to discover a soul in Crete and lead the way up. Don't dodge Crete. If in this city we have not found our Crete,—the area of human need that belongs to us,—then we are not quite Christians until we find it.

One other thing I think Titus said when Paul's letter came. I suspect he thought to himself: "Paul is right. The ultimate test of a man's faith in God is its power to see him through a hard place." Perhaps we have not been sympathetic enough with Titus. Create was a hard place, so hard and the people so unlovely that I suspect moral indignation had a good deal to do with Titus' first attitude. It would have been such a relief to his sense of what was fitting to tell them what he thought of them—liars, beasts, gluttons—and then leave them so. How natural! Many of us here, I suspect, are tempted to deal with some situation which we face by that cheap and easy method of moral indignation. It is much easier to denounce than to build.

Consider the church, for example. Nothing is easier than to berate the church. Sectarian, obscurantist, belated, out of touch with the major movements of thought and life in our time—the churches do face the most perilous situation they have faced since the Protestant Reformation. Here is a chance for irresponsible critics to revel in denunciation, and they are taking full advantage of the opportunity. But they get us nowhere. The situation calls for another attitude altogether—for Tituses who will stay in Crete, not content with Crete, not complaisant about Crete, but building the better Crete that is to be. As Paul said, to "set in order the things that were wanting."

When one is in Crete how much easier it is to be indignant than to be constructive!

Most of us, however, face this problem in much more intimate relationships. You know your Crete; I know mine. And we know that our serious inward problem is somehow to keep Crete from becoming our spiritual enemy and to make it our spiritual friend.

An eminent expert on child psychology was called in some time ago to help a young boy who every night dreamed of a frightful tiger. Night after night that dreadful vision came, and the repetition of the fear was shattering the lad's nervous system. So one evening the psychologist gathered the lad into his lap and said to him, "See here, my boy, I understand that every night you meet a tiger. Now, really, he is a nice, friendly tiger and he wants you to like him, so the next time you meet him just put out your hand and say, 'Hello, old chap,' and you will see." So the boy crawled into bed and fell into his restless, apprehensive, tossing sleep. But presently he stirred and thrust a small hand out from under the bedclothes and said softly, "Hello, old chap." Then his frightened breathing quieted into the restfulness of natural sleep. Away at the center of his life he had made friends with his tiger.

That is about the hardest thing some of us have to do: to take a situation that we hate, and say: I am not going to let you be my spiritual enemy; you shall not scare me nor intimidate me nor embitter me nor crush me; like the dragons in old myths, which, boldly faced, turned out to be princesses in disguise, you yet shall be my friend. Happy is the man who so transforms his Crete! Happy is the man who so makes friends with his tiger!

41

6

The Use and Misuse of Power[1]

A VERSE IN DR. Moffat's translation of the Book of Ecclesiastes accurately describes the intent of our morning's thought. Says the ancient Jewish writer, "Thoughtfully I pondered what goes on within this world whenever men have power over their fellows." We are introduced here to an area of experience without the thoughtful pondering of which it is impossible to understand human life. No moral test can be much more severe than the temptation to misuse power over our fellows. Yet every normal human being desires to possess such control; the will to power in the human ego is universal and imperious.

Freud goes wrong when he tries to reduce all the urgent motives of the self to what he calls *sex*. Deeper than that, interpenetrating that, and sweeping a wider range of compulsion, is another element, the will to power. Men do not usually seek money for itself; money is power. Men commonly do not seek knowledge for itself; knowledge is power. Historically the experience of love has found its thrill in no small measure in the fact that it is a conquest; it gives power over another. All the deep desires of the self which seek position, prestige, popularity, which love to sway people whether with charm of personality, strength of mind, or external possession, reveal how insistently our ego longs for power over our fellows.

We are not saying that this in itself is wrong but, rather, that the crucial test of character commonly comes at precisely the point where this strong demand of the ego begins to be satisfied. Power's possession is a heavy moral strain. For one thing, it opens the door to self-indulgence— a dangerous door to have opened. Many people cannot withstand its lure.

1. From *The Secret of Victorious Living* by Harry Emerson Fosdick, Copyright 1934 by Harper & Brothers. Copyright renewed © 1962 by Harry Emerson Fosdick. Reprinted by permission of HarperCollins Publishers.

As soon as they begin to see that door swinging wide, they walk straight in. Moreover, power's possession creates the thirst for more power. The feel of power in the hand that wields it is overwhelmingly attractive, so that the power habit, like the drug habit, easily impels one to seek an increase of the dose. And power's possession can unconsciously but dreadfully harden a man's heart. When one has power over his fellows, one finds it difficult to understand how his fellows live and then, later, one may find it difficult to care how they live. Another phrase from the Old Testament, in the prophecies of Micah, Dr. Moffat has translated thus:

> Woe to men who on their beds
> some mischief plan,
> and carry it out when morning comes,
> because they can!

That is an obbligato on what an endless series of ruthless deeds—"because they can"!

Here, then, is a fact of incalculable significance to personal and social life. Every young person here today desires power, and the forms in which you seek it may be so wholesome that all of us would heartily wish you success; only, we who are older know this also, that the day when you possess it will be not the end but the beginning of your problem.

At this point we run into an interesting contrast between the habitual attitude of Jesus and of ourselves. We constantly marvel at people who win spiritual victory despite adversity. How do they do it? we say. Starting with so little, cramped by penury of circumstance, overcoming powerful obstacles, and yet despite it all carrying off a spiritual triumph—how do they do it? But Jesus habitually marveled at people who carried off a spiritual victory in spite of prosperity. How can they do that? said he. How can a rich man enter the kingdom of God? he cried; "It is easier for a camel to go through a needle's eye." The rich man has such power over his fellows, the doors are so open to self-indulgence, the possession of power gives such opportunity to grasp more power, and riches so separate a man from understanding and sympathizing with his fellows—how can one, said Jesus, win *that* victory? Indeed, the Master marveled so at such a triumph that at the end of his discussion of it he said in explanation, "With men this is impossible; but with God all things are possible." Here is an interesting contrast between Jesus and ourselves. Jesus had thoroughly pondered, as perhaps we have not, what goes on within this world whenever men have power over their fellows.

We cannot, however, push this matter off into a corner as though it applied to one class of people only, like the rich. Obviously it concerns every one of us. Nothing, for example, gives one such intimate, interior, and dominant power over another as love. When we are loved, we are trusted with terrific power over our fellows, so that one who habitually deals with the confidential interests of individuals is likely to think of this first when he ponders what goes on in this world through the misuse of power. Charles Kingsley, asked the secret of his radiant and useful life, is said to have answered, "I had a friend." That is very fine, but many a bedraggled spirit comes to see the minister who, asked the secret of his sorry state, gives precisely the same answer. He too had a friend—who misused the power that friendship gives.

Let each of us, then, get himself or herself into the center of this picture. We have power to help people, to hurt people, to lift them up, to make their days hard and their nights long-drawn-out and anxious. Let us get our thoughts for a while off our weakness. We think of that too much anyway. Let us get our minds upon our power. We have some somewhere over our fellows.

This truth applies not only to each of us but in a special sense to our generation as a whole. We are in the midst of a widespread, deep-seated revolt against misused power. The steadiness of the American people through these years of strain, their refusal to follow demagogues or trust in violence, their fortitude and sportsmanship and even good humor in desperate circumstances, seem to me beyond all praise. Nevertheless, let none of us be fooled by that. We are facing an indignant and determined revolt against misused power. In 1928 in this city, I addressed a convention of representatives of one of our greatest industries. We were then at the flood tide of what looked like prosperity and, under circumstances very different from today's, I spoke to them on the same subject which occupies our thought now. No nation, I tried to say, had ever been trusted with such power as we then possessed. We were the creditor nation of the world and incredibly well-to-do. When one went to a country like Arabia, the problem was penury and want. When one went to a country like China, the problem was lack—lack of food, lack of a means of communication, lack of literacy. But when one came back to America, the problem was plenty. We had already passed out of the economy of want into the economy of abundance. We had means to produce more than we had use for. It was natural, I tried to say, to be self-congratulatory under such conditions, but, as a matter of fact, that was the most dangerous position which any nation could ever face. For the tragedies of history had been the tragedies of misused power. The catastrophes of history had not arisen mainly from the weak—no, from the strong. As individuals and as classes they achieved power and then, with the power they had, they grasped more power until in political or economic or military might they bestrode the world. Then they could not handle the power they had. They committed suicide with it. The terrific temptations associated with its possession were too much for them. The lust for power, the greedy employment of it, the desire to exploit rather than dedicate it, the failure of intelligence and character in handling the complicated problems presented by it—how history repeats the tragedy of misused power!

I had almost forgotten that old speech until the other day one of the men who heard it reminded me of it. "So," he said, "it came out as you feared. We mishandled our power."

This range of facts presents the most serious and most disillusioning problem which society faces. Interested in politics and believing in political organization, we see rings like Tammany Hall in New York or the Republican machine of Philadelphia or of Chicago, achieving power and then mishandling it. Enthusiastic over organized labor and collective bargaining, we see the unions possessing tremendous power and too often misusing it. Believing in the church and under favorable circumstances rejoicing in signs of its increasing power, whether in history or in some contemporary exhibition of mishandled strength, we feel the force of Dean Inge's biting but unfortunately true statement that every institution, even the church, ends by strangling the ideas it was founded to protect. No wonder our forefathers based the Constitution of this nation on balanced checks. Our forefathers had suffered so terribly from misused power that they dreaded it above all else.

It comes, then, straight from our tradition that we should revolt against mishandled economic power. Only one cure is possible for that revolt. The sole defense of any economic order is to make it work for the welfare of the people. That, however, involves something deeper than external rearrangement of the economic system. No economic reorganization will work one bit better than our present methods do without something deeper, the Christianizing—let me use that word in a deep sense—the Christianizing of the meaning and use of power. Without that profound ethical transformation we may secure any kind of economic order we chance to fancy—reformed capitalism, socialism, fascism, communism—but, all alike, they will go to pieces in the end on the same rock, the misuse of power.

In trying to see what is implied in this crucial, personal and social problem, consider first how dangerous a folly it is to suppose that Christianity is primarily intended for the weak. Often we have heard that. Inadequate people, afraid of life, insufficient to deal with it, wanting comfort—Christianity is for them. They ought to go to church, we are told, and be comforted, but strong personalities, able to stand on their own feet, resolutely facing the world and successfully grappling with it—why should they want Christ? Every minister some time or other has had a strapping youth in his pride of his power talk like that. Yet all history is a continuous answer to it. We could get on fairly well, muddling along with the unchristian weak. It is not they who have drenched the world in blood and made the centuries sick with ruthlessness. It is not they who on their beds some mischief plan and carry it out when morning comes, because they can. The strong have done that. So the ethic of Jesus was directed primarily at the strong. "He that is greatest among you shall be your servant." Power possessed, dedicated, used, and, if need be, renounced—that is the central principle of the ethic of Jesus.

That was his personal problem. He had power to handle. Indeed he did. A personality that could do what he did to the world must have had strength to manage, and even for him it was difficult. Each of the temptations, which in symbolic form he described to his disciples, concerns that. Should he turn stones into bread - that is, should he use his gifts for material ends? Should he cast himself down from the temple top expecting to be unhurt—that is, should he use spectacular methods to win easy, popular success without traveling a hard road of suffering and sacrifice? Should he fall down and worship the devil in hope of gaining the kingdoms of the world—that is, should he use violence to win an earthly dominion? There swirled the temptations of the Master, where temptation swirls in every son of man, around his power. And out of his personal problem came his characteristic ethic of dedicated strength, which Paul correctly understood: "We that are strong ought to bear the infirmities of the weak, and not to please ourselves."

You see, the Master had every reason thoughtfully to ponder what goes on within this world whenever men have power over their fellows. Remember what Pilate said to him that last hour in the Prætorium: "Knowest thou not that I have power to release thee, and have power to crucify thee?" So! Even the crucifixion was a tragedy of misused power.

The Christian churches of this nation face no more imperative task than the persuasive presentation of this truth to the strong. Sometimes in this pulpit I am accused of neglecting the weak and their need of comfort. I am sorry. I am aware of that other side of the gospel: "Come unto me, all ye that labor and are heavy laden, and I will give you rest." How amazingly many-sided the Master was! But the crucial problem of this nation now is not centered in the weak; it is centered in the strong. What are we going to do with our power? Some of my very intelligent friends say that already in this nation we have entered a race between the Christianizing of power on the one side and violent class war on the other. I hope that issue is a long way off. But my friends are very serious. Look, they say, at any privileged class in history, like the kings of France from the Grand Monarch on. That was a typically privileged class in which the possession of power worked out its characteristic consequence: private luxury in the midst of public poverty, power's possession creating the thirst for more power and more power and still more, deafness to the cries of despair from the great masses of the people, blindness to the inevitable coming of a new day, stubbornness against social change that would affect their own power, until at last they had to be violently upset.

You too will see this in our time, my friends say. Go on teaching the Christian ethic to the powerful; they will not accept it. The Christian ethic means the social dedication of power, its use for the commonweal, and, if need be, its renunciation. No privileged class in history ever accepted that until it was coerced into doing so. So, they say, you will see that it will require a class war to settle this problem. There is more such talk going on in this country than many people dream.

You know what I think about war, every kind of war, and of all wars the most irretrievably sinister is a class war. If Daniel Webster, looking with dread on a possible civil war, could pray that his eyes might never rest upon "a land rent with civil feuds, or drenched, it may be, in fraternal blood," one surely would pray that about a class war. But then, you see, despite Daniel Webster's prayers, the Civil War did come and one of the reasons was that once more in history a powerful owning class would not let it go. Has something like that to happen in our day? I am sure it need not happen; but I am sure also that whether it happens or not depends mainly on people like ourselves, one way or another on the privileged side of the social order. How are we going to handle our power? "He that is greatest among you shall be your servant." How difficult it is for a man whose fingers have tasted the feel of power really to dedicate it, or, when the need arises, to renounce it for Christ's sake and man's!

Again, as we face this crucial personal and social problem, consider how clean a line our thought draws between the ethic of Christ and the ethic of the world. To have that line so cleanly drawn that there is no mistaking it is one of the deepest needs of modern Christianity. Many of us have confused Christ and the world, smoothed out the contrast between them, like chameleons have adapted our moral color to the life we crawl across, until it is difficult to tell the difference between the living of Christians and that of non-Christians.

Now, there are various ways in which one can distinguish the ethic of Jesus from the ethic of the world, but none, I suspect, cuts deeper into the quick than the one with which we are dealing. By and large, despite fine exceptions, the world as a whole is run by the power-ethic,

> That they should take who have the power,
> And they should keep who can.

Christ, however, stands for the love-ethic—generous, sacrificial, outgoing love expressed in dedicated power. That *is* a contrast. It represents a conflict which we ministers face in one experience exceedingly difficult to endure. We see youths trained in Christian families and schools, sensitive, idealistic, boys and girls who seem to us the pride of the church and the hope of the world. Then we see these young people going out from home, church, and school, those comparatively sheltered areas where the love-ethic has been fairly established, into the world at large. That is not run by the love-ethic, but by the power-ethic. So these young men and women come back to us to say, We cannot be Christians out there; that is another world; we can make the love-ethic work within certain sheltered areas like the home, but Christ is not the lord of the great world; Nietzsche is, with his ethic of power.

Sometimes we ministers are told that social questions are not our business. I beg of you, think that through again. To train boys and girls in the love-ethic of Jesus and then send them out into a world of war and racial prejudice and social injustice, where the love-ethic is pounded to pieces by the power-ethic of a pagan society—that will not do! The Christian church has a tremendous stake, involving its very existence, in the social question; for this world cannot permanently go on half under a love-ethic and half under a power-ethic. They are mortal enemies. One or the other in the end will win a general victory, and if at last the great world as a whole should fall under the sway of the power-ethic, that would reduce to utter futility a few individuals here and there with the love-ethic.

This, then, is the crux and conclusion of the whole matter. Our truth comes up to the doorsill of every man's conscience. I have not tried to be comforting this morning. If this sermon is not a challenge it is a failure. It challenges my own life as much as any man's. It walks straight up to the doorsill of every conscience and says, You have power; what are you doing with it? More persons ruin their lives with their power than with their weakness—be sure of that! More persons help ruin their generation with their power than with their weakness—be sure of that! As for being Christians, never think of Christianity primarily as medicine for weakness. It is more than that. To be a Christian means to take in your strong hands the love-ethic and go out into this pagan world to live by it, believe in it, adventure on it, sacrifice for it, until we make it victorious in the institutions of mankind. And that is costly. Yet difficult and costly as it is, power in the hands of love is always the most beautiful thing in the world. And any kind of power—personal charm, intelligence, skill, leadership, possessions—in the hands of love is the most convincing thing in the world.

7

The Unknown Soldier[1,2]

IT WAS AN INTERESTING idea to deposit the body of an unrecognized solider in the national memorial of the Great War, and yet, when one stops to think of it, how strange it is! Yesterday, in Rome, Paris, London, Washington, and how many capitals beside, the most stirring military pageantry, decked with flags and exultant with music, centered around the bodies of unknown soldiers. That is strange. So this is the outcome of Western civilization, which for nearly two thousand years has worshiped Christ, and in which democracy and science have had their widest opportunity, that the whole nation pauses, its acclamations rise, its colorful pageantry centers, its patriotic oratory flourishes, around the unrecognizable body of a soldier blown to bits on the battlefield. That is strange.

It was the war lords themselves who picked him out as the symbol of war. So be it! As a symbol of war we may accept him from their hands.

You may not say that I, being a Christian minister, did not know him. I knew him well. From the north of Scotland, where they planted the sea with mines, to the trenches of France, I lived with him and his fellows—British, Australian, New Zealander, French, American. The places where he fought, from Ypres through the Somme battlefield to the southern trenches, I saw while he was still there. I lived with him in his dugouts in the trenches, and on destroyers searching for submarines off the shores of France. Short of actual battle, from training camp to hospital, from the fleet to No Man's Land, I, a Christian minister, saw the war. Moreover, I, a Christian minister participated in it. I too was persuaded that it was a war to end war. I too was a gullible fool and thought that modern war could

1. From *The Secret of Victorious Living* by Harry Emerson Fosdick, Copyright 1934 by Harper & Brothers. Copyright renewed © 1962 by Harry Emerson Fosdick. Reprinted by permission of HarperCollins Publishers.

2. An Armistice Day Sermon.

somehow make the world safe for democracy. They sent men like me to explain to the army the high meanings of war and, by every argument we could command, to strengthen their morale. I wonder if I ever spoke to the Unknown Soldier.

One night, in a ruined barn behind the lines, I spoke at sunset to a company of hand-grenaders who were going out that night to raid the German trenches. They told me that on the average no more than half a company came back from such a raid, and I, a minister of Christ, tried to nerve them for their suicidal and murderous endeavor. I wonder if the Unknown Soldier was in that barn that night.

Once in a dugout which in other days had been a French wine cellar I bade Godspeed at two in the morning to a detail of men going out on patrol in No Man's Land. They were a fine company of American boys fresh from home. I recall that, huddled in the dark, underground chamber, they sang,

> Lead, kindly Light, amid th' encircling gloom,
>   Lead thou me on.
> The night is dark, and I am far from home, -
>   Lead thou me on.

Then, with my admonitions in their ears, they went down from the second- to the first-line trenches and so out to No Man's Land. I wonder if the Unknown Soldier was in that dugout.

You here this morning may listen to the rest of this sermon or not, as you please. It makes much less difference to me than usual what you do or think. I have an account to settle in this pulpit today between my soul and the Unknown Soldier.

He is not so utterly unknown as we sometimes think. Of one thing we can be certain: he was sound of mind and body. We made sure of that. All primitive gods who demanded bloody sacrifices on their altars insisted that the animals should be of the best, without mar or hurt. Turn to the Old Testament and you find it written there: "Whether male or female, he shall offer it without blemish before Jehovah." The god of war still maintains the old demand. These men to be sacrificed upon his altars were sound and strong. Once there might have been guessing about that. Not now. Now we have medical science, which tests the prospective soldier's body. Now we have psychiatry, which tests his mind. We used them both to make sure that these sacrifices for the god of war were without blemish.

Of all insane and suicidal procedures, can you imagine anything madder than this, that all the nations should pick out their best, use their scientific skill to make certain that they are the best, and then in one mighty holocaust offer ten million of them on the battlefields of one war?

I have an account to settle between my soul and the Unknown Soldier. I deceived him. I deceived myself first, unwittingly, and then I deceived him, assuring him that good consequence would come out of that. As a matter hard-headed, biological fact, what good can come out of that? Mad civilization, you cannot sacrifice on bloody altars the best of your breed and expect anything to compensate for the loss.

Of another thing we may be fairly sure concerning the Unknown Soldier—that he was a conscript. He may have been a volunteer but on an actuarial average he probably was a conscript. The long arm of the nation reached into his home, touched him on the shoulder, saying, You must go to France and fight. If some one asks why in this "land of the free" conscription was used, the answer is, of course, that it was necessary if we were to win the war. Certainly it was. And that reveals something terrific about modern war. We cannot get soldiers—not enough of them, not the right kind of them—without forcing them. When a nation goes to war now, the entire nation must go. That means that the youth of the nation must be compelled, coerced, conscripted to fight.

When you stand in Arlington before the tomb of the Unknown Soldier on some occasion, let us say, when the panoply of military glory decks it with music and color, are you thrilled? I am not—not any more. I see there the memorial of one of the saddest things in American history, from the continued repetition of which may God deliver us!—the conscripted boy.

He was a son, the hope of the family, and the nation coerced him. He was, perchance, a lover and the deepest emotion of his life was not desire for military glory or hatred of another country or any other idiotic thing like that, but love of a girl and hope of a home. He was, maybe, a husband and a father, and already, by that slow and beautiful gradation which all fathers know, he had felt the deep ambitions of his heart being transferred from himself to his children. And the nation coerced him. I am not blaming him; he was conscripted. I am not blaming the nation; it never could have won the war without conscription. I am simply saying that *that* is modern war, not by accident but by necessity, and with every repetition that will be more and more the attribute of war.

Last time they coerced our sons. Next time, of course, they will coerce our daughters, and in any future war they will absolutely conscript all property. Old-fashioned Americans, born out of the long tradition of liberty, some of us have trouble with these new coercions used as short cuts to get things done, but nothing else compares with this inevitable, universal, national conscription in time of war. Repeated once or twice more, it will end everything in this nation that remotely approaches liberty.

If I blame anybody about this matter, it is men like myself who ought to have known better. We went out to the army and explained to these valiant men what a resplendent future they were preparing for their children by their heroic sacrifice. O Unknown Soldier, however can I make that right with you? For sometimes I think I hear you asking me about it:

> Where is this great, new era that the war was to create? Where is it? They blew out my eyes in Argonne. Is it because of that that now from Arlington I strain them vainly to see the great gains of the war? If I could see the prosperity, plenty, and peace of my children for which this mangled body was laid down!

My friends, sometimes I do not want to believe in immortality. Sometimes I hope that the Unknown Soldier will never know.

Many of you here knew these men better, you may think, than I knew them, and already you may be relieving my presentation of the case by another picture. Probably, you say, the Unknown Soldier enjoyed soldiering and had a thrilling time in France. The Great War, you say, was the most exciting episode of our time. Some of us found in it emotional release unknown before or since. We escaped from ourselves. We were carried out of ourselves. Multitudes were picked up from a dull routine, lifted out of the drudgery of common days with which they were infinitely bored, and plunged into an exciting adventure which they remember yet as the most thrilling episode of their careers.

Indeed, you say, how could martial music be so stirring and martial poetry so exultant if there were not at the heart of war a lyric glory? Even in the churches you sing,

> Onward, Christian soldiers,
> Marching as to war.

You, too, when you wish to express or arouse ardor and courage, use war's symbolism. The Unknown Soldier, sound in mind and body—yes! The

Unknown Soldier a conscript—probably! But be fair and add that the Unknown Soldier had a thrilling time in France.

To be sure, he may have had. Listen to this from a wounded American after a battle. "We went over the parapet at five o'clock and I was not hit until nine. They were the greatest four hours of my life." Quite so! Only let me talk to you a moment about that. *That* was the first time he went over the parapet. Anything risky, dangerous, tried for the first time, well handled, and now escaped from, is thrilling to an excitable and courageous soul. What about the second time and the third time and the fourth? What about the dreadful times between, the long-drawn-out, monotonous, dreary, muddy barrenness of war, concerning which one who knew said, "Nine-tenths of War is Waiting"? The trouble with much familiar talk about the lyric glory of war is that it comes from people who never saw any soldiers except the American troops, fresh, resilient, who had time to go over the parapet about once. You ought to have seen the hardening-up camps of the armies which had been at the business since 1914. Did you ever see them? Did you look, as I have looked, into the faces of young men who had been over the top, wounded, hospitalized, hardened up—over the top, wounded, hospitalized, hardened up—over the top, wounded, hospitalized, hardened up—four times, five times, six times? Never talk to a man who has seen that about the lyric glory of war.

Where does all this talk about the glory of war come from, anyway?

"Charge, Chester, charge! On, Stanley, on!"
Were the last words of Marmion.

That is Sir Walter Scott. Did he ever see war? Never.

And how can men die better
    Than facing fearful odds,
For the ashes of his fathers,
    And the temples of his Gods?

That is Macaulay. Did he ever see war? He was never near one.

Storm'd at with shot and shell,
Boldly they rode and well,
Into the jaws of Death,
Into the mouth of Hell,
    Rode the six hundred.

That is Tennyson. Did he ever see war? I should say not.

There is where the glory of war comes from. We have heard very little about it from the real soldiers of this last war. We have had from them the appalling opposite. They say what George Washington said: it is "a plague to mankind." The glory of war comes from poets, preachers, orators, the writers of martial music, statesmen preparing flowery proclamations for the people, who dress up war for other men to fight. They do not go to the trenches. They do not go over the top again and again and again.

Do you think that the Unknown Soldier would really believe in the lyric glory of war? I dare you; go down to Arlington and tell him that *now.*

Nevertheless, some may say that while war is a grim and murderous business with no glory in it in the end, and while the Unknown Soldier doubtless knew that well, we have the right in our imagination to make him the symbol of whatever was most idealistic and courageous in the men who went out to fight. Of course we have. Now, let us do that! On the body of a French sergeant killed in battle was found a letter to his parents in which he said, "You know how I made the sacrifice of my life before leaving." So we think of our Unknown Soldier as an idealist, rising up in answer to a human call and making the sacrifice of his life before leaving. His country seemed to him like Christ himself, saying, "If any man would come after me, let him deny himself, and take up his cross daily, and follow me." Far from appealing to his worst, the war brought out his best—his loyalty, his courage, his venturesomeness, his care for the downtrodden, his capacity for self-sacrifice. The noblest qualities of his young manhood were aroused. He went out to France a flaming patriot and in secret quoted Rupert Brooke to his own soul:

> If I should die, think only this of me
> > That there's some corner of a foreign field
> That is for ever England.

There, you say, is the Unknown Soldier.

Yes, indeed, did you suppose I never had met him? I talked with him many a time. When the words that I would speak about war are a blistering fury on my lips and the encouragement I gave to war is a deep self-condemnation in my heart, it is of that I think. For I watched war lay its hands on these strongest, loveliest things in men and use the noblest attributes of the human spirit for what ungodly deeds! Is there anything more infernal than this, to take the best that is in man and use it to do what war does? This is the ultimate description of war—it is the prostitution of the noblest powers of the human soul to the most dastardly deeds, the most abysmal cruelties of which our human nature is capable. That *is* war.

Granted, then, that the Unknown Soldier should be to us a symbol of everything most idealistic in a valiant warrior, I beg of you, be realistic and follow through what war made the Unknown Soldier do with his idealism. Here is one eyewitness speaking:

> Last night, at an officers' mess there was a great laughter at the story of one of our men who had spent his last cartridge defending an attack. "Hand me your spade, Mike," he said; and as six Germans came one by one round the end of a traverse, he split each man's skull open with a deadly blow.

The war made the Unknown Soldier do *that* with his idealism.

"I can remember," says one infantry officer, "a pair of hands (nationality unknown) which protruded from the soaked ashen soil like roots of a tree turned upside down; one hand seemed to be pointing at the sky with an accusing gesture. . . . Floating on the surface of the flooded trench was the mask of a human face which had detached itself from the skull." War harnessed the idealism of the Unknown Soldier to do *that*!

Do I not have an account to settle between my soul and him? They sent men like me into the camps to awaken his idealism, to touch those secret, holy springs within him so that with devotion, fidelity, loyalty, and self-sacrifice he might go out to war. O war, I hate you most of all for this, that you do lay your hands on the noblest elements in human character, with which we might make a heaven on earth, and you use them to make a hell on earth instead. You take even our science, the fruit of our dedicated intelligence, by means of which we might build here the City of God, and, using it, you fill the earth instead with new ways of slaughtering men. You take our loyalty, our unselfishness, with which we might make the earth beautiful, and, using these our finest qualities, you make death fall from the sky and burst up from the sea and hurtle from unseen ambuscades sixty miles away; you blast fathers in the trenches with gas while you are starving their children at home by blockades; and you so bedevil the world that fifteen years after the Armistice we cannot be sure who won the war, so sunk in the same disaster are victors and vanquished alike. If war were fought simply with evil things, like hate, it would be bad enough but, when one sees the deeds of war done with the loveliest faculties of the human spirit, he looks into the very pit of hell.

Suppose one more thing—that the Unknown Soldier was a Christian. Maybe he was not, but suppose he was, a Christian like Sergeant York, who at the beginning intended to take Jesus so seriously as to refuse to fight but afterward, otherwise persuaded, made a real soldier. For these Christians do make soldiers. Religion is a force. When religious faith supports war, when, as in the Crusades, the priests of Christ say, "Deus Vult"—God wills it—and, confirming ordinary motives, the dynamic of Christian devotion is added, then an incalculable resource of confidence and power is released. No wonder the war departments wanted the churches behind them!

Suppose, then, that the Unknown Soldier was a Christian. I wonder what he thinks about war now. Practically all modern books about war emphasize the newness of it—new weapons, new horrors, new extensiveness. At times, however, it seems to me that still the worst things about war are the ancient elements. In the Bible we read terrible passages where the Hebrews thought they had command from Jehovah to slaughter the Amelkites, "both man and woman, infant and suckling, ox and sheep, camel and ass." Dreadful! we say, an ancient and appalling idea! Ancient? Upon the contrary, that is war, and always will be. A military order, issued in our generation by an American general in the Philippines and publicly acknowledged by his counsel afterwards in a military court, commanded his soldiers to burn and kill, to exterminate all capable of bearing arms, and to make the island of Samar a howling wilderness. Moreover, his counsel acknowledged that he had specifically named the age of ten with instructions to kill every one over that. Far from launching into a denunciation of that American general, I am much more tempted to state his case for him. Why not? Cannot boys and girls of eleven fire a gun? Why not kill everything over ten? That is war, past, present, and future. All that our modern fashions have done is to make the necessity of slaughtering children not the comparatively simple and harmless matter of shooting some of them in Samar, one by one, but the wholesale destruction of children, starving them by millions, impoverishing them, spoiling the chances of unborn generations of them, as in the Great War.

My friends, I am not trying to make you sentimental about this. I want you to be hard-headed. We can have this monstrous thing or we can have Christ, but cannot have both. O my country, stay out of war!

Cooperate with the nations in every movement that has any hope for peace; enter the World Court, support the League of Nations, contend undiscourageably for disarmament, but set your face steadfastly and forever against being drawn into another war. O church of Christ, stay out of war! Withdraw from every alliance that maintains or encourages it. It was not a pacifist, it was Field-Marshal Earl Haig who said, "It is the business of the churches to make my business impossible." And O my soul, stay out of war!

At any rate, I will myself do the best I can to settle my account with the Unknown Soldier. I renounce war. I renounce war because of what it does to our own men. I have watched them coming gassed from the front-line trenches. I have seen the long, long hospital trains filled with their mutilated bodies. I have heard the cries of the crazed and the prayers of those who wanted to die and could not, and I remember the maimed and ruined men for whom the war is not yet over. I renounce war because of what it compels us to do to our enemies, bombing their mothers in villages, starving their children by blockades, laughing over our coffee cups about every damnable thing we have been able to do to them. I renounce war for its consequences, for the lies it lives on and propagates, for the undying hatreds it arouses, for the dictatorships it puts in place of democracy, for the starvation that stalks after it. I renounce war and never again, directly or indirectly, will I sanction or support another! O Unknown Soldier, in penitent reparation I make you that pledge.

8

Let's All Be Realistic[1]

PRACTICALLY EVERY YOUNG PERSON of my acquaintance who makes any pretense of thinking is trying hard to be realistic. By temperament he may be romantic and idealistic but, if he is, he tries not to let any one know it. Realism is the word today—clear-eyed, unblinking recognition of life's stern and ugly facts, with no fooling of oneself. Our ancient forefathers feared devils as the cause of evil, and every generation dreads its special demons, but ours are of a kind that the mid-Victorians, for example, never would have recognized as devils at all. Pleasing sentimentality, wishful thinking, idealizations, comforting faiths, satisfying optimisms—these are the devils of the new generation. Nothing will do today except realism.

In the realm of theology, for example, the liberals are being soundly trounced by a group of men who call themselves realists. The trouble which the realists find with the liberals is serious. Against the background of the old theology, with the wrath of God and fear of hell in the ascendency, the liberals reacted to the opposite extreme. They ceased being grim and became sentimental. They streamlined their theology to reduce wind resistance. With God pictured as a very kindly and affectionate father, with evil understood as only the shadow cast by the sunshine of the good, with progress on this evolving earth happily automatic and inevitable, and with hope for everybody in the world to come, liberals retreated into make-believe and, when they thought about the dark side of life, agreed with Tennyson to "cleave ever to the sunnier side of doubt." Well, the realists are fed up the cleaving to the sunnier side of doubt. They say, and I think rightly, that this world is a much wilder, fiercer, profounder place

1. From *The Power to See It Through* by Harry Emerson Fosdick. Copyright 1935 by Harper & Brothers. Copyright renewed © 1963 by Harry Emerson Fosdick. Reprinted by permission of HarperCollins Publishers.

than such superficial liberalism ever took account of, and, in view of the factual conditions existing today, they cry, Let us quit this infatuation with the sunnier side of everything and be realistic!

One does not have to live, however, in any special field like theology to feel the pressure of this prevalent demand. No man can escape it. Even when he is unaware of it, it presses on him like the atmosphere, over fourteen pounds to the square inch. Our modern novels and dramas strain after realism, especially in realms like sex, crime, and psychopathic abnormality. In many of our new biographies it is obvious that nothing makes a biographer so happy as to find some forgotten area of his hero's life where he can exploit a hitherto unsuspected sin or psychoanalyze an unguessed perversion. Even in our new autobiographies the influence of this *Zeitgeist* is manifest in a type of exhibitionism which a generation ago would have been incredible. As for our new music, where are the tunes and melodies and harmonies of our sentimental forebears? Such music, we are told, does not correctly represent the way the world actually sounds. The world is factually full of cacophonies, discontinuities, feverish and raucous noises; let even music be realistic! Everywhere one looks, one finds this demand for realism.

Many years ago there sat in the Congress of the United States a North Carolina mountaineer who represented Buncombe County. He was a long-winded, platitudinous speaker, and toward the close of the debate on the Missouri question, when the House was clamoring for the vote, he insisted on making a verbose address, on the ground that he had to make a speech for Buncombe. Unwittingly he put a new word into our English dictionaries; you find it there, "buncombe." And of late years another word has derived from that, "debunk," to deflate sentimentality, strip romantic disguises from ugly facts, and force people to be realistic. That word represents an influence so prevalent in our time that even trying to live a Christian life requires that one should understand it and come to terms with it.

No such movement would have gotten under way had it not been needed. Healthy realism is a great asset. Indeed, is not the Bible one of the most realistic books in the world? There is no need this morning to select a special text. The whole Bible is a text. Pick out, if you can, a single area of human life about which the Bible does not talk candidly. Its frankness about sex passions is notorious, from gross stories like that about Judah and Tamar to murderous tragedies like David's love for Bath-sheba. No modern war diary can be much more realistic about the brutalities of battle than the Bible is in many a passage. As for human abnormalities, have you recently read Paul's catalogue of the pagan vices in his letter to the Romans? Or if you have thought that the Bible is a book of wishful thinking, have you read the way the early Christians used to cheer themselves with memories of the heroes of the faith who were stoned, sawn asunder, slain with the sword? Or if any one supposes that the religion of the Bible in its origin is sentimental, let him read the story of the crucifixion. That starting point and abiding center of Christianity should assure us that when it comes to realism the Bible overpasses us. No, my friends, these spiritual humming birds, who flit about the Bible and suck sweetness here and there from the Twenty-third Psalm or the thirteenth chapter of First Corinthians, do not understand the Book. If it were only with a view to comprehending the Scriptures, one might cry, Let us all be realistic!

This matter, however, is much more urgent on our lives than that. Here in this Christian sanctuary, where often, I doubt not, our souls are tempted to retreat into vague idealism, let us consider certain areas of life with which as Christians we should be concerned and where there is no chance of getting anywhere if we are not realistic.

For one thing, we never will escape from our breakdown of moral standards in the relationships between men and women unless we achieve realism. After a recent peace sermon, a young man said to me, "I know one major reason why I am against war," and when I asked him what it was, he put his finger on a very realistic fact: war kills off the men—10,000,000 known dead soldiers, 3,000,000 additional supposed-dead soldiers in the World War. Start with more women than men in a population anyway and where does that leave us? Will you realistically think through the effect of that fact on personal morals? What is the use of sentimentally lamenting the appalling increase of homosexuality on one side or promiscuous sensuality on the other if we go on with war? Then, after war comes the economic debacle, and among other catastrophes this means millions of young people who dare not marry. We have been listening lately to a series of addresses on Christianity's stake in the economic situation, one of the most stimulating courses we have ever had, but some things I would have thought of saying first no one has thought of saying yet. Christianity's stake in the economic situation, for one thing, is all tied up with what the economic situation does to millions of young people who love each other and cannot marry.

One young man of unimpeachable character and ability, two years out of college with never a steady job yet, tried to tell me the other day that he was endeavoring to make the best of it, to keep his chin up, not to let the disappointment and the strain break his morale. Then he started another sentence. "I said to my girl," he began. I don't know yet what he said to his girl for, despite his determination to keep his chin up, he broke down when he started on that. Nothing much more arouses one's indignation than elderly sentimentalists who, softly cushioned themselves, shake their heads over the informal *liaisons* into which young people enter on every side, and ask me whether I do not think it lamentable. Of course I think it lamentable and I would do anything in my power to keep my young friends from getting into these alleys that lead only into misery. But the more important fact is that the young people themselves think it lamentable. They too want homes. They too want children. Do we elderly headshakers think the young people like this situation? But if we of the older generation are going on with war and with an economic order which gives to youth no opportunity or security, we cannot expect high standards of personal morality except in a selected group. That is the realistic fact.

Again, we will never get rid of war itself unless we stop being sentimental about it. War is supported among the great masses of the population mainly by sentimentality—martial music, gay uniforms, massing of the colors, the romanticizing of what goes on in war and, above all else, by emotional appeals to patriotism, as though patriotism and war were synonymous. I think some of the pleas for militarism this last Armistice Day—alas, some of them from Christian pulpits!—were about as sentimental slush as a man could listen to. Yes, and a New York newspaper that reported them gave us on the same day an editorial on a most realist piece of news about war. It said that the War Department now has a proposal before it that henceforth all American soldiers shall be tattooed in four places. The reason for this is that in the last war the soldiers were blown into such small pieces that, poor fellows, their tags were lost so that they could not be identified. Now the hope is that if we tattoo each American boy in four places, on both shoulders and both hips, there may be some chance of finding enough of him so that his family can be told of his death. That is war and if we could get people realistically to see that that *is* war we might get some concerted good sense about it.

Even yet, however, there are lovely ladies who will say sweetly to a man, "Wouldn't you die for your country?" I know the answer to that. Yes, I'd *die* for my country. But that is not the realistic question about war. The realistic question is: Would you *kill* for your country, screw your bayonet into another man's abdomen, bomb a city and indiscriminately murder mothers and children, let loose poison gas into a population, and so on and so on? To such a realistic question I have a realistic answer: No, I am not willing to do that for my country and, for one reason, because all the evidence points conclusively to the fact that such mass murder does no benefit to my country but only plunges her along with her enemies into irretrievable disaster, so that anybody who realistically loves his country will strive to defend her, not by war—you cannot defend any good thing by war—but against war. That is the realistic fact.

Again, we certainly need realism in looking on and dealing with the economic situation in this country. If we continue thinking in selfish class terms, being loyal to class interests, fighting for class privileges, owners and while collar workers on one side, mechanics and hand laborers on the other, possessors of our natural resources and our great agglomerations of machines on one side, the disinherited upon the other, we are bound to have two powerful economic groups—alas, one sees their outlines growing clearer now—ready to join in a class war which may ruin our democracy. That is the realistic fact. Here, this morning, practically all of us are naturally allied with one class rather than the other. That is the tragedy in Protestantism. But all the more on that account, we ought to say to our consciences some realistic things. Beware in days like these how we think selfishly in class terms and fight for our class privileges. Beware, for example, how we talk about the glory of the liberties bequeathed us by our sires and about the necessity of retaining them, in a country where today millions of our fellow citizens already are convinced that through economic impoverishment all the liberty that amounts to anything has been taken from them.

There was a famous actress once, Charlotte Cushman, who used to greet her friends at her Newport Villa by saying, "This is Liberty Hall; every one does as *I* please." So! I speak for workers, for the poor and the disinherited of this nation. When they hear a preacher in a church like this plead for the retention of our liberties, when they hear of an organization, sponsored by the powerful, going out to fight for the retention of our liberties, they think they hear the accent of that actress; they think we mean America is to be Liberty Hall, where everybody does as we please.

If we are on the more fortunate side of this economic issue and have any realism, we had better use it now. Of course, we ought to be concerned about liberty. There never was a time in the world's history when eternal vigilance was more surely the price of it. But if we are going to have liberty in this country we must win it, not for a class, but for the whole people, and it must be real liberty, based upon ever-increasing equality of condition and distribution of property, without which there is no liberty that is worth the name. That is the realistic fact.

Certainly, we all need realism in dealing with our individual problems. The psychiatrists constantly use the phrase, 'flight from reality.' It describes a process involved in practically every psychopathic abnormality. Think of the most dreadful things that can befall us in mental unbalance and, in so far as they are acquired, all of them happen in personalities escaping into make-believe from some reality that they do not want to face and do not know how to handle.

When one thinks of these many fields where realism is indispensable and then hears a young person say that, as for him, he proposes to be a realist, one prays that he may succeed.

Nevertheless, it is too much to expect that even so fine a thing as realism, when it becomes a fad, when as a vogue it runs through a whole generation, from novels that grovel in the gutter to philosophies that forget the soul, it is too much to expect, I say, that such a popular fashion should be without its exaggerations and aberrations. Every *Zeitgeist* is caricatured. You young people in particular are not in much danger of being sentimentalists. That is not the style. One knows well how cordially you have agreed with what we have been saying about the need of realism in one field after another. That is why one is concerned about you. You are sold on realism. Then watch your step, for realism is doing lamentable things to some people who are not handling it well. Realism is like arsenic—it is a tonic in grains and a poison in ounces.

Let me put it personally. As a Christian preacher I am doing my best to be realistic in this pulpit during these difficult days, but I have an understanding with my soul about what realism means, and that, in brief, I venture to share with you.

For one thing, realism is degraded when it slips down into the idea that only ugly things are real. Some people are so afraid of being sentimental and idealistic that they manage their thinking and their living as some men write their novels, as though sewers were the only real things and mountain streams were not real too. A literary critic, dealing with a book by Mr. H. L. Mencken, said that Mr. Mencken's method seemed to be "to collect every kind of folly, ineptitude, perversion and general idiocy out of the daily, weekly and monthly minor press of America, and then to ask the American public what they think of such horrors and stupidity." Whether or not that is fair to Mr. Mencken I shall not try to say, but any one with half an eye can find plenty of realism of that character.

If some one says that the trouble with that is lack of idealism, I answer, No, the trouble with that is lack of realism. Slums are real but so are humble and beautiful homes like those from which some of us derived. Sewers are real but so is a brook I know

> In the leafy month of June,
> That to the sleeping woods all night
> Singeth a quiet tune.

Judas Iscariot is real but so is Jesus Christ. If a man is going to be a realist, let him go through with it!

When Napoleon's dragoons stabled their horses in Milan before Da Vinci's painting of the Last Supper, I suppose they thought they were hard-headed realists. They were good representatives of some present-day realism. But now, when Napoleon's dragoons are dead as the dodo and the thing they stood for is the contempt and ridicule of thoughtful men, the spiritual meanings of the Last Supper which Da Vinci painted shine with undimmed reality in the minds of millions.

Let all realists consider.

Again, realism is degraded when it squeezes the possibilities out of a situation and so, leaving only the actualities, says that they alone are real, whereas the fact is that the most vital reality in any situation is its possibilities.

Less than forty years ago a young man went into a public library in Dayton, Ohio, and borrowed a book by a German named Lilienthal, who had succeeded in flying in a glider. Orville Wright, sitting till long past midnight enthralled by that book, is worth considering. What were the realities in that situation? What if one had had eyes to see! All the possibilities were part of the realities!

The common idea, therefore, that realism and hopefulness are antithetical terms flies in the face of the facts. The trouble with many of our so-called realists is that they are not realists at all but actualists. That is, they squeeze the possibilities out of every situation and call the stark remainder the real, when the stubborn fact is that the most significant factor in any human situation is to be discovered in the possibilities. Who, then, are the true realists? Not the cynics and the pessimists! Rather, scientists who foresee a new idea coming around the corner and head toward it; men of social vision who understand that the most significant fact about today is that it is pregnant with unborn things whose time will come; millions of thoughtful people everywhere with their eyes on the possibilities in persons, families, businesses, schools, social causes, giving to them creative faith; and men of the New Testament's faith, saying, "Now are we children of God, and it is not yet made manifest what we shall be." If a man is going to be a realist, let him go through with it!

Once more, realism is degraded when it becomes materialistic, physically-minded, as though men were body and not soul, and needed merely or mainly new physical implements to employ instead of deeper faiths and motives to employ them with. I am jealous about that fine word 'realism' and do not like to see it walked off with as it so commonly is today by people holding a low view of human nature, as though they said: Come now, be realistic; man is a brute. We who believe profoundly in the supremacy of the spiritual life, who see no hope for the race except in deepening quality there, and who have seen the high meanings of the spiritual life unveiled in Christ, are commonly dismissed as sentimentalists and wishful thinkers. But consider the facts. Can you imagine any wishful thinking more incredible than this, that regarding man as "a peripatetic chemical laboratory driven about by a sex impulse," as another put it, we should suppose that he could work anything except disaster with the tremendous powers which science confers? A peripatetic chemical laboratory driven about by a sex impulse is not made either happy or useful by being supplied with dynamite.

Yet that idea is no unfair caricature of the program for humanity which some realists unconsciously hold. One wishes one could ask them a simple question: What are the two realms in which man today faces his most difficult and dangerous problems? The answer is clear: the realm of international relationships, involving war, and the realm of economics. Then one would ask another question: What are the two realms where science has put into man's hands the most tremendous power? A similar answer comes: The international realm with its new intercommunications and engines of war, and the realm of economics. That is to say, wherever science gives man the most power, there man faces his gravest problems— problems that science creates but does not solve and for which there is no solution save in qualities of mind and character within man himself. That is the realistic fact. The essence of man's salvation lies not merely in his relations with nature but in his relations with himself—great faiths to impel him, great ideals to allure him, great principles to guide him. That is the realistic fact.

Here, then, is the gist of the matter, that the dominant modern mood is undoubtedly realistic but that realism means different things to different people. Among the saddest sights I know are some men and women, thoroughly cynical, disillusioned and sophisticated, living on a materialistic philosophy of the universe without and of their lives within, who, as another has said, "have become inured to spiritual despair," and whose pride "has made a pact with desolation." They commonly go about, calling themselves realists. Yet this is a universe which already has produced personality and across the centuries has moved man up a spiral, coming ever back to old problems but on a higher level. It is a universe where the beautiful is as real as the ugly, where the most significant factor in every situation is its potentialities, and where with each new stage in human life the center of the problem shifts still more to the quality of man's mind and character. Surely, in a universe like that, being realistic leads to deeper levels of thinking and living than our superficial exhibitions of it would suggest. Indeed, for my part, I do not see how one can think realistically in such a world without seeing Spirit to be the ultimate reality and on every side perceiving the unmistakable intimations of the living God.

Carlyle, walking in company with Robert Browning, once stopped before a wayside crucifix in France and, looking at the figure on the cross, addressed him, saying, "Ah, poor fellow, *your* part is played out." Upon the contrary, I suspect that that Man upon the cross was one of the great realists of history and that his day has barely dawned.

9

The Ghost of a Chance[1]

A DISTURBING PICTURE HAUNTS the imagination of many thoughtful observers of our time. It is the picture of our children or of their children after them sitting amid the wreckage of our Western civilization vainly wishing that they might get back again the chance we have in our hands now.

If we feel indisposed to entertain that picture, we may at least agree that it is the more intelligent and thoughtful persons of our generation who are most disturbed by it and the careless and thoughtless who fear it least. To say that it is impossible is nonsense. Too many times in history the children of great civilizations—Egypt, Assyria, Persia, Greece, Rome—have sat amid the wreckage of their power, wishing they could get back again the chance their fathers threw away, for us to suppose that such a fate cannot befall us.

This kind of situation is dramatized for us in one of the most picturesque scenes in the Old Testament—Saul going down to the witch of Endor's cave crying, "Bring me up Samuel." One moonlight night on Mount Tabor I saw the unforgettably impressive setting of that ancient scene. Far across the plain of Esdraelon, shining in the moonlight, one could see Mount Gilboa, where long ago Saul's army had encamped. Here in the foreground, three miles away, the lights of the little village of Endor, still called by the same name, were shining clear. Once could vividly picture Saul, perhaps on such a night as this, slipping away from his army in disguise, skirting the hosts of the Philistines, appearing at the witch of Endor's cave, and there in desperation over his situation pleading

1. From *The Power to See It Through* by Harry Emerson Fosdick. Copyright 1935 by Harper & Brothers. Copyright renewed © 1963 by Harry Emerson Fosdick. Reprinted by permission of HarperCollins Publishers.

with that ancient medium for a chance to speak with the dead prophet again—"Bring me up Samuel."

The impressive point is that Saul had had Samuel. He had had Samuel for many years and had disregarded and humiliated him. Samuel, the prophet, had picked Saul out to be the king of Israel, had tried to stand beside him and counsel him, had offered him his friendship and his wisdom; and Saul had thrown him over, had dropped the old pilot, had floundered on alone with growing folly and misfortune until now, when the final crisis comes and Samuel is dead, he wants the ghost of his old chance back again.

How familiar and how tragic that situation is! To have a great opportunity, to be careless about it and lose it and then want the ghost of it back again—how human that is! How many men, nations, and civilizations have gone down to Endor's cave crying, "Bring me up Samuel"!

Any one who knows human life knows that husbands and wives here this morning are saying that. They had every opportunity for a beautiful marriage and a lovely home but one or the other, or both of them, have tossed aside the sanctities of family life or handled with ill-tempered fingers the fineness of family relationships, and now, in a crisis too imminent to be avoided, we can see them slipping down to the witch of Endor's cave, craving the ghost of their old chance back again.

One knows also that persons here are acquainted with Endor's cave in their moral life. A man thirty years of age is under anxious watch-care in a New York hospital. He started drinking ten years ago. He is an alcoholic now, desperately trying to keep his footing on the steep and slippery incline whose bottom is a drunkard's grave. It is not pleasant to hear him as he talks about the chance he had a decade since, with a free, unfettered life, and cries, "Bring me up Samuel."

Look far enough and you will find whole nations in Endor's cave. They had their chance. Once they rode high on the saddle of the world but the insane game of war has been played with disastrous consequence for them, and because they live closer than we do to the ruins of old empires, from Tyre to Rome, which once bestrode the world and fell, they are not so childishly optimistic as we. They are wondering today whether they will ever get the ghost of their old chance back again.

The witch of Endor's cave is very populous. How many of us can remember chances lost, even this last year, which we wish we had back again! As to the basic principle which underlies all this we would agree.

If any man, nation, or civilization has a fine chance, then let the most be made of it, for it is fairly easy to keep an opportunity but it is desperately difficult to recover one. How one wishes that simple, basic truth could be made plain to individuals, to say nothing of civilizations!

You young men and women from our own families, for example, have a great chance. You have in your hands today the heritage of fine opportunity—not so hard to keep, if you will, but desperately difficult to get back again if once you lose it.

This is true about reputation. As I recall my youth, I think the importance of good repute was not adequately stressed. Character is what a man is, they said, and reputation is what people think he is; take care of the first and the second will care for itself. Now, however, when I see a youth with a clean name, no tarnish on it yet, I think how easily that can be lost and how many would give almost everything they possess to have it back again. So Robert Burns wrote the following epitaph for himself:

> The poor Inhabitant below
> Was quick to learn and wise to know,
> And keenly felt the friendly glow
>   And softer flame;
> But thoughtless follies laid him low,
>   And stain'd his name.

What is true about reputation is true about character. There are, in general, two types of life story—some start with a heavy handicap and work up, and some start with a great opportunity and throw it away. As for the first, a generation ago you could have seen, washing dishes in a Pittsburgh hotel kitchen, a young Hungarian peasant lad just over, unable to speak English. What chance had he? Well, some time since I gave the hand of fellowship to that boy, welcoming him into the communion of the Christian church. He worked by day and studied at night. When he graduated from the night high school, he took as the subject for his oration the opportunities America gives to the boys who come to her shores. He worked his way through one of our colleges and graduated an honor man, worked his way through the Harvard Law School, and into the membership of a New York law firm, and some of you may have cases with him, for all I know, little thinking that once he was a kitchen boy in a Pittsburgh hotel. That is one kind. He had a slim chance but he made the most of it.

Here is the other—a man whose name once was known throughout this country as a leader in the student Christian movement. He had every chance and, for a while a shining light, he is now a profane, contemptible wreck of a man, eking out a miserable existence in the back areas of the city. To see him is to hear the prayer, "Bring me up Samuel."

Now, one thing always lies behind this tragic experience in Endor's cave. Some one says, Sin. Yes, but that is too general. Always a silly optimism lies behind it. Say what we will about the unsupportable dreariness of life without hope, the fact remains that when hope goes to seed in foolish optimism the consequences are disastrous. Imagine going to Saul in those first days of his early victories and saying to him: Saul, you are making a fool of yourself; Samuel is the greatest opportunity you have; make the most of him or, if not, some day you will go down to some witch of Endor's cave, wanting the ghost of this chance back again. Saul would not have believed it. He would have "hoped for the best." He would have thought that everything would come out right. That attitude needs resolute tackling for it is one of the most prevalent in the United States. As a people we are tempted to silly optimism.

For one thing, we had a gigantic continent to exploit and the psychological results of that have been tremendous. We could waste our coal, waste our forests, spend our natural resources like drunken sailors, but everything would come out all right. Imagine America ever going down to the witch of Endor's cave wanting the ghost of her chance back again—impossible! But it is not impossible. It is inevitable unless we can be cured of our fatuous optimism.

Moreover, predisposed to a Pollyanna attitude by our resourceful continent, we have been carried further by our faith in inevitable progress. Many Americans who have given up almost all the rest of their religion—faith in God, the soul, and immortality—still believe with utter credulity in the inevitability of progress. Their philosophy of history is that we are on an escalator going up; if we should run we would go faster but, anyway, willy-nilly, no matter what we do, tomorrow we will be higher than today. That is a disastrous absurdity. Ask Greece; ask Rome. Regress is as possible as progress. It all depends on whether a nation successfully utilizes her opportunity while she has it.

Moreover, predisposed to a Pollyanna attitude by our great continent and carried further by this faith in automatic and guaranteed progress, we crown our optimism with a comfortable religion. Americans are noted around the world for having worked out the most comfortable religion on earth. When I listen to some of the characteristic productions of the churches I am sick at heart. Religion for comfort only—that is it. All too little realistic grappling with stern facts! All too little facing of difficult issues! All too little that is costly as though men had a serious sense of human destinies hanging in the balance! Religion for comfort only! A great deal of our American faith amounts to little more than this: that God is like a father with his children in a boat; he lets his children steer; sometimes to train them he lets them steer in perilous places but, just as a father when a storm rises and the rocks are near, will take the tiller and steer to safety, so God in every pinch of peril will recover us; whatever we do, everything will come out all right in the end; trust him for that. That is a dangerous religious falsehood. Look down the shores of history and see. What are those wrecks beaten to pieces on the rocks? Man after man, nation after nation, civilization after civilization, that had their chance and rose to prominence and power, growing wayward and throwing their opportunity away, are now hulks beaten to pieces on the reefs of history. God does let his children wreck their boats.

Around the nave of this church, on the capitals of the pillars, are carved scenes from the life of Jeremiah. I wish they might break into speech. We need his voice in America today. He lived and worked when the Jewish people were on the verge of their great catastrophe, the Exile. Everybody else was optimistic. They would tinker up this political alliance or that; they would trust God, whatever happened, to recover them in the end. As Jeremiah said, "They have healed the hurt of the daughter of my people slightly, saying, Peace, peace; when there is no peace." He alone was a realist. For forty years of prophethood he stood among his people, the one man in Judah who saw the facts and courageously declared them. He hated the message he had to deliver as any man hates to be sobering when he would far rather be cheerful. He said it was like a fire in his bones and that he could not contain it. But in the end what he foresaw came to pass and that fatuously optimistic people, throwing its chance away, went into the Endor's cave of the Babylonian Exile, crying, "Bring me up Samuel."

When I say that we in America need Jeremiah's voice, I am no croaking raven, crying, "Nevermore." Our Samuel is not dead yet. That is why it is worth while talking about him. We still have a glorious opportunity. It is in our hands, but now is the time to emphasize that fact. If on this road of foolish optimism we go much further, there is no power in heaven above or the earth beneath that will keep us, too, from Endor's cave.

Consider, for example, that we still have a chance to stop war. The more one knows about it the slimmer he sees the chance to be, but we still have a chance to stop war. Still the memories of our people can vividly recall the ugly and brutal hell that war is. Still books and plays keep vividly in the imagination of the populace the obscene abominations that war involves. Still straight-shooting thinkers plead for a pacifism which will refuse in the name of patriotism to support again the unspeakable damnation of a war. Yes, and the international agencies which grew out of our first passionate reaction against the Great War, the League of Nations, the World Court, and disarmament conferences, are still struggling hard to keep the candle of reason burning in a windy world. We have yet a chance to stop war and we had better take it because another world war would rob our children of everything that we have cared for most. But sometimes when I talk with Americans about this, watch their apathetic, indifferent attitude, even to great matters of public policy like the World Court, I am dismayed.

In 1890 the United States appropriated not quite $25,000,000 for its army; for 1934 the expenditure was over $243,000,000. In 1890 the appropriation for the navy was barely $22,500,000; for 1934 the expenditure was over $297,000,000. And that is going on all over this poverty-stricken earth. We are traveling precisely the same road which all the civilizations before us have traveled and with our sentimental optimism we will not believe it. If we are to have peace we must care about peace more than we have been caring, care for it sacrificially as our fathers used to care for causes which they died for. All too commonly we picture peace as a dove or as a beautiful maiden scattering largess from her ample cornucopia. That is no figure for peace. When peace comes she will not arrive as a dove or as a carefree beauty but as one who has been despised and rejected of men, a man of sorrows and acquainted with grief. We have our choice—to care about peace with some serious sense that civilization is in the balance, or else to have our children cry for the ghost of our chance again.

Once more, we still have a chance to build a humane and equitable economic life that will minister to the welfare of all people. I do not see how any one can look across the world today without perceiving that it is a narrow chance. For see the picture: communism rising as a prodigious world power and all the capitalistic nations arming themselves to the teeth to fly at each other's throats and tear each other to pieces. Many people think of ministers of religion as visionary idealists and of business men as hard-headed realists. Upon the contrary, I should like nothing better than to help some of my business friends to be hard-headed realists just now. For capitalism is on trial. That is the realistic situation. Our whole capitalistic society is on trial; first within itself, for obviously there is something the matter with the operation of a system which over the Western World leaves millions upon millions of people out of work who want work and millions more in the sinister shadows of poverty. Second, capitalism is on trial with communism for its world competitor. Now, I do not like communism; I love liberty too much. I cannot stomach such suppression of free speech, free assembly, free labor, as communism involves. But this verbal damning of communism and capitalism hinges on one point. Can capitalism adjust itself to this new age? Can it move out from its old individualism, dominated by the selfish profit-motive, and can it so create a new cooperative epoch with social planning and social control, that it can serve, better than it has, the welfare of all the people? If it can, it may survive. If it cannot, some form of coercive collectivism will be forced upon our children. Be sure of that! Today we have our chance to build a fair, democratic economic life but, if we lose it, tomorrow our children will be wanting the ghost of that chance back again.

The issue of all this is a deep need which I urge on my conscience as I urge it on yours. We need a rebirth of citizenship, a rebirth of public spirit, a renaissance of spiritual life and ethical Christianity that will issue in social-mindedness. With prosperity selfish individualism is natural. When wealth is plentiful each one is tempted to struggle for as large a share as possible for himself. But that is not our situation now. Some of you here this morning are suffering cruelly in this depression. Some of you whom I know personally, accustomed to plenty, are in a situation where penury is lurking around the corner. And the factors which caused that are not individual but social; they are not even merely national—they are world-wide.

Selfish individualism for man or nation in this new world is downright insanity. There may have been a time when a man could be the master of his own fate, but now a man's welfare or a man's disaster depends on world-wide conditions, which he cannot handle for himself, so that only social-mindedness, cooperatively handling them together for the good of all, can meet the issue. John Wesley once said, "I look upon the world as my parish." Unless we can achieve that kind of public spirit, with some intelligence to make it effective, nothing can save us.

Bring this truth for a moment down to our individual consciences. Though Jeremiah was trying to save the Jewish people from their fate, his nephew Baruch—the private secretary who preserved the records of his ministry—was tempted to selfish individualism. Member of a great family, with as good a chance as any one to serve his private ambition, he saw his own brother achieve political prestige and was tempted to a selfish life. Then Jeremiah, seeing how desperately critical the social situation was, challenged him with words that I wish could be burned into the conscience of this country: "Seekest thou great things for thyself? seek them not."

Centuries afterward a boy on the Cornell campus wandered into a religious meeting out of curiosity just as the words were being spoken—"Seekest thou great things for thyself? seek them not." It was the turning point of that boy's life, as it had been, long before, of Baruch's, and with some importance to Christianity withal, because that boy was John R. Mott. I challenge my conscience and yours with those words today. This generation is no flower garden to dally in. Today our chance to build a more decent world, tomorrow our children wanting the ghost of it back again! Seekest thou great things for thyself? seek them not.

If this sermon has seemed depressing, I beg of you to notice that our message is a lesson, not in gloom but in appreciation. What it says to every man or nation is: Appreciate your Samuel; while you have any Samuel, appreciate him! A more practical message could hardly be brought to us. How fortunate some of us are—home, friends, repute, character, opportunity—and for all the criticalness of the social situation, a magnificent chance left yet to build a warless and humane world. How many Samuels stand close beside most of us! God keep us, every one, from throwing the chance away. God save us, every one, from Endor's cave.

10

Every Man's Religion His Own[1]

IN THE NEW TESTAMENT the Christian gospel is spoken of in two con-
trasted ways. On the one side, it is an objective, external fact; whether
accepted or rejected, there it stands, a message to mankind through an
historic personality. So the Book of Revelation calls it "the everlasting gospel" and Paul refers to it as "the gospel of God" and "the gospel of Christ."
Paul calls it by another name, however, suggestive of another range of
meaning, when in his letter to the Romans he writes, "according to my
gospel." So, when Christianity came into Paul's mind and, like the ocean
flowing into a special bay, took the contour of his experience, not only did
something profoundly important happen to Paul, as we have always understood, but something profoundly important happened to the gospel.
As Paul looked at the result, he could call it, indeed, "Christ's gospel," but
also "my gospel"—that is to say, Christ's gospel as it has taken shape in me,
as I have been able to apprehend it, seen with my eyes and applicable to
my life—*my* gospel.

If this were merely an historic matter, we could content ourselves
with studying, as scholars do, the changes of category and color that were
impressed upon the Christian message when it passed through the mind
of Paul. But this is more than an ancient matter. Who of us can consider
his own religious problems or watch the souls of men struggling with belief and disbelief and not see how many of our difficulties spring from this
contrast: on the one side, the historic gospel, the official gospel, established
Christianity, and, on the other side, what is real to me in Christianity, what
gets me and makes a difference to me—*my* gospel.

1. From *The Power to See It Through* by Harry Emerson Fosdick. Copyright 1935 by
Harper & Brothers. Copyright renewed © 1963 by Harry Emerson Fosdick. Reprinted by
permission of HarperCollins Publishers.

Let us start by noting that something always does happen to Christianity when it comes into a new life. We commonly emphasize the transforming experience that befalls the soul. See, we say, from St. Augustine and St. Francis of Assisi to John Bunyan and Kagawa of Japan, when Christianity comes into men it radically changes them. But here is a companion truth: in St. Augustine and St. Francis, John Bunyan and Kagawa of Japan, Christianity flowed into diverse contours of mind and character and shaped itself to intellectual forms and practical expressions intensely individual and unique. Surely, something transforming happened to the men but something transforming happened also to the gospel. There is a sense in which there is a new kind of Christianity every time it flows into a new soul.

Certainly that was true in the case of Paul. Every New Testament scholar understands what is meant by "Pauline Christianity." It was not the same as the Christianity of James or John; it was not identical with Peter's. The sun falls through a prism into diverse colors. A tree puts forth its leaves, no two of them alike. So, even at the first, New Testament Christianity was not a unanimous and indiscriminate affair. It kept flowing into fresh personalities and becoming a new thing in each new soul.

Even before one goes further with this matter, it ought to have significance for some one here, especially some young, independent spirit, resentful at the endeavors of the elders to run him into predetermined molds, particularly wary, it may be, about putting his neck, as he figures it, into the noose of official Christianity. Friend, you have that figure wrong. Religion is not like a noose; it is like music. To be sure, music has basic and external factors in it which cause it always to be music and not something else, but it has also this constantly revivifying attribute that each new musician who is possessed by it makes it a new thing. Palestrina could have said, My music. Bach, Beethoven, Mozart, Mendelssohn, Wagner, César Franck—the merest amateur in appreciation knows the difference. Whenever music flows into the contours of a new artist, it becomes a fresh, original, individual thing. So is real Christianity. The Master never tried to make James like John or John like Peter. Individuality is of the essence of religion. I would not for anything run you into a religious mold, but if the great realm of spiritual life revealed in Christ could find in you a fresh, original expression, so that of some of it you verily could say, My gospel, that would be a major event in your life story.

With so much clear, let us pass to a further aspect of the matter. By its essential nature, religion is a kind of experience which, if we are to possess it at all, must be possessed by each man for himself. We fool ourselves about the things we can publicly inherit. Gratefully lumping in a general mass the high traditions of the race and calling them ours, we forget that there are realms of experience which by no possibility can be inherited. In them each new man, as he arrives, must be a personal discoverer. Real estate can be handed down from one generation from another but not friendship. To be sure, our inheritance can help us there, leading us to opportunities for friendship else impossible, but always the inevitable moment comes when, if I do not claim the privilege so that for myself I can say, My friend, then no matter what the tradition of friendship may be, I have no vital portion in it.

Sometimes this seems about as solemn a fact as life presents us with. Some things can be done once for all and we reap the benefit, no matter what we do. Columbus discovered America; it need not be done again. Edison discovered electric light; that is a gain for us all, willy-nilly. But soon one's thought passes over the boundaries of such public inheritance to those realms where, no matter what has been done in the past, it is of small account to me if I do not personally rediscover it, appropriate it, possess myself of it, and intimately live by it. All the courage of the past means naught to a man who cannot say, *My* courage. All the prayers of the past cannot nourish the spirit that never prays. There are no proxies for the soul. Only what is mine is really mine. The profoundest experiences of the spirit must be reproduced in each new man. No substitute can take my place in loving Shakespeare or delighting in nature. I can have no surrogate in worshiping God or caring for my fellow men.

Indeed, is it not clear that the supreme hours in human life come when some universal experience impinges upon our individual experience and becomes our very own? All men must die; that is a universal. Then some day the inevitable hour arrives when it ceases being merely universal and becomes individual—I must die. In that hour there are no proxies for the soul.

Love is a universal. We had known the tradition of love from our youth up and many a story of it and poem about it we had read. Then the hour came when it was no longer merely universal but particular. Love became our very own. In such hours there are no substitutes for the soul.

Surely, this applies to the Christianity of some one here. Multitudes of people in Christendom have no more Christianity than they can outwardly inherit—its forms and customs. Yet, living in a world where the spiritual life revealed in Christ is available, it is a tragedy not to have some of it for one's own and be able to say of its inner faiths, its deep resources, its saving virtues, That is mine.

Indeed, such are the intellectual problems of some of us that, if we are to have any Christianity at all, we must have it on our own terms; we must give up all Christianity unless we can thus be independent about it and have our own kind, even though it differs from the official brand. Surely, that was true of Paul. No sooner had Christ's commanding presence come into his life than, he tells us, he consulted with no man but went off to Arabia alone. He had, for himself, to think through this new experience and, when he returned, he brought back Christianity, indeed, but Pauline Christianity, his very own.

If that attitude was necessary even in those days, when official standardization had so little affected the gospel, how much more is it needed now! Some of us would find our whole lives profoundly changed if once we thoroughly understood the implications of this approach to being Christian. "I do not see," says a recent letter, "how people can believe the Apostles' Creed." "What do you make," says another, "of all this mass of sectarian ecclesiasticism?" You see, such minds are confronting the official gospel, established Christianity, and because it is not theirs they stand outside it.

Let a man who has been a minister of Christ for over thirty years say, I do not see, either, how people believe all the Apostles' Creed or consent to the sectarian churches. Surely, if Paul were here, far from consenting to our formal creeds and official churches, he would go again to some Arabia and think this thing through for himself, go down into the inner elements of Christ's message to discover what does verily belong to him there, apprehended by his mind and applicable to his life.

My grandsire was a stalwart Christian, but my Christianity is not like his. To be sure, it is like his in the same sense in which music is always music, whoever interprets it, or nature's beauty nature's beauty still, whether Homer sing of "the wine-dark sea" or Shelley celebrate the west wind on an autumn day. Surely, my grandsire's Christianity and mine are of kin but how different—in intellectual formulation, in practical expression, how profoundly different!

This, which is true of individuals, is true also of generations as a whole. Go back to some ancient day in Europe when, let us say, within thirty-four years the Black Death carried off twenty-five million of the population, when misery reached depths beyond imagination's fathoming, when Christianity, having no visible hopes on earth, concerned itself overwhelmingly with post-mortem otherworldliness. That is not our Christianity; it cannot be. Here is the healthy side of modernism. We have broken up the idea that Christianity is like an old copy book in school with a perfect, copperplate piece of writing on the page's top which we must repeat and repeat with linear exactness down the page. Vital Christianity never was like that. Was St. Francis a copy of St. Augustine? Is Sir Wilfred Grenfell a copy of Phillips Brooks? Are all of them together merely copies of Jesus? Such souls in religion have been as gloriously diverse as artists have been in art.

Here in this church many people have joined with us who came at first shyly and hesitantly, wondering whether they had a right to a place in the organized company of Christ. They said in effect: We do not accept the official creeds; we cannot believe all that the official church seems to teach, but here at the center of our lives is that much of Christianity we have found very real, by which we are trying to live, for which we will gladly stand; have we a right in the Christian fellowship? One of the most notable results of this church's policy is found in souls like that, scores of them, among the most exhilarating characters and the most effective workers in our fellowship. For even a little Christianity personally possessed is worth an infinite amount of Christianity externally copied.

Let us press on now from this to a matter immediately suggested by it. In a day of trial and strain it is only that much of the gospel which has become *my* gospel which can stand the storm of doubt and trouble. A few years ago, for example, Bertrand and Dora Russell blew across this country like a high wind, arousing everywhere the publicity which sensationalism can always evoke. And this was their message, that marital fidelity is now an obsolete ideal, that husbands and wives should freely grant each other extra-marital *liaisons*, that jealousy about such *liaisons* is the sign of a narrow mind, that now at last the hour had struck for emancipation from such obscurantism, and that they, Bertrand and Dora Russell, were in their own relationships exhibiting their gospel's truth. So they talked and the repercussions of their influence were tremendous. Only a week ago I ran upon another sample of it. To be sure, within the last few months Bertrand and Dora Russell themselves have come to the end of their matrimonial rope in one of the most scandalous divorce actions in recent English history. But some of us did not have to wait for that before we knew that they were absolutely wrong. And if asked how we could be so sure, the answer would go back not so much to general argument about the psychological factors in marriage, although they seem obvious enough, but even more it would go back to our personal experience of what a great home is like—*my* family life, as I knew it when I was a boy and as I have known it since. A deep conviction about the home, able to stand the storms of modern doubt and the persuasiveness of clever argument, is that much of the general truth about the family that has become one's very own.

If, then, in the realm of religion some one asks how it is that in this terrific generation, when every form of unbelief has pitilessly beaten on the Christian faith, some of us, shielded by no orthodoxy from the full force of the storm, have still maintained a Christian faith, the best answer, I suspect, was given by Canon Streeter of the University of Oxford. He kept his faith, he said, though often sorely tried, because he had an inner experience which he knew a materialistic interpretation of the universe was powerless to explain. Some of us have had all the theology we possessed stripped from us and every argument we had been accustomed to use in the defense of our faith wrested from our hands. What a generation it has been in which to keep one's faith! But always in a pinch there was that unshaken core of solid fact, an inner experience which we knew a materialistic interpretation of the universe was powerless to explain—my gospel!

As for trouble, that always reveals the difference between a Christianity affixed to us and a Christianity possessed by us. I do not need to tell you in days like these how easily the things not our very own peter out in a crisis. It is when the storms fall that the Pauls stand out and if one asks why the Pauls stand out, the answer is not so much that they believe in *the* gospel—millions do that—as that a vital part of the gospel has become so really theirs that, though the tempests beat, they can say, This verily is mine.

Hear, then, the conclusion of the matter, that without such recognition of the individuality of religious experience there can be no genuine religion but with the recognition of it there does come also a serious peril. Suppose we should hear a man say that he loved nature and that far from being a borrowed experience it was his very own; we should be glad of that. But suppose we should learn that this man, though he had means and opportunity to acquaint himself with nature in all her varied moods on sea and mountain, never left New York and that when he meant by his experience of nature was only what he got in Central Park. That would trouble us. What a pity, we would say, that a man who has in him the capacity to love nature and has this solid core of real experience in Central Park should not extend it! Has he not read Masefield on the ocean or Wordsworth on the hills? Have not Keats and Shelley awakened his discontent with this too-limited delight in nature and made him want to go adventuring for larger views and deeper insights? To be sure, an independent mind will not subjugate itself to authority but there are two kinds of authority. Keats and Shelley do not ask a man to put out his eyes in order to use theirs. Keats and Shelley open a man's eyes to see what else he had not seen. What is the matter with a man, then, who, when he has a real experience in a great realm of human life, does not want more?

That parable certainly applies to some of us. For here is the unhealthy side of modernism. Accentuating individualism in Christian faith and experience, we have done well but, in consequence, too many modernists, possessing only a little real religion, as though all the nature that a man knew were in Central Park, have settled down with that, content, complacent, sometimes intellectually supercilious, saying, My gospel. Friends, you would not take a cupful of scientific knowledge and, saying, My science! be content as though it were the whole. You would be humble about that and pray for more.

So I raise with you the question of your Christianity. Is ours the only bay into which the great sea of God has flowed that we should be satisfied with it? No one ever understands what the church rally means until he sees her in this regard. The real church—ideal, spiritual, catholic, universal—is trying to keep all the bays in mind, to comprehend them all and not forget the ocean. For our individualistic Christianities are minute and partial. Some individuals are all for personal religion; that is real to them. Some are keen about the social gospel; that grips them. Some are mystics and prayer is their native speech. Some are ethicists and the gist of their gospel is, "By their fruits ye shall know them." Some come at religion by way of the intellect, head first; it is philosophy to them. Some come with broken lives; for then it is forgiveness and renewal. How partial we are and how incomplete our particular outlooks on the sea!

Sometimes in imagination I behold the church—as I wish in this closing moment of our worship you might behold her—pleading with us as though she said, Prize, indeed, your individual Christianity, but humbly, mind you, humbly and with tolerance for others and, above all, with penitence profound that when you say, *My* gospel, it falls so far short of being *the* gospel.

11

What Is Our Religion Doing to Our Characters?[1,2]

S OME YEARS AGO IN the American College at Beirut, Syria, I addressed an audience of students in which, so they said, there were representatives of sixteen different religions. One could fairly feel the rival faiths bristling at each other. I still can see in my mind's eye a Moslem from Upper Egypt, a fierce devotee of Islam, who had come to the college at Beirut determined that he would never give in to the influence of Christianity. He was there, and others like him, on guard against this preacher from the West who probably would argue for his religion against theirs. And I can feel yet the tense quietness of the audience at the first sentence. It ran like this: "I am not going to ask any one here to change his religion but I am going to ask every one here honestly to face this question, What is your religion doing to your character?"

To be sure, it was a Protestant Christian from the West who asked it but, even so, what escape did that offer to the Moslem from Upper Egypt? He had come in, a fierce partisan of his faith, ready to defend it against all rivals; but this was another matter—what was his religion doing to his character?

Every Sunday in this congregation are representatives of all the major religious backgrounds of the West and some from the Orient, and today, this first Sunday of the Lenten season, I propose asking that same question again. We are not suggesting that any one here change his religion, but this is a larger matter which outflanks our partisanships and takes us all in: what is our religion doing to our characters?

1. From *The Power to See It Through* by Harry Emerson Fosdick. Copyright 1935 by Harper & Brothers. Copyright renewed © 1963 by Harry Emerson Fosdick. Reprinted by permission of HarperCollins Publishers.

2. Preached on the first Sunday in Lent.

rifice but a privilege—there is the authentic mark of a genuine Christian experience. You would not consider a man a true lover of music who was morose about it. You would not believe a man who said he loved nature but was habitually gloomy over it. Any genuine experience in a high realm of the spiritual life is evidenced by radiance and gaiety and joy. What, then, is our religion doing to our characters?

With this as an illustration of our meaning, let us go further. Religion can be not only one of the most depressing but one of the most belittling influences in life. An essential factor in religion is the sense of sacredness and what religion does to character depends largely on what the sense of sacredness attaches itself to. In the realm of religion, as everywhere else, there are small matters—"mint, anise and cummin," Jesus called them—on which religion can lay its sanctifying hand until they become huge and towering. Among the most tragic factors in history is the propensity of religion to make things matter terribly that intrinsically do not matter in the least. Some may say: This has been the work of little men and in any realm they would have been little anyway; religion did not make them so. True! but they would not have been so dangerous if they had not been religious. Religion can make triviality terrific. Meanness in other realms has at least a fair chance to be recognized as such, but religion can sanctify meanness, make little things holy until strong, deep loyalties adhere to them. Small men, in the name of God, can even harass the Christ and raise the storm that breaks at last on Calvary.

The consequence is that, both in individuals and in whole generations, religion, far from promoting good character, can supply and has supplied substitutes for good character. To be sure, the bandit reputed to have hoped for pardon and for heaven because he had been careful never to commit a murder on a Friday, is an extreme example, but he is an example of something which every religious man needs to watch his step about—substituting things technically religious for the solid virtues of honest character. How Jesus did, to use the current phrase, keep cracking down on *that*. There is hardly a page of the Gospels where he is not talking about that—"Woe unto you, scribes and Pharisees, hypocrites! for ye tithe mint and anise and cummin, and have left undone the weightier matters of the law, justice, and mercy, and faith."

The pity of such trivial religion is that its possessors miss the enlarging influence which religion at its best has always exerted on life. What great souls it has produced! A friend once told me that he had heard one of the leading Buddhists of India say that Gandhi was a great Buddhist, that he had heard one of the leading Moslems of India say that Gandhi was a great Moslem, that he had heard one of the leading Christians of India say that Gandhi was a great Christian. That is, Gandhi has a religion, which has expanded his range until he strikes the note of catholicity and universality. Lord Reading, when he was Governor-General of India, had trouble enough with Gandhi but his comment after his visit with him is said to have been: "I do not agree with all his opinions, but I am a purer man for having met him." Whether in individual lives like that or in great historic movements of thought where the prophets of religion gave us our first hopes and our driving ideals of human brotherhood—all mankind one family under one God—high religion has created great souls and great ideas. What, then, is our religion doing to us?

At no time in history can largeness have been more called for than it is today. Magnanimity, generosity, tolerance, catholicity, universality, breadth of vision, inclusiveness of sympathy and understanding—how profoundly they are needed! These wretched prejudices, partisanships, parochialisms that so split the nations and the world are ruining us. A great religion producing great spirits—one can fairly see the whole world saved by that. What is our religion doing to us?

With this much said, let us go further, for religion can be not simply a depressing and belittling force, but one of life's most enfeebling, debilitating influences. Surely, some one says, That cannot be; whatever else religion does, it produces power and, even when it goes wrong, it still backs men up with the sense of divine assistance and confirmation and so releases confidence and strength. Religious faith assures us that there is a world unseen, intangible, and real. Religion says to us that over and through this visible system of external circumstance there is a world invisible and ideal. Just as truly as we can see a man's body but never can see his thoughts, his loves, his creative motives, which are the man himself, so this universe at large, which the eye beholds, is only the outward integument of something deeper—invisible, spiritual, eternal. That, says our critic, is of the essence of religious faith and to say that that is enfeebling and belittling in incredible; it is a fountainhead of transcendent power in living.

To this argument I answer: You are right about that essence of religion and you are right that, well handled, it does produce powerful character. But, for all that, when it is misused, even that essence of religion is one of the perils of mankind. For see what a lotus-land of easy retreat is offered by this belief in a world beautiful and spiritual. So, from the stark and ugly facts of life demanding our intelligent and sacrificial attention, we can run away to a land of pure delight. The man who wrote "Way down upon the Swanee River, far, far away" had never been there. He simply searched an atlas until he found a name liquid and rhythmical, and then he dressed it to fit into the picture that had charmed his imagination. To multitudes of people the religious life is a Swanee River to the lovely thought of which they run away when life is difficult. We may well ask ourselves what our religion is doing to our characters in this realm?

To be sure, there is a kind of faith in a world spiritual and real to which a man can wholesomely retreat, not weakly running away to it but ascending into it and coming back again powerfully equipped for life. Music means that to some of us. It is not a lotus-land; it is no Swanee River; it is a real world where here and now to which we go and from which we return with vision cleared, faith renewed, and power replenished.

As we were entering the war in 1917, the English poet, John Masefield, fresh from the trenches in France, visited America. He was under no illusions about war and described it in the strong language of a captain who had been three years on the Somme front: "Modern warfare is damned dirty, damned dull, and damned dangerous!" But a friend of mine also heard him say that, passing through the front-line trenches before an attack, he had heard English soldiers quietly repeating to themselves Gray's "Elegy Written in a Country Churchyard":

> The curfew tolls the knell of parting day,
> > The lowing herd winds slowly o'er the lea,
> The ploughman homeward heads his weary way,
> > And leaves the world to darkness and to me.

What strange, dual, bifurcated creatures we are, living in two worlds! So in peace time, many of life's experiences can be dirty, dull, and dangerous. How impossible, then, some of us would find it to live well without that other kind of world, spiritual and ideal, to which we can ascend to gain strength for grappling with the tasks of life!

Indeed, is there anything much more significant than those souls, deep in the secrets of religion, whose faith in an ideal and spiritual world is the creative source of their social passion? Let a man have an ideal world that is real to him, in which, let us say, all souls are loved by God and all personalities are sacred, and that vision, far from being a lotus-land, will not let his thought or effort rest save in a transformed earth. There is, for example, one section of this city, extending from 59th Street to 86th and from Central Park to the East River, which includes one of the wealthiest sections of the world. They say that the annual maintenance of some of the apartments there amounts to $45,000 a year, and yet in that district is "Slum Area #5" in which there are 32,000 rooms without windows or with windows opening only on a five-foot shaft through which no gleam of sunshine can ever come, where tonight thousands of America's little children will sleep. What is America's religion going to do to America's character about situations like that—be a lotus-land to run away to from the horrid thought of such impoverishment or an inward standard of duty, an impulse of motive, a source of power for changing social conditions which make it possible? Jesus also had a living faith in a spiritual world, ideal and eternal, but it was no lotus-land for him. When he spoke of it he shook the conscience of the centuries with his words, "Seek ye first his kingdom, and his righteousness."

Religion is ambiguous in still another realm. Strangely enough, it can on one side produce fine humility or, on the other, appalling self-centeredness and egoism. One has only to listen to some selfish hymns to see that. Indeed, there are prevalent ideas of divine guidance by which eternal God is so reduced as to become an individual's valet, giving him direction, so one famous, present-day religionist declares, as to the color of the tie he shall put on in the morning. So can a great matter—God's guidance of personal life—be made the minister of egregious self-centeredness.

Such egoistic religion is easy to explain, for religion teaches us that there is a will of God and that we can know and do it. If some one claims that as a glorious faith, I agree. In the midst of a world which so often seems chaotic, to believe in an Eternal Purpose unifying life and putting meaning into it is glorious. Nevertheless that belief is also dangerous. If one handles it as Jesus did, making oneself small and the Eternal Purpose great, saying, "Not my will, but thine, be done," it builds magnificent character. But belief in the will of God can be perilously handled in another way altogether. One can start, that is, with one's individual opinions and convictions and then identify the will of God with them; once can start with one's self-centered interests or with one's emotional "hunches" and identify the will of God with them. So, instead of humbly enlarging oneself through vision of the Eternal Will one uses the Eternal Will as a "yes man" to confirm and validate one's own ideas and feelings. God can become the egoist's rubber stamp of cosmic approval. *There* is an opportunity for colossal pride and egotism.

How has God stood it in Christian history? The Christian record should have been a symphony played upon the theme of the thirteenth chapter of First Corinthians, but it has been anything but that. In bigotry, intolerance, persecution, all in the name of the will of God, it has been dreadful. That the patriarch of Alexandria kicked to death the patriarch of Constantinople over a difference of doctrine is, as everybody who knows church history understands, far too typical. When, now, this is brought down to date, it changes its form but not its substance. I crave for myself and for you, this Lenten season, a fresh vision of the will of God that will bring us to humility and penitence. It is a tremendous experience to get a glimpse of what really is the will of God. It is not God's will that these wretched nationalisms should continue, and armaments mount, and war ravage the earth. It is not the will of God that his children should suffer the limitations of penury and the humiliations of inequality which now ride mankind the like the Old Man of the Sea. It is not God's will that personality, the most potent and promising creation we know of in the cosmos, should in any one remain enslaved by sin or conquered by trouble. The will of God for the world and for our lives within it does not consent to any deplorable *status quo* but involves disturbing, forward-looking ideas which require strong vision to see, faith to believe, and courage to stand for. God's will, when it is truly known, produces no egoism. It carries men out of themselves, makes them forget themselves; it rebukes and chastens, humbles and dedicates them.

In what clear contrast with self-centered religion stands the quality of Jesus! His first principle of religious faith and conduct was not *God for me*, but *My life for God*. Such an attitude reorients life and brings with it humility, not pride; magnanimity, not arrogance; self-sacrifice, not expectation of immunity from trouble. It sees in true proportion God's eternal will and man's earthly life and does not mistake their relative importance. It leads its possessor habitually to Gethsemane's prayer and commonly to Calvary's cross.

What deplorable consequences in character have come and still are coming from religion! What moral tragedies befall when, even in this realm, the perversion of the best becomes the worst! I commend you, therefore, to your prayers for a religion which will be in you light, not darkness—elevating, not depressing; enlarging, not belittling; empowering, not enfeebling; God-centered, not self-centered. The profoundest need of the world is such character produced by such religion.

12

On Being Christians Unashamed[1]

A T LEAST ONE KINDRED element joins Paul's generation with our
own; there were plenty of things in Paul's time, too, of which to be
ashamed. Paul was ashamed of himself, first of all, and of many of his
friends. He was ashamed of the Christian churches of his period, with
their divisions and quarrels, mortified by the way in which his own people
and nation were behaving, and of Gentile civilization he said as blistering
things as ever have been said of public morals anywhere. One suspects
that out of this experience of general disgust with a disgraceful generation
Paul's resounding affirmation arose concerning one thing which called
for no shame. "I am not ashamed," he wrote to the Romans, "of the gospel
of Christ."

Granted sensitiveness of conscience, how can any one of us read the
morning paper without being morally humiliated? Of what sordid details
is the minor news compounded! And as for the major news, with nations
plunging headlong into war, with societies surrendering priceless human
freedoms, with the return of barbaric extremes of racial prejudice, with
bloody civil war abroad, the meanness of partisan politics at home, and
needless poverty everywhere, does not mankind present a disgraceful
spectacle? It is true, is it not? that when we are not doing anything else we
spend a good deal of time being ashamed.

This capacity to feel moral shame, while it is one of the distinguish-
ing faculties of human nature and ennobling in many of its uses, can easily overplay its hand and well-nigh ruin us. Moreover, it is ruining many
people today. Sensitive of conscience and not caring deeply about the
world, they are so ashamed of the human spectacle that they are disheart-

1. From *Successful Christian Living* by Harry Emerson Fosdick. Copyright 1937 by
Harper & Brothers. Copyright renewed © 1964 by Harry Emerson Fosdick. Reprinted by
permission of HarperCollins Publishers.

ened, humiliated, and dismayed. Read Santayana's *The Last Puritan* and see. When a man is fine, as Santayana is, all the more he may be shamed by the world until chronic disgust becomes his habitual mood.

Some of us who are older can remember times when disgust was not our chronic mood at all. We thought of mankind in elevated terms and supposed that everything was getting bigger and better. Far from shame, enthusiasm was our mood. We joined in Browning's singing,

> How good is man's life, the mere living! how fit to employ
> All the heart and the soul and the senses forever in joy!

Well, times change. Most of the Browning circles have broken up. Read our modern poetry, novels, drama, and see the prevalent mood of disgust and disillusionment.

When I cannot stand it any longer, when I have been disgusted with things that a man ought to be disgusted with until I have reached the saturation point, I find myself seeking recovery of spirit by recalling some things that do not cause shame. The Ninth Symphony, so conducted by Toscanini that we came down from hearing it as from a Transfiguration mountain, trailing glory into the common street—that was something, at any rate, which man had done, of which we need not be ashamed. Or the tennis champion in the Middle West who lost his right arm in an accident and then relearned tennis with his left arm and became a champion again—there is a brave conquest of calamity, of a kind one sometimes sees, of which one need never be ashamed. So in these days, we find ourselves almost of necessity seeking some things we can glory in.

But these, you see, are times; they are details picked up here and there. What if there is within our reach something more than that—a whole philosophy of life, a majestic movement of the human spirit inspired by the Divine, which we can claim for our own and glory in? *That* was Paul's affirmation. He had found something which put elated significance into the whole of life. "I am not ashamed of the gospel of Christ: for it is the power of God unto salvation to every one that believeth."

Let us see what that means and, like Paul, let us make it our personal confession!

For one thing, I am not ashamed of the gospel of Christ as a message of monotheism. It is that to start with. It is, I think, the most distinguished announcement in human history of one God, Father of the whole human family. One ought not to be ashamed of that. If ever this embittered world needed to recover the meaning of monotheism, it is today.

One of the most thrilling adventures of the human mind has been the endeavor to see this cosmos as one system, one integrated and coherent universe. To the wondering eyes of primitive man the stars were first like swarms of flies and then like marshaled armies marching. But now go to the Planetarium and see! Apparent chaos has been conquered by man's mind and order reigns. Whatever else this amazing cosmos is, it is one system, unified, integrated, coherent—from top to bottom, from center to circumference—one vast whole.

We never succeed, however, in getting the whole cosmos really together on a materialistic basis only. For the most amazing thing in this universe is not matter but mind. The visible stars are marvelous enough but they are not so marvelous as the invisible mind that comprehends them. And this mind, which has conquered chaos, must not be left out of the explanation of the very universe which it has, as it were, created. That is the assertion of monotheism. It is the high refusal of the human intellect to leave out of the explanation of the universe the most momentous factors here—mind, spirit, creative purpose. Until these have been brought into the very center of the explanation we have not got our universe together. I am not ashamed of monotheism. It is the most adequate statement of the truth we have. From all detours philosophy keeps coming back to it, teased by the fact, as Jesus the physicist says, that this universe is more like a great thought than like a great machine. Indeed it is—one Power, one Mind, one God. That insight alone gives us a real universe.

Even more does one glory in monotheism when one thinks of its moral implications. Has some one here been thinking that, after all, monotheism is an ancient achievement of thought? Rather, monotheism is so new that it has barely gotten started, and the people on earth today who really believe it are so few that mankind is sick for the lack of them. For monotheism is the doctrine that all men and all women, of all nations and all races, have one Father and are one family. How many really believe that? "I bow my knees unto the Father, from whom every family in heaven and on earth is named"—how many do that? "I saw, and behold, a great multitude, which no man could number, out of every nation and of all tribes and peoples and tongues, standing before the throne"—how many see that?

Even in popular Christian thinking the common supposition prevails that the primary enemy of monotheism is intellectual doubt. No, the major antagonists of monotheism today are not intellectual but moral and social. Nationalism and racialism are the great denials of monotheism. And they do deny it terribly. With fearful explicitness of prejudice and slaughter, they say to all the world, There is not really one God and one human family. And amid the consequent storms, which all but beat our common life to pieces, like a beacon shines the gospel, to believe and practice which is the hope of the world—one God, one Father of all, one family. A man ought not to be ashamed of that. Whatever hopeful future there is on earth belongs to that. One wishes that gospel could be shouted from the housetops.

For another thing, I am not ashamed of the gospel of Christ in its insistence on the tragic sinfulness of man and his desperate need of interior salvation. I can remember days when that deep and tragic message about man could easily be side-stepped and forgotten. We did not think ill of mankind. Leaders of thought like Herbert Spencer told us that progress was a beneficent and inevitable necessity, and poets like Tennyson assured us that "the thoughts of men are widen'd with the process of the suns." In those days we felt as though on the broad bosom of an ample river we floated to some heavenly ocean, the predetermined goal of human perfection. Of course, if we pulled hard on the oars we might get there sooner; still, whether we pulled on the oars or not, we were bound to arrive anyway, because we were afloat on a strong current of inevitable progress.

That was a fool's paradise, you say. Indeed, it was! Inventive science had given us some new and startling contrivances, like railroads, which predisposed our minds to temporary optimism. Now, however, it is plain that no contrivances can save us. Our need is far too deep. Like Roman candles and skyrockets, our mistaken dreams of salvation by ingenuity have gone off, and some of us begin to see again the abiding stars.

The gospel of Christ always has been right about the deeper matter. There is no such thing as inevitable progress. This is a tragic world where what man sows he reaps. The eternal laws of cause and consequence turn not aside for any man or nation, and history is the record of the rise and inexorable fall of societies and empires that tried to build on the foundations of unrighteousness. It cannot be done.

We thought that science might save us, but see how we ruin ourselves with the very implements that science gives! We thought that education might save us, but see to what more accomplished and destructive devil-try the trained mind turns its evil instincts! We thought that patriotism might save us, but see the murderous consequence which now we face! No! Something greater than science, deeper than education, more inclusive than patriotism, must save us. I am not ashamed of the gospel of Christ.

Indeed, in these difficult days one seems to discover its deep meaning all over again. In the gospel stands the most sober, realistic statement of the tragic need of man that the race has ever faced. Why should we balk at the great word "salvation" in view of our desperate want of it? Does not scientific medicine set itself to save us from disease? Do not schools exist because we need salvation from ignorance? Do we not institute philanthropies and pioneer more equitable economic orders because we need to be saved from poverty? Salvation is the chief preoccupation of all intelligent and earnest minds. But behind disease, ignorance, poverty, and running through the causes which produce and perpetuate them, is this deeper thing, the tragic selfishness of the unredeemed human soul. That is the sober, realistic fact. So the gospel of Christ has always taught. We may well be ashamed of much that is associated with the history of organized Christianity and with much that goes on in the churches today, but the gospel of Christ—*that* presents the soberest statement of realistic human need the world has ever faced.

For another thing, I am not ashamed of the gospel of Christ in its insistence on the prodigious lifting power of vicarious sacrifice. Vicarious sacrifice is the most impressive fact in the moral world. What one of us has not been saved from something because another, who did not need to do it, voluntarily took on himself our calamity or sin and by self-sacrifice redeemed us? And wherever that spirit of the cross appears and the ancient words come alive again, "He saved others; himself he cannot save," there is the most subduing, humbling, impressive fact we see. How can a man be ashamed of that?

This last week we buried Mrs. Anne Macy, Helen Keller's lifelong friend and teacher. Nearly fifty years ago, a little girl barely seven years of age—imprisoned behind doors so firmly locked it seemed they could not be unclosed and walls so high it seemed they could not be overpassed—was given to the care of this sacrificial teacher. For Mrs. Macy too had met blindness and, having partially surmounted it, vicariously gave herself to the blind. How subtly she passed through those fast closed doors! How marvelously she overpassed those high, strong walls and became to that imprisoned child the great emancipator! Years went by and Helen Keller passed her entrance examinations to college. Years went by and Helen Keller graduated from college *cum laude*. More years passed and Helen Keller was a world figure, known by every one. Still in the background was this magician, this self-effacing teacher, putting her life into another's and liberating it. It is one of the most amazing stores in the human record. And so powerful is such sacrifice that, because of this example of what can be done, new hopes have come, new methods, new open doors for blind and deaf folk everywhere, and the story has no end. Once more vicarious sacrifice works its miracle. How can one be ashamed of that?

To be sure, our world is disgraceful with the opposite of it, man's callous selfishness. Has some one here supposed that Paul, a man of piety and faith, must have been, therefore, a sentimentalist and looked at life through rosy spectacles? You should read the whole of this first chapter of the letter to the Romans, where our text appears. It is one of the most vehement eruptions of disgust with human life ever written. Listen to Paul in his denunciatory summary of humankind, "filled with all unrighteousness, wickedness, covetousness, maliciousness; full of envy, murder, strife, deceit, malignity; whisperers, backbiters, hateful to God, insolent, haughty, boastful, inventors of evil things." So he goes on, paragraph after paragraph, and at times is so specific about human perversity that I could not quote him here. He is no sentimentalist. He wears no rosy spectacles. But ever and again, in this same letter, he takes, as it were, the shoes from off his feet, for the place whereon he stands is holy ground. He comes within sight of the cross. He sees that most moving exhibition of self-sacrifice in history. He feels the lift of that power, which could save the world if we would let it. And before the marvel and mystery of that he bows in awe.

Like the law of gravitation running through the physical world, the law of vicarious sacrifice runs through the spiritual. No scientific medicine, no high education, no great music, no social progress, no lovely home, has ever come save as some one has voluntarily taken on himself a creative task. That is true of the cross on Calvary. That is true of Noguchi, going to South Africa to find the secret of a human plague and dying in consequence. That is the law of the spiritual world. If some one here is almost letting go and sliding to the dogs but still is held back from the last surrender, what is holding you is some one's vicarious love and sacrifice on your behalf. That is the most powerful force in the spiritual world. One should not be ashamed of it.

Once more, I am not ashamed of the gospel in its emphasis on what it calls the eternal purpose which God purposed in Christ. That is to say, before the gospel urges us to do something it tries to get us to see something, to see something everlastingly so about this universe: namely, that our world is not a feckless wanderer, coming from nowhere and going nowhither, but that an eternal purpose runs through it in which we can invest our lives, with which we can coöperate, and so be, as Paul said, "God's fellow-workers."

In this regard, the process of great religion is much like the process of great science. For great science also at the first stands aloof from practical problems, goes apart from the too clamorous demands of the world, and in isolation from the strife of tongues seeks to discover something everlastingly so about this universe. And, lo! when that has been discovered, the by-products begin to come, amazing by-products, from seeing something true, so that the face of the world is changed. So the gospel begins by asking us to *see* something, an eternal purpose through this universe with which we can coöperate .

Personally, I deeply need to see that. All the substitutes for it in our generation have blown up and gone to pieces. Only a few years past, nontheistic humanism was acclaimed as the great new religion. Never mind about God, it said; never mind about what this universe really is; let us blow on our hands anyway and save mankind. But in morals and in social hopes, as much as in science, what the universe really *is* is the basic matter. What if the universe is only chance and chaos? Suppose Schopenhauer is right, that all human history is nothing but a tragi-comedy played over and over again with some slight changes of scenery and costume? Then what is the use of blowing on our hands? Only one philosophy can undergird a long sustained and arduous investment of self-sacrifice—the idea that there is something at the heart of this universe greater than ourselves, a Power that makes for righteousness with which our little lives can ally themselves and coöperate.

One of the most surprising confirmations of this in our times has come from communism. That is the last place I expected such confirmation from. The communists started by saying they were atheists. We naturally supposed they meant that the universe in their eyes was without source, without purpose, without goal. But now the truth comes out as communist writings become available. The communists leaders say stoutly that they do not believe in mere mechanistic materialism. They go beyond it. They believe in dialectical materialism, which apparently teaches that, while there can be no such God as we believe in, history is so channeled, society by its own nature is forced to flow in such currents, that the kind of society they want is predicted and furthered by the nature of things. So they find cosmic backing from beyond themselves to make their enterprise reasonable. "Dialectics"—I quote a communist—"gives the proletariat the certainty of victory, it is to a certain extent *the guarantee of this victory*." So the communists threw theistic religion out of the door only to find that part of it came back through the window. For all their talk about atheism, they cannot make sense of their arduous, sacrificial enterprise without having a cosmic backing.

That is an amazing confirmation of what Christianity has always said, that the only philosophy which makes long sustained and sacrificial labor reasonable is one recognizing something greater than ourselves in which we can invest ourselves and with which we can be fellow-workers. Well, then, if we are going to have *that*, why not have it at its best—the living God and his eternal purpose purposed in Christ? I am not ashamed of that.

We have picked four elements, out of many in the gospel, in which to glory, and, so doing, we have been attacking the timid, negative, apologetic attitude on the part of multitudes of Christians, as though they were half ashamed of being Christian. When one listens to the resounding cries of those who serve other causes—as though it were a glory to say, I am a Nazi, I am a fascist, I am a communist—one sees how outclassed we Christians are with our apologetic attitudes. I have dared to hope that some of us might go out from this service today with our heads higher, with more confidence and assurance saying, I am a Christian. Let that banner catch the winds once more! One God and one human family, the deep need of man for interior transformation and the Spirit that can meet it, the powerful lift of genuine self-sacrifice, the stimulating message of the eternal purpose which God purposed in Christ—what a gospel! When we see it burst into a life, when it is incarnate, from Christ to his humblest disciple, we cannot be ashamed of *that*.

13

The Church Must Go Beyond Modernism[1]

IF WE ARE SUCCESSFULLY to maintain the thesis that the church must go beyond modernism, we must start by seeing that the church had to go as far as modernism. Fifty years ago, a boy seven years of age was crying himself to sleep at night in terror lest, dying, he should go to hell, and his solicitous mother, out of all patience with the fearful teachings which brought such apparitions to the mind, was trying in vain to comfort him. That boy is preaching to you today and you may be sure that to him the achievements of Christian modernism in the last half century seem not only important but indispensable.

Fifty years ago the intellectual portion of Western civilization had turned one of the most significant mental corners in history and was looking out on a new view of the world. The church, however, was utterly unfitted for the appreciation of that view. Protestant Christianity had been officially formulated in prescientific days. The Augsburg Confession was a notable statement but the men who drew it up, including Luther himself, did not even believe that the earth goes round the sun. The Westminster Confession, for the rigorous acceptance of which the Presbyterian rearguard still contends, was a memorable document but it was written forty years before Newton published his work on the law of gravitation. Moreover, not only were the mental patterns of Protestant Christianity officially formulated in prescientific days but, as is always true of religion, those patterns were sacred to their believers and the changes forced by the new science seemed impious and sacrilegious.

Youths like myself, therefore, a half century ago faced an appalling lag between our generation's intellect on one side and its religion on the

1. From *Successful Christian Living* by Harry Emerson Fosdick. Copyright 1937 by Harper & Brothers. Copyright renewed © 1964 by Harry Emerson Fosdick. Reprinted by permission of HarperCollins Publishers.

other, with religion asking us to believe incredible things. Behind his playfulness the author of *Through the Looking Glass* had this serious matter in mind when he represented the White Queen as saying to Alice, "I'm just one hundred and one, five months and a day." Said Alice, "I can't believe *that!*" Said the Queen pityingly, "Can't you? Try again: draw a long breath, and shut your eyes." So the church seemed to be speaking to us.

Modernism, therefore, came as a desperately needed way of thinking. It insisted that the deep and vital experiences of the Christian soul with itself, with its fellows, with its God, could be carried over into this new world and understood in the light of the new knowledge. We refused to live bifurcated lives, our intellect in the late nineteenth century and our religion in the early sixteenth. God, we said, is a living God who has never uttered his final word on any subject; why, therefore, should prescientific frameworks of thought be so sacred that forever through them man must seek the Eternal and the Eternal seek man? So we said, and, thanks to modernism, it became true of many an anxious and troubled soul in our time that, as Sam Walter Foss expressed it,

> He saw the boundless scheme dilate,
>   In star and blossom, sky and cod;
> And as the universe grew great,
>   He dreamed for it a greater God.

The church thus had to go as far as modernism but now the church must go beyond it. For even this brief rehearsal of its history reveals modernism's essential nature; it is primarily an adaptation, an adjustment, an accommodation of Christian faith to contemporary scientific thinking. It started by taking the intellectual culture of a particular period as its criterion and then adjusted Christian teaching to that standard. Herein lies modernism's tendency toward shallowness and transiency; arising out of a temporary intellectual crisis, it took a special type of scientific thinking as standard and became an adaptation to, a harmonization with, the intellectual culture of a particular generation. That, however, is no adequate religion to represent the Eternal and claim the allegiance of the soul. Let it be a modernist who says that to you! Unless the church can go deeper and reach higher than that it will fail indeed.

In the first place, modernism has been excessively preoccupied with intellectualism. Its chosen problem has been somehow to adjust Christian faith to the modern intellect so that a man could be a Christian without throwing his reason away. Modernism's message to the church has been after this fashion: When, long ago, the new music came, far from clinging to old sackbuts and psalteries, you welcomed the full orchestra and such composers as Palestrina, Bach, Beethoven, to the glory of God; when the new art came you did not refuse it but welcomed Cimabue, Giotto, Raphael, and Michelangelo, to the enrichment of your faith; when the new architecture came, far from clinging to primitive catacombs or the old Romanesque, you greeted the Gothic with its expanded spaces and aspiring altitudes; so now, when the new science comes, take that in too, and, however painful the adaptations, adjust your faith to it and assimilate its truths into your Christian thinking.

Surely, that has been a necessary appeal but it centers attention on one problem only—intellectual adjustment to modern science. It approaches the vast field of man's experience and need head first, whereas the deepest experiences of man's soul, whether in religion or out of it, cannot be approached head first. List as you will the soul's deepest experiences and needs—friendship, the love that makes a home, the enjoyment of music, delight in nature, devotion to moral causes, the practice of the presence of God—it is obvious that, whereas, if we are wise, we use our heads on them, nevertheless we do not approach them mainly head first, but heart first, conscience first, imagination first. A man is vastly greater than his logic, and the sweep and ambit of his spiritual experience and need are incalculably wider than his rational processes. So modernism, as such, covers only a segment of the spiritual field and does not nearly compass the range of religion's meaning.

Indeed, the critical need of overpassing modernism is evident in the fact that our personal spiritual problems do not lie there any more. When I was a student in the seminary, the classrooms where the atmosphere grew tense with excitement concerned the higher criticism of the Bible and the harmonization of science and religion. That, however, is no longer the case. The classrooms in the seminary where the atmosphere grows tense today concern Christian ethics and the towering question whether Christ has a moral challenge that can shake this contemporary culture to is foundations and save us from our deadly personal and social sins. So the world has moved far to a place where mere Christian harmonizers, absorbed with the intellectual attempt to adapt faith to science and accommodate Christ to prevalent culture, seem trivial and out of date. Our modern world, as a whole, cries out not so much for souls intellectually adjusted to it as for souls morally maladjusted to it, not most of all for accommodators and adjusters but for intellectual and ethical challengers.

When Paul wrote his first letter to the Corinthians, he said that he had become a Jew to the Jews that he might win the Jews, and he intimated that he had become a Greek to the Greeks that he might win the Greeks. "I am become," he said, "all things to all men, that I may by all means save some." That is a modernistic passage of adjustment and accommodation. But that is not all Paul said. Had it been all, Paul would have sunk from sight in an indistinguishable blend with the Greco-Roman culture of his day and we should never have heard of him. When he wrote the second time to the Corinthians he said something else:

> Come ye out from among them, and be ye separate,
> saith the Lord,
>   And touch no unclean thing.

Church of Christ, take that to yourself now! Stop this endeavor to harmonize yourself with modern culture and customs as though they were a standard and criterion. Rather, come out from among them. Only an independent standing-ground from which to challenge modern culture can save either it or you.

In the second place, not only has modernism been thus predominantly intellectualistic and therefore partial, but, strange to say, at the same time it has been dangerously sentimental. The reason for this is easy to explain. One of the predominant elements in the intellectual culture of the late nineteenth and early twentieth centuries, to which modernism adjusted itself, was illusory belief in inevitable progress. So many hopeful and promising things were afoot that two whole generations were fairly bewitched into thinking that every day in every way man was growing better and better. Scientific discovery, exploration and invention, the rising tide of economic welfare, the spread of democracy, the increase of humanitarianism, the doctrine of evolution itself, twisted to mean that automatically today has to be better than yesterday and tomorrow better than today - how many elements seduced us in those romantic days into thinking that all was right with the world!

In the intellectual culture to which modernistic Christianity adapted itself, such lush optimism was a powerful factor, and the consequences are everywhere present in the natural predispositions of our thought today. In the little village of Selborne, England, the visitor is shown some trees planted by a former minister near his dwelling, so that he might be spared the view of the village slaughter-house. These trees are suggestive and symbolic of the sentimental illusions we plant to hide from our eyes the ugly facts of life. Especially we modernistic Christians, dealing, as we were, with thoughts of a kindly God by evolution lifting everything and everybody up, were deeply tempted to live in a fool's paradise behind our lovely trees!

For example, modernistic Christianity largely eliminated from its faith the God of moral judgment. To be sure, in the old theology, the God of moral judgment had been terribly presented so that little children did cry themselves to sleep at night for fear of him and of his hell. Modernism, however, not content with eliminating the excrescences of a harsh theology, became softer yet and created the general impression that there is nothing here to fear at all. One of the most characteristic religious movements of the nineteenth century heralded this summary of faith:

> The Fatherhood of God.
> The Brotherhood of Man.
> The Leadership of Jesus.
> Salvation by Character.
> The Progress of Mankind—
> onward and upward forever.

Well, if that is the whole creed, this is a lovely world with nothing here to dread at all.

But there *are* things here to dread. Ask the physicians. They will tell us that in a law-abiding world are stern conditions whose fulfilment or non-fulfilment involve bodily destiny. Ask the novelists and dramatists, and at their best they are not lying to us as they reveal the inexorable fatality with which character and conduct work out their implied consequence. Ask the economists. They will tell us there are things to dread which lead to an inevitable economic hell. Ask even the historians and they will talk at times like old preachers about the God of moral judgment, as James Anthony Froude did when he said, "One lesson, and only one, history may be said to repeat with distinctness: that the world is built somehow on moral foundations; that, in the long run, it is well with the good; in the long run, it is ill with the wicked."

Indeed, cannot we use our own eyes to see that there are things here to fear? For this is no longer the late nineteenth and early twentieth centuries. This is the epoch after the first world war shook the earth to its foundations, and the God of judgment has spoken. My soul, what a world, which the gentle modernism of my younger ministry, with its kindly sentiments and limitless optimism, does not fit at all! We must go beyond that. Because I know that I am speaking here to many minds powerfully affected by modernism, I say to you as to myself: Come out of these intellectual cubicles and sentimental retreats which we build by adapting Christian faith to an optimistic era. Underline this: *Sin is real.* Personal and social sin is as terribly real as our forefathers said it was, no matter how we change their way of saying so. And it leads men and nations to damnation as they said it did, no matter how we change their way of picturing it. For these are times, real times, of the kind out of which man's great exploits have commonly been won, in which, if a man is to have a real faith he must gain it from the very teeth of dismay; if he is to have real hope, it must shine, like a Rembrandt portrait, from the dark background of fearful apprehension; if he is to have real character, he must achieve it against the terrific down-drag of an antagonistic world; and if he is to have a real church, it must stand out from the world and challenge it, not be harmonized with it.

In the third place, modernism has even watered down and thinned out the central message and distinctive truth of religion, the reality of God. One does not mean by that, of course, that modernists are atheists. One does mean, however, that the intellectual culture of the late nineteenth and early twentieth centuries, in which modernism adjusted itself, was predominantly man-centered. Man was blowing on his hands and doing such things at such a rate as never had been done or dreamed on earth before. Man was pioneering new truth and building a new social order. You young people who were not here then can hardly imagine with what cheerful and confident trust we confided to man the saving of the world. So the temptation was to relegate God to an advisory capacity, as a kind of chairman of the board of sponsors of our highly successful human enterprise. A poet like Swinburne could even put the prevailing mood into candid words:

> Thou art smitten, thou God, thou art smitten; thy death is upon thee, O Lord.
> And the love-song of earth as thou diest resounds through the wind of her wings—
> Glory to Man in the highest! for Man is the master of things.

Look out on the world today and try, if you can, to repeat those words of Swinburne and still keep your face straight! At any rate, if ever I needed something deeper to go on than Swinburne's sentimental humanism, with man as the master of things, it is now—a philosophy, namely, a profound philosophy about what is ultimately and eternally real in this universe. We modernists were so disgusted with the absurdities of the old supernaturalistic theology that we were commonly tempted to visit our distaste on theology as a whole and throw it away. But theology means thinking about the central problem of our existence—what is ultimately and eternally real in this universe. And in the lurid light of days like these it becomes clearer, as an increasing number of atheists are honestly saying, that if the eternally real is merely material, if the cosmos is a physical fortuity and the earth an accident, if there is no profounder reason for mankind's being here than just that at one stage in the planet's cooling the heat happened to be right, and if we ourselves are "the disease of the agglutinated dust," then to stand on this temporary and accidental earth in the face of this vast cosmos and try lyrically to sing,

> Glory to Man in the highest! for Man is the master of things,

is an absurd piece of sentimental tomfoolery. And because I have been and am a modernist it is proper that I should confess that often the modernistic movement, adjusting itself to a man-centered culture, has encouraged this mood, watered down the thought of the Divine, and, may we be forgiven for this, left souls standing, like the ancient Athenians, before an altar to an Unknown God!

On that point the church must go beyond modernism. We have been all things to all men long enough. We have adapted and adjusted and accommodated and conceded long enough. We have at times gotten so low down that we talked as though the highest compliment that could be paid Almighty God was that a few scientists believed in him. Yet all the time, by right, we had an independent standing-ground and a message of our own in which alone is there hope for humankind. The eternally real is the spiritual. The highest in us comes from the deepest in the universe. Goodness and truth and beauty are not accidents but revelations of creative reality. God is! On that point come out from among them and be ye separate! As the poet imagined Paul saying:

Whoso has felt the Spirit of the Highest
    cannot confound nor doubt Him nor deny:
yea with one voice, o world, tho' thou deniest,
    Stand thou on that side, for on this am I.

Finally, modernism has too commonly lost its ethical standing-ground and its power of moral attack. It is a dangerous thing for a great religion to begin adjusting itself to the culture of a special generation. Harmonizing slips easily into compromising. To adjust Christian faith to the new astronomy, the new geology, the new biology, is absolutely indispensable. But suppose that this modernizing process, well started, goes on and Christianity adapts itself to contemporary nationalism, contemporary imperialism, contemporary capitalism, contemporary racialism—harmonizing itself, that is, with the prevailing social *status quo* and the common moral judgments of our time—what then has become of religion, so sunk and submerged in undifferentiated identity with this world?

This lamentable end of a modernizing process, starting with indispensable adaptations and slipping into concession and compromise, is a familiar phenomenon in religious history. For the word "modernism" may not be exclusively identified with the adjustment of Christian faith and practice to the culture of a single era. Modernization is a recurrent habit in every living religion. Early Protestantism, itself, emerging along with a new nationalism and a new capitalism, was in its day modernism, involving itself and us in entanglements and compliances with political and economic ideas in whose presence we still are tempted to be servile. Every era with powerful originative factors in it evokes from religion indispensable adaptations, followed by further concessive acquiescences, which in time must be superseded and outgrown. Early Christianity went out from an old Jewish setting into a new Greek culture and never would have survived if it had not assimilated into its faith the profound insights of Greek philosophy. So in the classic creeds, like that of Nicæa, we have a blending of the old faith with the new philosophy, and in that process John and Paul themselves had already played a part. But, alas, early Christianity in its adjustment of its faith to Greek culture did not stop with adaptation to the insights of philosophy. At last it adapted itself to Constantine, to the licentious court, to war, to the lucrative enjoyment of imperial favors, to the use of bloody persecutions to coerce belief. One after another, it threw away the holiest things that had been entrusted to it by its Lord until, often hardly distinguishable from the culture it lived in, it nearly modernized itself into moral futility. Lift up that history, as it were in a mirror, in which to see the peril of our American churches.

It is not in Germany alone that the church stands in danger of being enslaved by society. There the enslavement is outward, deliberate, explicit, organized. Here it is secret, quiet, pervasive, insidious. A powerful culture—social economic, nationalistic, militaristic—impinging from every side upon the church, cries with persuasive voices, backed by all the sanctions and motives most urgent to the self-interest of man, Adjust yourself, adapt yourself, accommodate yourself!

When Great Britain was as mad about the Boer War as Italy is mad today about the Ethiopian War and all the forces of propaganda had whipped up the frenzy of the people to a fever heat, John Morley one night in Manchester faced an indignant, antagonistic crowd, and pleaded with his countrymen against the war. This in part is what he said: "You may carry the fire and sword into the midst of peace and industry: it will be wrong. A war of the strongest government in the world with untold wealth and inexhaustible reserves against this little republic will bring you no glory: it will be wrong. You may make thousands of women widows and thousands of children fatherless: it will be wrong. It may add a new province to your empire: *it will still be wrong.*" John Morley did not call himself a Christian. He called himself an agnostic. But he was far nearer standing where Christ intended his church to stand than the church has often been.

We modernists had better talk to ourselves like this. So had the fundamentalists—but that is not our affair. We have already largely won the battle we started out to win; we have adjusted the Christian faith to the best intelligence of our day and have won the strongest minds and the best abilities of the churches to our side. Fundamentalism is still with us but mostly in the backwaters. The future of the churches, if we will have it so, is in the hands of modernism. Therefore let all modernists lift a new battle cry: We must go beyond modernism! And in that new enterprise the watchword will be not, Accommodate yourself to the prevailing culture! but, Stand out from it and challenge it! For this unescapable fact, which again and again in Christian history has called modernism to its senses, we face: we cannot harmonize Christ himself with modern culture. What Christ does to modern culture is to challenge it.

14

Why Worship?[1]

To begin with, here are two or three quotations from prominent modern intellectuals, which, to say the least, strike one as queer. Professor Wieman of the University of Chicago says about worship, "There is no other form of human endeavor by which so much can be accomplished." Professor Hocking of Harvard, speaking of the finest things in human experience, such as recreation, friendship, love, beauty, says in italics, "*Worship is the whole which includes them all.*" And Professor Tawney of the University of Illinois exclaims about worship, "It is indeed so important that one finds oneself sometimes wondering how any of us can afford to do anything but educate ourselves in this art." Even here in a service of Christian devotion, such words from philosophers sound extreme and strange. Can it be that worship is as important as all this?

To be sure, the Bible is full of it, from the Old Testament's typical call, "O magnify the Lord with me, and let us exalt his name together," to great passages in the New Testament proclaiming God as Spirit, so that "they that worship him must worship in spirit and in truth." Moreover, man everywhere appears as a worshiping creature. Some of us have prayed with Buddhists in their temples, bowed with Confucianists in their shrines, knelt with Moslems in their mosques, worshiped many a time in synagogues, and with all sorts of Christians have shared devotion. What does all this mean? Why do people worship? What does it do? It must do something.

Thinking of worship in its primitive forms, one may give it a primitive explanation and with the skeptical Latins say, *Timor deos fecit*—Fear made the gods. That, however, does not cover the case. Worship is like

1. From *Successful Christian Living* by Harry Emerson Fosdick. Copyright 1937 by Harper & Brothers. Copyright renewed © 1964 by Harry Emerson Fosdick. Reprinted by permission of HarperCollins Publishers.

agriculture, in primitive days primitively carried on but so universal and indispensable that the most modern and sophisticated societies cannot outgrow it. "Fear made the gods" may explain some worshipers, but not President Eliot of Harvard, remembering the days when Phillips Brooks conducted worship in the university chapel and saying, "Prayer is the greatest achievement of the human soul." Can it be that worship is as important as that?

We do not treat it so. We Christians, who occasionally or even customarily are found in the sanctuary, do not take worship so seriously as *that*. As for the world outside, few practices seem to the average man farther from the vital centers of human need or less applicable to the critical problems of mankind's peril. Yet, here today we are worshiping, while men of intellectual light and leading say that there is no other form of human endeavor by which so much can be accomplished. How can this be?

Let us confess that many people, some of whom are doubtless here, get little or nothing out of worshiping. The reasons are not far to seek. For one thing, while such folk come to church, they may not worship. A prevalent American disease has been called "spectatoritis." We go to see football games played, but do not play ourselves; to hear dramas performed, but do not share in the performance. In one realm after another we are only spectators. So in church we watch the ministers and the choir indulge in prayer and praise. Thus to go to church is an external act, but genuinely to worship—to be lifted by the companionship of kindred and aspiring souls until the spiritual tides rise within, and reefs and sandbars which lower moods could not surmount are overpassed and the soul sails out into God's great deep—is an inward, creative experience. Many receive little or nothing from their formal devotions because they suffer from spectatoritis.

Others receive little from what they call worshiping because they do not fulfil the serious conditions for receiving anything. They saunter in, saunter through, saunter out. Great things, however, are greatly arrived at. We cannot saunter in to a Beethoven symphony, saunter through, and saunter out, or, if we do, it will amount to nothing. One of our leading psychologists tells of a country boy, unversed in music, who, coming to live in Boston, early in his stay attended a concert by the Symphony Orchestra. It meant nothing to him. It might as well have been produced by tom-toms and harmonicas for all he received from it. Yet around him he saw people to whom such music was like the breath of life, and he determined that if music could mean so much to others he would find the secret of it for himself. For a full season, therefore, he attended concerts of the orchestra, each evening taking with him a musical friend. Gradually the light began to break, some here, some there, until a new world opened up before that youth, a marvelous world of which he is now the grateful citizen, and which he might easily have missed. He took music seriously enough to fulfil the conditions of understanding and of enjoying it. Do we suppose that we can worship the Most High God in spirit and in truth on lesser terms?

Furthermore, many receive little from their worshiping and are discouraged concerning it because they expect a unanimous record of success. That, however, is too much to expect. James Russell Lowell once entered a European cathedral and had a high experience there, which in his poem, "The Cathedral," he has made immortal. Even to James Russell Lowell, however, that did not always happen. Once in Switzerland I climbed the Rigi. It was a foggy day upon the summit; we could not see fifty feet. Is the Rigi, then, a failure? If you have even been there when the day was clear and the vast horizons opened up their unforgettable panorama of majesty and beauty, you know that it is worth climbing the Rigi many times to get that view once. So to any soul worship is not always a success, but he who knows what can happen when the great hours come and the amplitudes of the spiritual life are open to one's vision, knows that its consequence is worth habitual continuance and patient waiting.

Well, this is the question: Is worship a realm of experience so supremely important? What is it, indeed, that we are looking for in worship? With multitudes of people the very nub of the problem lies there—they do not even know what they are looking for when they are worshiping.

In the first place, in worship we are reminded of values that the world makes us forget. The word itself means worthship, the recognition and appreciation of real worth. In this sense we all do inevitable and habitually worship, but see what the casual secular world does to this process in us! It puts first things last and last things first, makes the great seem small and the small great, often holds a penny so close to the eye that we cannot see the sun, and every day magnifies the transient and carnal at the expense of the abiding and spiritual, until our sense of worth is twisted and awry. Often in hours like that, when one can hardly tell what one is living for, one knows why the Psalmist cried, "My soul longeth, yea, even fainteth for the courts of the Lord." We do desperately need to be brought face to face with the Most High and there reminded of the real worths that this world makes us forget.

All this has been specially vivid to me since, some years ago, I visited the Orient. At home I had taken services of Christian worship for granted. They were as much a part of life as the hills and trees. In the Orient, however, I reached places where one could not take for granted an assembly of Christian people, meeting together in kindling aspiration and praise. I never shall forget, after returning home, the first stirring service of great worship. I felt like a branch, long fallen from a bonfire and well-nigh gone out, that now had been thrown back into the community of conflagration and had caught fire again. On a recent Sunday morning a missionary family spoke with me here. They had been seven years on a lonely outpost station and now, home on furlough, they had been attending their first service of worship. They were in tears. Once more to feel the assembly of the church around them and the "joy of united reverence," once more in a fellowship to be reminded of the high things that a man ought not to forget, was to them a renewing experience.

Recently one of our city's clergymen created a sensation by suggesting a moratorium on preaching. Probably he will not get it. It may be he would not like it if he did, but I think I know what he is driving at. He is concerned because the great multitude of our Christian people do not really worship. They must have some one forever talking to them. They do not know how to make high use of the power and joy of united reverence. His concern was justified.

Here in this church we are at work seven days and nights a week. On an average, ten thousand people enter our doors each week. We have only one sermon. That is not overworking preaching—thirty-five minutes of it in a week. I am not sure, however, that we are getting what we planned to get when we so arranged it—the worship of the people in the services where there is no preaching. I am concerned about you. Do not try to tell me that you do not need to worship. I know you too well. I know this city too well. You deeply need to be reminded of high and Christian things that they world makes you commonly forget.

In the second place, in worship one is carried far enough away from the close-ups of daily life so that one can see the horizons around his living and thus, reorienting himself, regain his sense of direction. Canon Streeter of Oxford said recently, "The greatest need of mankind today—socially and individually—is a true sense of direction." One does not go about achieving that merely by working harder, as though, lost in a fog, a boat tried to get its bearing by driving about more furiously. Nor does one get it by thinking more meticulously, as though, faced out of countenance already by the immediacies of this troubled time, we put our minds still more closely on them and analyzed them further. If we are lost in the woods, the one thing we must seek first is altitude. We must find a hill, if we can, and on it a high tree, but somehow we must get altitude so that around the confusing close-up of the woods we can see horizons and perspectives. Recovering the sense of direction is always a matter of elevation and vision.

Who does not need *that* today in his spiritual life? The canyons of these city streets sometimes become to us unbearable; the pressure and tension of their noisy restlessness we cannot endure. We must away where there are distance and altitude, sky and horizon. So one lives with the terrific problems of our time—personal and social, economic and international—until the whole world seems mad and all its ways incoherently insane. But coming, it may be, into a service of great worship, see what may happen to a spirit so confused! "O God, who art, and wast, and art to come, before whose face the generations rise and pass away"—what a world of long distances and vast horizons this is! The world speaks no such language.

> Before the mountains were brought forth,
> Or ever thou hadst formed the earth and the world,
> Even from everlasting to everlasting, thou art God!

So the transient and temporal are not all; the insanities of man many a time have reared themselves against the Most High, and still the Most High he is. "While we look not at the things which are seen, but at the things which are not seen: for the things which are seen are temporal; but the things which are not seen are eternal." So one can know the east from the west and the north from the south and take up his way again. "Strengthened with power through his Spirit in the inward man"—so there are resources which can enable one to carry on.

Forgive me if I make the matter seem easier than it really is. I know that effectively entering into worship and getting from it large consequence is not simple. There are many difficulties, theoretical and practical, in the conduct of public worship, which keep even the intelligent from understanding and the spiritual from profiting. We have to use symbolism, for example, and symbolism becomes obsolete and for many loses meaning. Nevertheless, do not miss a major matter because of a minor difficulty. You need spiritual altitude. Almost more than anything else in the world, for your living, day by day, you need spiritual altitude. And the casual secular world does not supply it, but rather bears you down with its externalisms and vicissitudes. As you care for your soul, therefore, have a hill to climb—a familiar hill habitually climbed—from which returning, to face once more the wrath of devils and the scorn of men, the great affirmations of the faith echo in your heart: "Therefore will not we fear, though the earth be removed, and though the mountains be carried into the midst of the sea. . . . The Lord of hosts is with us; the God of Jacob is our refuge."

In the third place, worship is an experience that rebukes the evil in one's life. Out in the world it is dangerously easy to get by with one's conscience. There are plenty of other people living worse lives than we are. There is ample moral darkness in which the gray shades of our compromises and surrenders do not show up. We are pretty good out in the world. But let a man really worship and his worse self comes face to face with his better self, and his better self comes face to face with something better still. That is a humbling experience without which there is no spiritual health. No man can be his best unless he stands over and over again in the presence of that which is superior to his best.

To be sure, the relationship of worship to the good life is not simple. Worship has often been used as a substitute for righteousness, as though God could be placated by pious observances and flattering praise. Alongside those passages in the Bible, therefore, where worship is exalted, one must in all honesty put others where it is vehemently condemned: Isaiah, crying against his people's ritual observances amid their cruel social injustices, and, saying in the name of God, "Who hath required this at your hand, to trample my courts?"; Micah, drawing his appalling picture of the worship of his day, saying in contrast, "What doth the Lord require of thee, but to do justly, and to love kindness, and to walk humbly with thy God?"; Jesus, saying, "If therefore thou art offering thy gift at the altar, and there rememberest that thy brother hath aught against thee, leave there thy gift before the altar, and go thy way, first be reconciled to thy brother, and then come and offer thy gift."

If any one here needs that kind of message, let him take it! Of all substitutes for a good life, worship is the most superstitious and hypocritical. "Be not deceived; God is not mocked" by empty hymns, anthems, and prayers. I suspect, however, that that kind of message is not the prime need of most of us. Who here commonly practices worship as a substitute for a good life? The realistic fact is that the modern man does not worship much at all.

At times, therefore, I should like to appeal to Jesus against the universal application of his own words. I think he would understand my meaning. Lord, I would plead, you say that if I come to worship at the altar and there remember that my brother hath aught against me, I am to leave my worshiping, first go be reconciled with my brother, and then come and worship. But I beg of you, let me worship a little first! For this man you call my brother I do not like. I am not sure I wish to be reconciled with him. He has wronged me, and I hate him. I cannot blow on my hands and go out to be reconciled with him. Something transforming must happen within me before I can do that. Let me worship a little first! For if I could worship until I saw myself so needing to be forgiven that I should be willing to forgive, if I could worship until I saw you upon your cross, even there forgiving, if I could be lifted a little above the rancor and vindictiveness of common moods, until pity for our kindred human frailty grew real to me and the love of God were shed abroad in my heart, then I might go out and be reconciled to my brother. Let me worship a little first!

The other day a man sent $12,000 to the United States Government in payment of duty on goods he had smuggled in. Why did he do that after he had gotten safely away with his theft? I happen to know about that—he had been worshiping. Once a journalist in this city checked out on a Sunday morning from his hotel with only a little money in his pocket, and, buying a deadly poison at a drugstore, started for the park to take it and die. But passing a church and seeing a crowd waiting, his journalistic curiosity was so aroused that he entered, and, to his astonishment, found himself being lifted by the worship of the congregation. When he went out he poured the poison down the nearest manhole, took a new grip on life, and a week later, his battle for a new character and a new career well started, he came to tell me about it. As he went out from that rememberable interview, I recall thinking that, after all, the poets are wiser than the cynics, and that more things are wrought by prayer than this world dreams of.

Finally, worship is an experience that rededicates life and so releases its power. You must have felt, as I have, that such a theme as we are dealing with runs so counter to the powerful drift and tendency of our time that it is hard to make headway with it in our thinking, and harder yet in our living. All the more because of this powerful, antagonistic drift, we need to apprehend the import of our truth. Professor Hocking is right in saying that all man's life can be reduced to two aspects, work and worship—what we do ourselves, and what we let the higher than ourselves do to us; what we actively labor at, and what we receptively are enriched by, what we are aggressive about, and what we are spiritually hospitable to; what belongs to us because we achieve it, and what we belong to because it has mastered our loyalties. This boat of human life is rowed with two oars—work and worship—and the trouble with many of us is that we are rowing with one oar, and, going around in circles in consequence, are getting nowhere.

If any of us are finding in life radiant meaning and clear direction, then somewhere, somehow, we have found values, greater than ourselves, to which we belong and our loyalty to which emancipates our powers. If some one says that this experience came to him outside the church, very well! The church's worship is the endeavor to make easily and habitually available to all people the liberating experience for which we plead, and while Isaiah had his in the temple, Jesus had his alike in the temple and on Galilean hillsides. Be sure of this, however, he who knows only the work side of life is a slave; it is worship, wherever you find it, that gives life elevation, emancipation, and release.

When we deal with the physical world, we grow great by the things we master. We say to this material power, Go, and it goes; and to that, Come, and it comes; and we grow powerful thereby. But when we deal with the spiritual world, we grow great by the things that master us, by the goodness, beauty, and truth that lay hold on us and to which we loyally belong. That experience is the essence of worship.

To be sure, there are modern endeavors to explain worshiping in terms of pathological psychology. When men grow weary of the gross and realistic world, so this explanation runs, they escape to the imagination of a superearthly world where all is right and God is love and goodness is triumphant, and in that visionary world of fiction and fantasy they find retreat from the too hard realism of their actual existence. To this I say in answer, Granted that worship, like everything else, can be perverted; granted that it can be pathologically misused. The Bible often grows fiery with blazing denunciations of that. But when a man like Isaiah goes into the temple, sees the Lord there high and lifted up, finds there the great loyalty to which his life belongs, and, saying, "Here am I; send me," comes out again to live one of the supreme lives of history, that and the reduplication of that across the centuries, in the supreme characters and careers of service, cannot be explained in terms of pathology—or, if it can, then may God make us all sick, for there is nothing this world needs much more! We verily are sick for the lack of this thing we have been pleading for, sick with complacency over things, sick with satisfaction concerning our technological mastery over material, sick for the lack of reverence toward things that ought to be revered, of adoration toward things that should be adored, of loyalty toward things alone worth living for.

Can it be that still this truth of which we have been speaking seems irrelevant to some? Some of us cannot live without great music, but there are others to whom it is irrelevant. Some of us cannot live without great books and the magnificence and loveliness of nature, but there are others to whom they are irrelevant. Some of us cannot live without great worship, but there are others to whom that is irrelevant too. Yet what a commentary such irrelevances are! "O magnify the Lord with me, and let us exalt his name together."

15

An Appeal from the Present to the Future[1]

S OME OF THE GREATEST books in the world's literature have been written for a curious and suggestive reason: men ahead of their time,
facing disbelief and opposition from their contemporaries, knowing that
they would not live to see the triumph of the cause they stood for, set their
faith down in a book. Thus they have borne witness against the blindness
of their own time and have appealed for their vindication from a hostile
present to the future.

So Job, facing the contradiction of his friends, cried,

> Oh that my words were now written!
> Oh that they were inscribed in a book!

So Jeremiah, despised and rejected of men, speaking the wisest words uttered in his time on public and spiritual issues, only to be scorned, heard
God say to him, "Write there all the words that I have spoken unto thee
in a book." So Isaiah's prophecies came to be preserved. Had his contemporaries believed him and followed his counsel, the chances are we might
hardly have heard of him. Constrained, as he was, however, by the antagonism of his own time to make appeal to generations yet unborn, he heard
the command, "Now go, write it before them on a tablet, and inscribe it in
a book, that it may be for the time to come for a witness for ever."

For such characters one feels instinctive admiration. To see a truth
which your contemporaries fail to see, to believe in its victory even when
you do not expect to witness it, and to put it in a book as an appeal to
future generations, shows moral vigor. I wonder if ever in history there
was greater need than now for this type of character.

---

1. From *Successful Christian Living* by Harry Emerson Fosdick. Copyright 1937 by
Harper & Brothers. Copyright renewed © 1964 by Harry Emerson Fosdick. Reprinted by
permission of HarperCollins Publishers.

Such men, whose quality we admire, were not, in the ordinary sense of the word, optimists. Certainly Job, Jeremiah, and Isaiah never had that reputation. Their dire denunciations of their people's sin and their realistic pictures of the consequence of evil make it impossible to ascribe to such prophetic souls soft and easy attitudes. They did not think that everything was coming out all right. They did not trust in any vague, ameliorative drift. They had not even heard the comfortable and fallacious doctrine of inevitable progress. They were exceptionally hard-headed men, living exceptionally difficult and painful lives, but they were strong in character and the cause they believed in they believed in so much that on its behalf they appealed to the future and fell on sleep leaving their faith in a book for their children's children to see.

Let us note the contrast between that type of character and some of our contemporary attitudes and tempers.

For one thing, in light of such characters we feel the contrast between strong patience and fretful impatience. One does not mean that these prophetic souls in a cheap sense were patient. Often they were tremendously impatient with the follies, sins, and cruelties of their generation, but in a profound sense a strong patience was part of their character. They did not give up a great matter because it failed to come off successfully all at once. Around their towering souls lesser men rose and fell away—men, that is, who thought that oaks should grow like mushrooms and who, when some great matter failed to take root and flourish, were ready to sign themselves, as one letter coming to me a week ago was signed, "duped, cheated, and embittered."

Isaiah tells us of impatient people in his day saying about God, "Let him make speed, let him hasten his work, that we may see it." Jeremiah in his time described impatient people as saying, "Where is the word of the Lord? let it come now." In Jesus' day, impatient people pressed around him, supposing "that the kingdom of God was immediately to appear." How natural, how familiar, and how contemporary that is! About international peace, a decent economic order, Christian union, and many other great causes, multitudes of people, disappointed with hope deferred, that makes the heart sick, are crying, Let it come now!

Over against such fretful impatience we set today another type of character, which says in effect, Probably I shall not live to see the triumph of my cause; nevertheless, I nail that flag to the masthead; for it I stand, in it I believe, on its behalf I work, and, as for its triumph, I entrust the vindication of my faith to the future—write that in a book.

Characters of such quality realistically fit this kind of universe. Far from being the sentimental optimists they sometimes are accused of being, they are the realists. For a fretful impatience is one of the most unrealistic attitudes a man can take in this kind of world. Leonardo da Vinci, about 1500, foresaw airplanes, drew pictures of them, and put them in a book! Think of the impatient cynics since, laughing that faith to scorn, crying, Let it come now and let us see it! Well, four centuries and more have passed and Leonardo has been vindicated. He was the realist. Always the strong, wise, patient, farseeing people have been the realists.

At this point we run on one of the basic mysteries of the universe, which I do not pretend to understand. If God was going to make the cosmos, why didn't he make it, as Aladdin built his palace, with magical swiftness, finishing it overnight? I do not know. But, obviously, the method of creation in this cosmos is of another kind altogether, so that of every great matter Keats' description of the Grecian urn holds true—"Thou foster-child of Silence and slow Time." That puts on us a heavy strain. We are in a hurry. We think too much of ourselves to wait for the fulfillment of our desires some centuries after we are dead. This universe is not scaled to the short measurements of our desires. It is far too big a task for some of us to live in a world to whose God a thousand years are but as yesterday when it is past, and as a watch in the night.

In some valleys in the Tyrolean Alps it takes four hours for sunrise. Four hours the cosmos works in bringing up the dawn. But a few years ago some cinema men took a moving picture of that sunrise which is run off, they say, in ninety seconds for the delectation of the crowds. That is our way. We say to the universe, Hurry up! How natural it is! Yet we might well seek the wisdom of the long look and the patient mind. After all, not the impatient cynics but Isaiah, Jeremiah, Jesus, and the Leonardo da Vincis have been realistically right.

In the light of such strong characters we feel a contrast, also, between essential belief in the power of right and lack of that belief. Most people, I suspect, think of right as good, beautiful, lovely, ideal, but not as powerful. They leave out of their concept of right one factor which has always been present in the thinking of strong characters. In Victor Hugo's "Hernani" is a splendid passage which we might summarize by saying, Nothing in this world is so powerful as an idea whose time has come. That conviction has always belonged to strong characters. They have been certain that the adjective "mighty" belongs with the word "right" and the adjective "self-defeating" belongs with the word "wrong." Lowell put it,

> Truth forever on the scaffold, Wrong forever on the throne,—
> Yet that scaffold sways the future, and, behind the dim unknown,
> Standeth God within the shadow, keeping watch above his own.

For the time being we may omit the divine guarantee of the victory of the right.

> Truth forever on the scaffold, Wrong forever on the throne,—
> Yet that scaffold sways the future—

stop it there if you will. Even on the basis of observed human fact how often that has been the case!

Can we not, for example, observe the self-defeating nature of wrong in the case of war? War is wrong—that is clear. But something more than that is clear, which was not evident a few years ago—war is self-defeating; it is suicidal; no one can really win a war; the more war flourishes the more it fails; the bigger wars grow, the more intolerable they become; the more we improve the implements of war, the more they ruin those who wield them. War is not simply wrong, it is a *cul de sac*; there is no thoroughfare down that road. If some one says that in the world today war seems very powerful, I answer, Of course, and if, because of that and because a first experiment with a League of Nations has not made the war system collapse like Klingsor's palace before the magic spear in Parsifal's hand, you are out of hope, then you *are* out of hope. But some of us are not. War is self-defeating. War itself makes war on war. The more I watch the accursed thing, the more I echo Carlyle's words, "No Lie can live for ever." I do not expect to see peace splendidly victorious in my lifetime, but if wagering were possible I would wager with you. I would put it in a book. War will be subdued along with torture chambers, religious persecution, slavery, and many another curse that once possess the earth.

Recall that day when Gladstone allied himself with the Liberal Party in Parliament and, in the face of the bitterest opposition, made his brilliant appeal for Lord Russell's Reform Bill. "You cannot fight against the future," said he. "Time is on our side. The great social forces which move onwards in their might and majesty, and which the tumult of our debates does not for a moment impede or disturb—those great social forces are against you; they are marshalled on our side; and the banner which we now carry in this fight, though perhaps at some moment it may droop over our sinking heads, yet it soon again will float in the eye of heaven ... perhaps not to an easy, but to a certain and to a not distant victory. He turned out to be realistically right. Lord Russell's party was overturned but the next year an even more sweeping Reform Bill was passed and put into effect.

In light of such characters, one feels a further contrast between clear insight into the momentous forces in a generation's life and lack of such insight. Almost never has a noisy thing in any generation been the really significant event. In what generation has the future ever belonged to the blatant, the ostentatious, the spectacular? Always the incredible has happened and some idea, some movement so obscure that contemporaries have almost missed it, has turned out to be the major factor in the epoch. Pick out any significant era in human history and it is a safe generalization that the great mass of its people had not the faintest idea what was important there. What turned out in the end to be of world-transforming consequence was so quiet, so unostentatious, that contemporaries well-nigh missed it.

For myself, then, I cannot realistically be a cynic. I cannot believe that this generation is utterly different from every other. I hear the raucous noises which fill the public places of the world, but when I think of what our children's children will say about this age when they look back on it, I am sure we would be utterly astounded could we listen. Always it is what the contemporaries miss that turns out to be important.

So in his time Kepler was content to say that since God had waited thousands of years for an observer of his stars, he, Kepler, could afford to wait a century for a reader. So Spinoza was banished from his home city because he was unorthodox, and after his death it was almost a hundred years before people dared mention his name with respect, much less acknowledge their indebtedness to him. So Milton got a paltry ten pounds for "Paradise Lost," and Mozart, dying in poverty, was buried in a pauper's grave. As for Socrates and Jesus, think what their contemporaries did to them!

See all this, the cynic says, What is the use, then, of believing or endeavoring great things? To which I answer, Friend, these things that the contemporaries missed were going to be the masterpieces of the world. It takes a long time for a masterpiece to win its way into the acceptation of mankind but when it is there it stays. Ten thousand lesser things rise and pass away but the masterpieces stay. Great things come slowly but they last.

Therefore pray for eyes lest we should miss the really momentous affairs of our day. Be sure of this, they are not spectacular or noisy. They are not in the limelight on the public stage. What if the great thing in our time were not violent nationalism but the slowly emerging idea of a world community? What if the great thing in our time were not economic chaos but the slowly growing idea of a new, amazing technology, socially employed to abolish poverty? What if the great thing in our time were not our miserable religious partisanships but the slowly growing possibility of a more united Christendom? What if our children's children, looking back, should say, This was the creative movement of that age to which the future was to belong? Should *that* be so, our generation would be running true to history. For my part, I am willing to write that in a book.

In light of such characters we see a still further contrast between deep faith in a divine Coöperator and lack of such faith. In this is involved the essential meaning of belief in God. If the universe were merely materialistic, how could we wager anything on the future? All the dice would be loaded against us. Then we little people, blowing on our hands and trying to do something, would be pitting our small strength against the dead-set and vast indifference of the universe. Even if we won a victory it would be only temporary. We could not ultimately whip an antagonistic universe—be sure of that! But if at the center of creation there is a Spirit and purpose with which we can coöperate and so become in Paul's great phrase, "God's fellow-workers," then we can wager our lives upon the future. Such confidence, I think, is the essential meaning of belief in God.

Some of us as children became aware of a purpose in our home, an underlying intention in the family, that we should be educated and that, thus competently trained for some special work, we should live useful and creative lives. That undergirding purpose in the family did not take responsibility from us; it put responsibility upon us. We worked hard, but always with this stimulating fact in view—we were coöperating with a purpose greater than our own, by which everything we contributed was caught up, backed up, and carried on. We never would have gotten anywhere without *that*. And now in maturity we face a similar situation in the universe. In this age-long and tremendous task of building here a decent earth for men to live upon, are we human beings merely going it alone in a cosmos that cares naught for us and ultimately will wreck our work? Is there not an eternal purpose by which what we sow is caught up, backed up, and carried on?

Let no one here dismiss this profound problem from his philosophy of life as a light matter. Whenever any one becomes socially in earnest so that he finds himself nailing some flag to a masthead, saying, I never expect to see the victory of this cause in my lifetime but I wager my life that the future belongs to it, he faces the need of that philosophy. Every great character in history who has sacrificially appealed from a hostile present to the future has, so far as I know, believed in some kind of cosmic backing, whether he called it "philosophic dialectic" or God.

Who does not need that? Sometimes the human river runs in smooth courses, but then come rapids and cataracts and in the tumult of the time men are tempted to cry, This is the end of the world! Yet commonly such days have been the beginning of new eras, with new prospects and new courses. Suppose you had been a Hebrew in Egypt under Pharaoh, trying to make bricks without straw, when Moses rose in indignation against an intolerable situation and killed a taskmaster—how could you have guessed what would come of that? Suppose you had been a Jew in Palestine when the great prophets taught, who, far from seeming great to their contemporaries, were derided and scorned; when Jerusalem fell before invading armies and the prophets were powerless to do more than keep a small remnant true to their spiritual heritage—how could you have guessed what would come of that? Suppose you had been at Calvary when the power of the Roman Empire was concentrated on the fearful business of putting a glorious life to a disgraceful end—how could you have foreseen what would come of that? In a thousand troubled eras, when the hearts of men turned to water in them for fear, how could we have previsioned the outcome? Yet always the outcome has been a new epoch with larger prospects, new hopes. Our human life is a river; rapids and cataracts do not stop it—you can put that in a book.

Two travelers, one a veteran and the other a novice, were climbing the Pyrenees. At night they were caught on one of the peaks and had to sleep upon a ledge. Toward morning a storm came up and the howling wind that the old Latins called *Euroclydon* wailed fiercely among the heights. The frightened novice waked his friend and said, "I think it is the end of the world!" "Oh, no," said the veteran, "this is how the dawn comes in the Pyrenees!"

To be sure, I am almost afraid to preach this sermon. I dread that some may think I mean that everything is coming out all right. Upon the contrary, our whole Western civilization may wreck itself. If it does, it will not be the first civilization gone to ruin, trying to escape the laws of God, in accordance with which what men and nations sow they reap. So Egypt fell and Assyria and Greece and Rome. Yet even that was not the end of the world. It takes more than such rapids and cataracts to stop the river. Modern life has richer hopes and possibilities than Egypt could have guessed or Rome have dreamed. Many a time civilizations have fallen and the fierce *Euroclydon* has howled across the world, but still the dawn was coming up, and the only realists of the time were those who kept their eyes on the things to which the future belonged.

Take a fresh look, then, at the universe! This, I think, is the inner-most fact about it: it is built up of and replete with law-abiding conditions, waiting to be fulfilled to bring amazing consequences. This afternoon I shall speak over the air, and then from places like South Africa and Chile, Alaska and Newfoundland, I shall hear from the auditors. Fifty years ago all the conditions which make that possible were in the cosmos waiting—waiting to be fulfilled to bring the amazing consequence. That kind of universe we inhabit. It is not the dour and dreadful thing discouraged souls suppose. The world is a bundle of potential miracles. The world is a cosmic pipe organ, on only a few of whose stops we have played while hundreds more are waiting. There is no telling what divine surprises are waiting. What a universe it is! How unworthy we are to live in it! How it calls for intelligence, for faith, for character—those three—without which it will give us nothing good but with which it will become indeed a bundle of progressive miracles!

16

Giving the Highest a Hearing[1,2]

A FTER THESE MANY MONTHS of comparative seclusion and quiet, you would hardly expect me on this first Sunday morning of our reunion to speak about the affairs of the world, with its social upheavals and clamorous problems—you have been living in that world yourselves. You might, however, expect me to speak about another realm, where I perforce have been, where one must stop being active and become receptive, stop being strenuous and become quiet, stop talking and listen.

Centuries ago Elijah had that experience. In the midst of a strenuous life, in a turbulent time, an emergency befell that put a stop to his active social struggle and led him on a long journey to the wilderness of Sinai. There, as though to picture his own life to him, the noisiest things in creation passed before him—a strong wind, an earthquake, a raging fire, and God in none of them. Then in the narrative come the words which to succeeding centuries have rightly seemed among the most significant in the ancient literature of religion: "And after the fire a still small voice. And it was so, when Elijah heard it, that he wrapped his face in his mantle, and went out, and stood."

So, long ago, a man came to the place where he gave the Highest a hearing.

Such is our predisposition that we naturally estimate listening to a still small voice as both more easy and less significant than dealing robustly and effectively with the world's hurly-burly. But even a moment's serious reflection indicates that giving the Highest a hearing is about as important an event as ever happens in human life.

1. From *Successful Christian Living* by Harry Emerson Fosdick. Copyright 1937 by Harper & Brothers. Copyright renewed © 1964 by Harry Emerson Fosdick. Reprinted by permission of HarperCollins Publishers.

2. The first sermon preached after a long, enforced vacation.

The turning points in scientific progress have been associated with it. One man, compelled by the prevalence of a pestilence to suspend his teaching labors at the University of Cambridge, and forced, like Elijah, to take a vacation in the country, sat in his garden and, seeing an apple fall, listened to a still small voice about what it meant. To scientists as to other people, this noisy world is a stimulating place in which to do things but a poor place in which to hear things. When, therefore, we trace back momentous scientific achievements to their creative origins, we commonly come to secluded and listening minds like Copernicus, or Newton, or Darwin, each in his own realm giving an idea a hearing.

Even more obviously is this experience associated with the turning points of man's spiritual progress. A new idea succeeds in catching the inner ear of some attentive soul and, lo! an era begins. It may be a carpenter who listens until the flowers on Galilean hillsides speak to him and he is captured and commanded by an inner voice so that he will die on Calvary rather than deny its imperious validity, and centuries afterwards men still know that if they would listen to what he heard they would find the things that belong unto their peace.

This profound, interior experience of sensitive audition to the Highest is not easy, nor is it a mystic matter isolated from the world. It goes to the very quick of life. Of all of us in this audience it is true that sometime or other, in a way large or small, we have had a spiritual disaster; some ethical failure, some moral tragedy has befallen us; and as we carry back our memory to the causative beginning of that lamentable time we know that it need never have happened if we had listened to an inner voice. To be sure, there were urgent clamors persuading us to what we did but there was another kind of voice—our better selves, our finer moods, our common sense, our consciences—divine mentors that almost always speak in a quiet tone. In this sense, the most deplorable tragedies that befall mankind come because we will not give the Highest a hearing. Even railroad crossings advertise the warning, "Stop, Look, Listen."

With this much preparation of our thought, let us now walk about our truth and see it, one aspect at a time. In the first place, we must take it for granted that the appeal of the Highest will habitually come to us quietly, modestly, without obtrusiveness. We might have made this world other than it is, with the loveliest things shouting at the top of their voices and evil things shy and retiring, but, as it is, the actual world behaves far otherwise. When the New Testament presents the divine method of approach to life, it pictures God as saying, "Behold, I stand at the door and knock: if any man hear my voice and open the door, I will come in to him, and will sup with him, and he with me." So the Divine is not obtrusive; he bursts into no man's life unbidden; he is reserved and courteous. He knocks at the door to see if any one, listening there, may care to welcome him.

How true to our experience this picture is becomes evident when we consider the divine voices in detail. Beauty does not shout at us. The fairest things we know are not clamorous—the loveliness of flowers, or of woods at sunset time, or of poems, or of moving symphonies, or of a mountain stream

> In the leafy month of June,
> That to the sleeping woods all night
> Singeth a quiet tune.

Consider how beauty stands upon our doorsills and knocks to see if some one within may be interested.

Our finest moods are not clamourous. Our worst moods are. Our tempers, passions, and despairs can blow like howling hurricanes and thunder like Jove, but when the hour of visitation from on high arrives and a nobler mood is sours, it almost always speaks with a still small voice.

Our consciences commonly are difficult to hear. Especially in the world's continuous din and furious explosions, a man must take heed if he is to hear his conscience speak. The young son of a friend of mine said once to his father, "What is conscience?" to which my friend answered, "I am not quite sure what conscience is, but, son, whenever that telephone bell rings, you take down the receiver and listen."

All the familiar appeals of the Highest speak in calm tones. The admonitions of experience, the reasonableness of common sense, the appeal of a new idea slipping silently into the mind, the call of a social need, described by Wordsworth as "the still, sad music of humanity," and even those more tremendous advents of God into select souls, to their own transformation and the shaking of the world—seldom are such approaches of the Highest noisy.

When, then, in such a boisterous world a man tries to keep his soul alive, he finds that one of the central problems is maintaining a sensitive ear for these quiet voices. If to any this fact seems a sweet and gentle thing to say, it shows how little its import is understood. The great characters of history that most have stood like towers of brass against the tumult of the world have so been built. Each of them had an inner voice so imperiously clear that when the pinch came and the cries of the crowd were against him, that voice was more commanding to him than all else. So in times like these, when strident voices make hubbub of the days and the ugliest things are often the loudest, and what men would have us think and do is dinned into our ears with noisy propaganda, there is desperate need of men and women who have learned this deep, essential art of spiritual life, giving the Highest a hearing. Only so come free souls, free in the only way souls can be free, their dominant control not clamor without but a voice within. So Elijah, of the still small voice, was the most titanic moral force in Israel's history for four centuries.

In the second place, note that however practical we make this truth and however far from creed and church we carry its illustration, we are dealing here with the essence of religion. If nothing else were accomplished this morning, I should be glad for the benefit of some to translate the meaning of prayer into the terms of this truth. Few things make more evident our obsession with strenuousness, activity, aggressiveness, than our habitual treatment of prayer as though it meant mainly or merely our talking to God. Even when we pray, many of us will not drop our aggressive self-assertiveness. But look at the Hebrew prophet: "After the fire a still small voice. And it was so, when Elijah heard it, that he wrapped his face in his mantle, and went out, and stood." *There* was momentous prayer, with momentous social consequences, but Elijah was not talking; he was listening.

You will understand, then, that our appeal in this matter is no mere modernist endeavor to escape the intellectual difficulties involved in self-assertive praying. Rather, this is part of the great tradition. As the ancient Psalmist said, "I will hear what God the Lord will speak." To be sure, this is not the only kind of prayer. Communion with God is a great sea fitting every bend in the shore of human need. But he who never listens when he prays never prays. Here is a meaning of prayer which makes it an indispensable attitude of the soul. In a very noisy world prayer is giving the Highest a hearing.

Indeed, here is a function of the church which, recovered and exalted, would enable us to meet one of the deep needs of human life. Men and women desperately need help in giving the Highest a hearing. One evening I had finished my serious reading and was casually scanning the advertisements of a magazine when to my surprise my eye fell on this statement about an insurance company: "We are an old, conservative company, operating on old-fashioned principles." "Why!" said I, "here is a strange thing; almost everything advertised today is praised because it is new. Buy this article, the advertisers say; it is the latest thing, in the most modern mode. But here is another note—'We are an old, conservative company, operating on old-fashioned principles.'" There may be things, then, which we profoundly need that are not merely modern. In automobiles we would wish the latest smartness, but not necessarily in insurance companies, on which security depends. So, while I am a modernist in religion to my finger-tips, if it be old-fashioned to conceive the central function of the church as helping men and women in a turbulent time to hear their divine voices within, whose quiet persuasion makes the best personal character and social progress that we know but whose appeal can be so easily drowned out by the world's uproar, then so be it!

None of us can easily learn this fine art of listening to the Highest. It takes technique; it requires practice; it calls for a fellowship of friends in kindred endeavor trying to make divine voices imperiously clear. Even listening to music is an art. But to listen to an inner voice that talks of high motives in a world ridden by low motives, of cleanness in an age blatant with uncleanness, of Christ in a social order that still crucifies him—in such a world, where the lowest so commonly is the loudest, we need a fellowship to help us give the Highest a hearing.

In the third place, not only personal religion but, to a degree that at first one might hardly guess, personal character is involved in our truth. If some one has been saying that it is possible to over-emphasize giving the Highest a hearing, that on that point the New Testament itself issues a warning which the preacher had better heed: "Be ye doers of the word, and not hearers only, deluding your own selves," I agree. Hearing truth without doing anything about it is a peril to character. But, after all, lack of aggressiveness is not our prevalent disease; activism is our chronic state of mind; whatever else we are, in church or out of it, we are doers. Without much fear of betraying this audience into a lack of balance, therefore, I plead that, while of course it is a danger to be a hearer and not a doer, for many of us it is even a greater peril to try to be doers—restless, impatient, aggressive doers—when all the time the interior voices of divine guidance have been drowned out in the world's uproar, so that like a ship with its compass out of order we go plunging strenuously on, off our course.

When we trace back great character to its genesis, we commonly come to a listening ear. We think, for example, that we know much more about child psychology than our forefathers did, but many a story in the Bible goes to the quick of a child's life. Once a young boy named Samuel, for whose coming his mother had prayed before he was conceived and who had been dedicated to the service of God while still she carried him beneath her heart, was taken to the temple to serve the altar. So, that little lad, thus prepared, heard God talking to him in the night. It is an old story but how timeless the record sounds—"And the Lord came, and stood, and called as at other times, Samuel, Samuel. Then Samuel said, Speak; for thy servant heareth."

Not only does the genesis of great character commonly go back to such experience, as many of us know well, but the maintenance of great character goes back to its repetition. Indeed, my sermon had come thus far on when I remembered that somewhere in William James' *Psychology* was a famous passage in which the essence of the will was interpreted in terms of the capacity to pay attention, so that when we try to understand what free will is—the power of choice—we come at bottom to this mysterious faculty within us by which we pay attention to one thing rather than another. So, turning to his *Principles of Psychology*, I found it: "Effort of attention is thus the essential phenomenon of will." That is to say, what we give habitual hearing to inevitably determines our choices.

Then to my surprised eyes the next sentences presented my sermon from a psychologist's point of view. For William James describes a man in a passion, the turbulence of cupidity or lust or temper noisy within him, in a fit mood to ruin himself withal, and fighting off all listening to the cool, calm voices of reasonable ideas. Concerning this familiar situation James says, "Passion's cue accordingly is always and everywhere to prevent their still small voice from being heard at all," to which he adds, "The strong-willed man . . . is the man who hears the still small voice unflinchingly."

That is pertinent to every one of us. That situation is reduplicated how continually in this company! On how many hearts are memories engraved of tragedy that need never have taken place had we but listened! What tragedies today are on their way, due to arrive tomorrow, that would never happen if some soul would now listen! Strange, penetrating word of the Master, so often quoted, so little understood: "He that hath ears to hear, let him hear."

Finally, I do not see how any man can maintain his courage and morale in a day like this if he hears nothing but the noisy voices. Recovery of morale is not commonly associated with uproar but with quiet places. So the twenty-third Psalm strikes a universal note—

> He leadeth me beside still waters.
> He restoreth my soul.

Elijah himself was a whipped and beaten man when he left for the wilderness, a disillusioned public servant, a tired liberal, a disheartened prophet ready to quit, but he heard something in that still small voice that sent him back to his work again like an army with banners, his soul restored. Far from feeling deserted, he was convinced now that there was a strong minority in Israel that had not bowed the knee to Baal, that the cause he had thought was lost need not be lost at all, that, though he had been defeated in a moral battle, he could still be victor in the moral war. He came back to fight again, confident that the future of the world belonged, not to the noisy forces, but to the still small voices.

Human history can be told in terms of the successive victories of quiet forces over their noisy enemies. Repeatedly in science, as well as morals, in politics as well as religion, some new idea has come so silently that it caught at first but the inner ear of one who listened and then was heard by but a few, like the twelve disciples about our Lord in Galilee, and all around these still small voices raged the antagonistic world. But again and again the ultimate victory has come, not to the shouts upon the street corner, but to the voice heard in the inner chamber, as Jesus said.

Has some one here been saying that the supreme need today is for courageous minds to build a better social order and a new international system? You know how cordially I agree with that. But because we do so desperately need men and women of undiscourageable faith and effort whom this world can neither whip nor tame, we need this deeper thing we have been speaking of.

> Breathe through the hearts of our desire
> Thy coolness and thy balm;
> Let sense be dumb, let flesh retire;
> Speak through the earthquake, wind, and fire,
> O still small voice of calm!

17

The Modern World's Rediscovery of Sin[1]

A TRAGIC FACT LIES behind the New Testament's understanding of Christ: "Thou shalt call his name Jesus; for it is he that shall save his people from their sins." So, like the Star of Bethlehem seen against the night, the very birth of Jesus is seen against the background of man's sinfulness.

In this regard a clear contrast exists between the Christianity of our fathers and the liberal Christianity to which most of us have become accustomed. To our fathers sin was a horrid reality, a deep-seated depravity in human nature in which from birth we all shared and from which only the grace of God in Christ could save us. The old theology was centered in that conviction, the old hymnology expressed it, and the old pictures of hell made lurid the endless horror of sin's consequence.

Liberal Christianity, however, has on the whole been complacent about human nature. Modernism grew up in an era when progress was in the air, with evolution as the process behind life and education as the means of liberating life. It was the time of fresh discoveries, idealistic hopes, alluring prospects, dominant optimism. So our liberal Christianity has everywhere been characterized by an ideal view of human nature. To be sure, there were failures to be outgrown, inadequacies to be overpassed, ignorance to be illumined, selfishness to be corrected, but no such tragic depravity at the heart of human nature as made Pascal call man "the glory and the scandal of the universe . . . a monster, even beyond apprehension." Now, however, we face a difficult era, with such cruel and depraved things afoot in the world as some of us have never seen before. I do not believe the old theology; I am glad many of the old hymns have

1. From *Living Under Tension* by Harry Emerson Fosdick. Copyright 1941 by Harper & Brothers. Copyright renewed © 1968 by Harry Emerson Fosdick. Reprinted by permission of HarperCollins Publishers.

been dropped from the hymnal never to return; the old pictures of hell are to me an incredible anathema. But how can one be content with this soft, sentimental, complacent type of liberalism that thinks comfortably of human nature? It is said that a modern teacher wrote an elaborate book on religion's meaning, and when his friends called his attention to the fact that in it he had not even mentioned sin, he said: "Oh well, there ought not to be any such thing." Say what we will about our fathers' incredible ways of stating the matter, they were infinitely more realistic about the facts of human nature than is such superficiality.

Today we and our hopes and all our efforts after goodness are up against a powerful antagonism, something demonic, tragic, terrific in human nature, that turns our loveliest qualities into evil and our finest endeavors into failure. Our fathers called that sin. If you have a better name for it, use it, but recognize the realistic fact.

Certainly, every path that man is traveling today leads to the rediscovery of sin. There is scientific inventiveness, for example. How full of hope for man's abundant life that once seemed! Here were gifts in endless affluence that he could use to build a better earth. But see to what tragic misuses they are put! We have achieved electric lights but they have not lighted the way to justice and brotherhood. We have mastered refrigeration but it has not cooled the angry passions of man's heart. We have built towering skyscrapers but they have brought us no nearer God. We have achieved giant power, but it never has been powerful enough to save a single man from his inner evil. Rather, we invent airplanes and get bombers, invent automobiles and get tanks, explore chemistry and get incendiary bombs, create world-wide intercommunications and use them to produce blockades and famines. We blame our forefathers for even believing in infant damnation, but we, as it were, with our organized starvation and our bombing of cities, have taken over the job ourselves, using for our purposes the very gifts that were to have saved us. There is something demonic in human nature that can use the best for the worst.

Or consider education. A century ago in Boston, Horace Mann believed that crime could be practically eliminated in this country by increase in the size and number of our tax-supported schools. Well, we have built tax-supported schools in size and number beyond anything that Horace Mann dreamed, yet we are not through with crime. Indeed, add up all that we spend in America on education. That is an immense sum. Add to that all we spend for churches. That is another great sum. Add to that all we spend for charity. That is another large sum. Yet when we have added them all together, we are told that crime in this country costs us $500,000,000 more than them all. Moreover, into that crime goes every educated ingenuity from which education was to have saved us. Here again the old proposition proves true that the worst calamities that fall on man come from a combination of high intelligence and low desires.

Or consider man's spiritual qualities: loyalty, responsiveness to great leadership, patriotism, the sense of community and fellowship. In themselves they are beautiful. Man as been saved from egocentric selfishness by his ennobling capacities to care for something other than himself in race and nation. Yet look across the world and see what this incomprehensible monster, man, is doing with them! Recently a Christian Japanese woman called upon me. She was one of the most surprised persons I ever talked with. She had just come from Japan and for the first time was seeing from an outside point of view what Japan is doing in China. She told me what one sees inside Japan—the unifying and adoring loyalty to the Emperor, the kindling consciousness of solidarity and community, the sense of Japan's sacred mission in the Far East, the high crusade to save the Chinese people from their false rulers, the aged and kindly mothers who arise in the early morning, even in winter, to speed with their prayers the brave young fellows going to the front. So all wars are fought, and the most damnable things on earth done, whether in China or here, not by stark evil only but by the finest qualities in us, twisted to unholy uses by this demon that our fathers called sin.

Surely our fathers were not shadow-boxing. We have mastered physical nature in ways they never dreamed, but we are still up against human nature. What to do about that? Physical nature is a realm of necessary law-abidingness, where we can trace cause and consequence and make ourselves masters of that outcome. But human nature presents us with something new and different—freedom, that high and terrible gift of freedom, that can take the holiest and make the worst out of it, and an inner wrongness that, so misusing freedom, brings to futility and grief the fairest hopes of men. I am sure that this view of human nature is the first step to a realistic outlook on what life is, and it can add the dimension of depth to our insights.

In the first place, it adds the dimension of depth to our thought of our social problems. All easy-going trust in social panaceas—as though, if we changed this circumstance a little here, or altered that environment there, or took a short-cut yonder, we would come to a happy social consequence—goes back to a radical failure to see that there is something wrong in human nature itself. If someone will not believe this because it sounds so much like the old theology, will you believe it if it is said to you in other terms by the new psychology? Early theologians called this inner depravity of human nature "original sin," and said we are all born with it. Freud calls it "the id," and he says we are born with it too. If you want to call this fact of primitive, selfish, and often perverted emotion, that makes war on ourselves and the world, "id" instead of "original sin," by all means do so, but recognize the realistic fact: A racial inheritance—Freud is right about that—rolling down from generation to generation, ruining all the fair hopes of men, and in the end the source of these tragic disappointments when our fine schemes of social reformation are wrecked.

How easily some people have supposed that the human problem could be solved! In 1893, Hiram Maxim, speaking of his new and terrible gun, said: "It will make war impossible." That is all he knew about human nature. In 1892 Alfred Nobel, the inventor of dynamite, said that his new dynamite factories might end war sooner than peace congresses. That is all he knew about human nature. This incomprehensible monster, man, has it in him to use for wholesale destruction things a thousand times worse than dynamite and Maxim guns.

Or carry our thought to a higher level. We tender-hearted liberal Christians, brought up in the humane tradition, deeply feeling the ills of the underprivileged, are constantly tempted to suppose that if only everybody were privileged that would solve the human problem. Now, I too hate these inequalities that curse our life. They are the shame of our civilization. I want decent housing for everyone, decent subsistence for all. No man worthy of the name can be content until we have a more equitable distribution of this world's goods. But as we hope to escape one of the most tragic disappointments in human history, let us not suppose that that alone will solve the human problem. It is difficult to be a good Christian if one is underprivileged, but do you think it is necessarily easier to be a good Christian if one has all the world's goods? Does the fact that one can live on Fifth Avenue or Park Avenue or Riverside Drive necessarily mean the solution of those elemental problems of human nature that, like God himself, are no respecters of persons? If you think it does, then you do not know some people on Park Avenue, Fifth Avenue, and Riverside Drive. We are going to run from one social disappointment into another until we see that behind all outward evils there is a need in human nature that only a profound spiritual renewal can meet. That is true not only of blind Bartimæus begging by the roadside but of Zacchæus in his counting house and Dives in his palace. That is true not only of a coarse woman of Samaria coming to draw water from the well; it is true of Nicodemus in his study, needing to be reborn.

Recognition of this tragic fact about human nature, far from being the beginning of discouragement, is the beginning of hope. The man who is afraid to face it shows himself unprepared to confront the realistic facts. But the New Testament, which from beginning to end faces it, far from being discouraged, is the most radiant and triumphant book in the world. For the New Testament started with the tragic fact: "Even when we were dead through our trespasses." That is where it started. And then it saw that a saving power had been released into the world through Christ, which could redeem individuals and move them over until they were no longer part of the problem but part of the answer, and then could take groups of people and move them over until on the whole they were no longer part of the problem but part of the answer. In that the New Testament saw the promise of a redeemed manhood. It started with the night and then it saw the Star and was glad. That is the realistic approach to life. As another put it: "To expect a change in human nature may be an act of faith; but to expect a change in human society without it is an act of lunacy."

In the second place, this truth adds the dimension of depth to our thought of ourselves. No man understands himself until he has seen that he shares this inner wrongness, from which he needs to be saved. Once, runs the old story, there was a religious hermit, so holy that the evil spirits sent to tempt him were discouraged. They could not break him down. They tried the passions of the body and failed, the doubts of the mind and failed again. Then Satan himself came and said to the evil spirits: "Your methods are crude. Permit me one moment." So, going to the holy hermit, Satan said: "Have you heard the good news? Your brother has been made Bishop of Alexandria." That got him. He, a poor hermit, and his brother, Bishop of Alexandria! Jealousy swept over him like a flood. He could stand almost anything except the success of his brother. What we are saying is that no man understands himself until he has faced the presence in himself of some such share in what our fathers called "original sin."

In this regard we often deceive ourselves because sin can take such a high polish. Sometimes sin is gross and terrible. It staggers down the street; it blasphemes with oaths that can be heard; it wallows in vice unmentionable by modest lips. Then prosperity visits sin. It moves to a finer residence; it seeks the suburbs or gets itself domiciled on a college campus. It changes all its clothes. It is no longer indecent and obscene; its speech is mild; its civility is irreproachable. But at heart it is the same old sin, self-indulgent, callous, envious, cruel, unclean. As anybody may easily observe, sin takes on a very high polish.

The tragedy in all of this is that my sin is not simply mine individually but may share in the corporate evil that is destroying the hopes of the world. For selfishness, carnality, cruelty, are not merely individual; they roll from generation to generation, spoiling all man's hopes, and my curse is that I can be part of this major problem of the race instead of part of the answer. Indeed, by nature I am part of the problem unless I am saved from being that by some power of spiritual renewal. All seers have said this. I would almost venture that every major work of literature in the world's history has been centered in this truth. Start with the great tragedies of Greece and think your way down through *Macbeth, Othello, Hamlet, Faust, Le Misérables, Romolo, The Scarlet Letter, Anna Karenina,* what you will. The great seers have faced the centrality of sin in human life, and our tragic capacity to be part of the corporate evil that spoils the world.

The recognition that this is true about man, far from being the beginning of discouragement, is the beginning of hope. This is what the New Testament is all about, trying to get man to take a serious view of himself and then seriously seek a cure for his malady. Go through this highly respectable congregation here and who of us does not need this? For some here have sinned secretly and are afraid it will be found out publicly, and their lives are anxious, wondering if and when the ambush may be sprung. And some here have sinned and they cannot forgive themselves, and, like a bell buoy tolled by the restless motion of uneasy waves, remorse is tolled by their tossing consciences. And some here have sinned and sin begins to grow habitual, so that, as one plus one plus one adds up an accumulating sum, sin mounts and mounts in size and in control. And some here have sinned and have tried to keep the consequence to themselves and they cannot; it overflows and hurts their family and friends, as though once more the innocent are nailed to the cross because of them. Every man or woman here understands what I am saying. This is not Greek to anyone. No one understands himself till he sees this. No one understands Christ's central meaning apart from this. It would be making earnest with the gospel indeed were we to take ourselves and his saviorhood thus seriously. As Clement of Alexandria said long ago about Christ: "He hath changed sunset into sunrise."

This leads us, in the third place, to note that our truth adds the dimension of depth not only to our thought of our social problems and ourselves but to our thought of Christianity and of Christ himself. Liberal Christianity in some of its forms has succeeded in reducing religion to little more than a kind of spiritual cosmetic, adding a touch of heightened color to a countenance not radically changed. For if one starts with a complacent view of human nature, religion inevitably becomes an addendum, comforting to some, reassuring to those who need it, but not an indispensable salvation. So men treat it as superfluous. But if what we have said today is true, then Christianity has a dimension of depth to it. It is an indispensable salvation from that inner curse that is wrecking human hopes.

Why should moderns shrink so from the word salvation? What is scientific medicine? It is salvation, and when a man takes the measure of disease and what it does to men, sees it flowing across the generations, bringing its recurrent miseries on humankind, he thanks God for the saving hope of surcease from pain, and cure for malady, that scientific medicine brings. Every major activity of man is concerned with salvation from human tragedy, and the Christian gospel has a specialty as real as scientific medicine. It came to save men from that inner wrongness that curses human life.

I should suppose we would feel the need of that today. The human drama is not playing itself out well and no mere shifting of the scenery will fix the drama up. Something profound must happen to the actors if it is to come out right. We need Christ's radical remedy for our radical disease: one God, high over all, in loyalty to whom we are saved from our ruinous idolatries, one human family of every tribe and nation, in devotion to which we are saved from our destructive nationalisms and racisms, and within ourselves the gospel of forgiveness and power—those two, forgiveness and power—by which, one by one, men and women are transferred from being part of the problem to being part of the solution.

In these terrific days especially we should not be content with formal religiousness. Saviorhood is the essence of Christ, and to face our deep needs in earnest, to repent sincerely and seek forgiveness and power, to take seriously him who for our sakes suffered, the just for the unjust, that he might bring us to God—that would be entering into the meaning of the gospel.

18

The God Who Made Us and the Gods We Make[1]

Throughout the Bible there are two ways of speaking about God that at first sight seem in direct opposition. On the one side is the theological affirmation, God is and he made us. On the other side is the psychological affirmation, We make gods and serve them. "In the beginning God created the heavens and the earth," so the Bible starts, but throughout its course we keep running on another point of view. "Where are thy gods that thou hast made?" says Jeremiah; or again: "Shall a man make unto himself gods?"

If this were only ancient history, we could let it lie, but few things go more deeply into our contemporary situation than this contrast between a theological approach to God—one deity who made us—and a psychological approach to those elements in life which gain our devotion and become our gods. God made us—that is theology. We make gods and worship them—that is psychology.

Much of the unreality of our religious experience springs from our failure to note this difference and face its implications. A friend of mine sometime since visited the Planetarium and came back deeply impressed by that visual exhibition of the universe's unity and order. "Man!" he said, "the word chance doesn't fit it! There's mind behind that!" So, he believes theologically in God. But does that necessarily imply anything about those inward deities that he really serves? Upon the contrary, that man conceivably might make drink his god, or lechery his god, or money his god, or nationalism, or race, his god. We theologically can believe in the God who made us, while all the time psychologically we are controlled and dominated by the gods we make.

Sometime since in a national poll 91 per cent of the ballots registered faith in God. One suspects that that average represents the American population as a whole. Man! they would say about this universe, the word chance doesn't fit it; there's mind behind that. Nevertheless, look at the American population! Do not all the political bosses believe in God? I never met a roaring, American militarist who did not believe in God. Sing Sing is not filled with atheists. Men who cherish bitter, menacing, anti-Semitism, one of the most malign influences in America, earnestly believe in God. And we Protestants would all consent: "I believe in God the Father Almighty, Maker of heaven and earth." This practical unanimity of consent to theological faith in the God that made us does not prevent our lives from being dominated psychologically by the gods that we make. Were Jeremiah to say to us again, "Shall a man make unto himself gods?" we should have to answer, Jeremiah, that is what we are doing all the time; there is no habit more familiar in human life.

This aspect of human nature, which is obscured for us because in our vocabulary the word "God" is restricted to the deity who made us, was very vivid to the early Christians in the Greco-Roman world, when polytheism was in full flower. Bacchus was not simply drunkenness; he was a god. Venus was not simply lust; she was a goddess. Mercury was not simply slick and crafty contrivance; he was a god. And Mars and the deified Caesar were gods, and all those major and dominating factors in life that take possession of men, control them, and call out loyalty, were deities in the Pantheon. The accumulated imagery of a rich mythology made easily vivid to those early Christians the situation we are trying to make plain to ourselves today—on the one side, the God who made men; on the other side, the gods that men make. Every day the early Christians could see gods that men made controlling the personal, religious, political, and international life of their time. The god question was critical with them. They had to choose between gods. Should they serve Bacchus or Venus or Mercury? Should they worship Caesar or become devotees of Mars? When instead they chose the God revealed in Christ, *that* was no mere matter of theology as so often it is with us, but was a profound inward, if you will, psychological matter that penetrated to the pith and marrow of their daily life.

The polytheistic language has now largely gone. Sometimes I think it is a pity. It is the only language that is fitted picturesquely to display what we confront in this modern world. To how many is the nation their real god—and that not alone in Nazidom. Let a man, indeed, look down inside his own life. Who is really God there? Commonly not the theological God, belief in whom we may have inherited or persuaded ourselves to by argument, concerning which the New Testament itself says: "The devils also believe, and tremble." Commonly some psychological god is the real one, claiming the honest-to-goodness allegiance of our lives. Until a man has faced the god question thus, he has not been serious about it.

Let us take a further step, and with greater precision try to describe those elements that constitute, in this deeper sense, a man's real god. Wherever a man discovers anything in life on which he relies, his central dependence and deepest satisfaction, and to which he gives himself, his central loyalty—that is his real god. Those two elements always constitute the essential psychological meaning of one's genuine god: one's central reliance and one's central devotion. "He restoreth my soul"—one way or another, a man soon or late says that of his real god. "Not my will, but thine, be done"—one way or another, a man says that to his real god. That is why we say that a man makes drink his god. It can mean his central reliance and his central devotion. That is why we say that a man makes science, or art, or music, or some humanitarian cause his god. It can become his main dependence and his main devotion. When the god question is thus described in inner and psychological terms, it is no matter simply for church on Sunday; it penetrates into the pith of every day's most common attitudes.

Indeed, let us light up this matter by considering what psychological atheism would mean. Theological atheism we often speak about. That means a materialistic philosophy that reduces the universe to the fortuitous self-arrangement of physical elements. But psychological atheism is much more intimate and penetrating. Psychological atheism means a day-by-day life that, whether its possessor believes in the theological God or not, never has found anything on which centrally it can rely, and to which centrally it can give itself. The psychological atheist has no God-experience within, no deep source from which he lives, no major loyalty for which he lives. That kind of life, where a man finds *nothing* that restores his soul, *nothing* that commands his devotion, is one of which it may be said that the man had better never have been born.

I should hate to be a theological atheist and think the universe a mere matter of chance, but if I had to choose, I had rather be that than a psychological atheist. Indeed, a whole sermon might well be preached about a religion for those people who cannot believe in God. There are such folk. They go to the Planetarium and return unconvinced. Even the order, unity, symmetry, law-abidingness and intelligibility of the cosmos leave them unpersuaded. They do not believe in the theological God. Yet how lovely some such folk are! How much we should hate to lose them from the circle of our families and friends! As one watches them one sees that while they do not have our theological God, in a profound sense they do have a psychological god. They have found in life a deep reliance and a deep devotion—some goodness, truth, or beauty they have found, some art, some science, some humane cause, some inner source of satisfaction from which to live, and some worth-while objective for which to live. I am sorry they do not believe in the Eternal God who made us, but sometimes I would like to show such people to some Christians, and say to the Christians, Look at them! There, at least, as far as it goes, is a genuine God-experience. There, at least, is a deity, such as it is, that really commands a man's life. And as for us Christians, professional believers in God, who have inherited a faith in God or persuaded ourselves of it by argument, see how ineffectual that mere theological God is until he has become what in Christ he always seeks to become, a real, interior God, our inner reliance and our day-by-day devotion.

The practical upshot of all this is that this genuine God-experience is never inherited. It seldom lies at the end of an argument. It comes as a satisfaction meeting a profound personal need. I suspect that few people ever get it who have not needed it in some difficult crisis. I know a man, for example, who was once a confirmed alcoholic. He drank one bottle of gin a day, and then two, and when he started to drink three he was concerned, and thought he would stop. He found he could not stop. That frightened him so that he went to the best medical experts he could find. They hospitalized him, diagnosed him, treated him, and finally came back with the verdict: He was a hopeless alcoholic. All his friends agreed with that; he was a hopeless alcoholic. All the experts agreed. And when he looked inside his own life, he had to agree. Now that man had always been an agnostic. He did not have the theological God. But in his crisis he needed God, some vital God-experience, a new reliance and a new allegiance. So, alone one day with all this converging testimony about his hopeless alcoholism pressing in upon him, he went down on his knees in a desperate endeavor to change gods—from Bacchus to God, from this god he had made, to the God who made him and could remake him.

Explain it as you will, that man has never taken a drink since. He says he has no desire for one. Were you to meet him you would never suppose that this distinguished-looking gentleman had ever been through anything like that. As for the medical men, like good scientists they confess that they are astonished. And as for his agnosticism, you should hear him talk about God—quietly, with a deep sense of mystery, not supposing that he knows much about theology but absolutely sure that whereas a power greater than himself had hold on him, another power greater than himself got hold of him. Since the God that made him has remade him, his God is real, a reliance, and a devotion.

Our experience need not be dramatic and critical like that, but there is nothing the church of Christ needs more deeply today than men and women who have done more than inherit a theological God. How *real* is your God? "He restoreth my soul"—does he mean that? "Not my will, but thine, be done"—does he mean that? "Be ye transformed by the renewing of your mind"—does he mean that?

Let us now take a further step and note the critical importance of this truth for the large affairs of the world today. Indeed, I suspect that this sermon started from my reading of Hitler's book, *Mein Kampf*. I picked up the unabridged edition of *Mein Kampf* rather casually, but when a man has once started it, how can he lay it down? Here is presented with amazing frankness a man's soul and his philosophy of life. At the very heart of it, beating like a pulse in every paragraph, is this fact: that man has a god. Every time he thinks of that god his soul tingles, and to that god he has given the last ounce of his devotion. *Mein Kampf* is a story of one of the most absorbing god-experiences in our generation. But the god is the Aryan race. The only hope of mankind, Hitler says, lies in the Aryan race. Every possibility of mankind's advancement hangs upon the supremacy and dominance of that race. The supreme crime is the pollution of the purity of that race with alien blood, and the one devotion most worthy of human allegiance is the spread, sovereignty, and power of the Aryan race. The only ultimate test of right and wrong, says Hitler, is whether a thing does or does not assist the ascending glory of that one supreme god. With unabashed frankness he praises organized lying, mendacious propaganda, fitted to the passion, prejudice, and ignorance of the mob, if only it will help that race. With unqualified candor he glories in what can be done with a population by systematic terrorizing, if only it will help that race. Again and again he uses the words "fanatic" and "fanaticism" about himself and about his followers as words of praise, especially when with unbounded rancor he reviles the Jews, because anything is right that helps the Aryan race. That end justifies every means. As for the state, his theory is that it is only the political instrument to make possible in the world the sovereignty and supremacy of that race.

Reading *Mein Kampf* makes one wish, indeed, that polytheistic language were native to our tongue. No other can adequately picture what we are facing in this generation. The gods are in the field. Mankind's central question is the choice of gods. Out of the heart of every other problem rises this problem: Who shall be our god—these deities that we have made, or the one God, who revealed himself in Christ?

Do not, I beg of you, leave that matter stranded overseas with Hitler. Hitler is not the only one who makes race his god. Mussolini is not the only one who makes a nation his god. Stalin is not the only one who makes an economic class his god. A capitalist can do that as thoroughly as a Communist. No city that Paul ever traveled through, filled with temples to the deities of the Pantheon, was ever more replete with altars than is this modern world. And now, as in ancient times, the Christian gospel, when it keeps its purity, comes to this generation, saying, There are the gods that you have made, but there is one God who made you—all races, all nations, all classes, all men. Not Mars or Caesar, but the God of all mankind revealed in Christ, he alone is God.

If we should take that seriously it would be no mere matter of theology. Should we be earnest about that, it would shape and mold our attitudes as individuals and our policies as nations. To the Christian pastors in the Reich prisons and concentration camps today, because, like the Christians of old, they cannot worship Caesar, the god question is very practical. The god question has no business not to be practical. See these gods that rend the world asunder! They cannot save mankind. As a matter of most practical fact, they cannot save mankind. Many people today talk as though the present situation were denying the Christian gospel. Rather, it is confirming the Christian gospel. See these alternative and substitute gods! "By their fruits ye shall know them." They cannot redeem the world. As a realistic fact only one God can save the world: the God of all mankind revealed in Christ.

Finally, let us come back to our own individual lives and contritely confess the superficiality of much of our popular Christianity. You recall Charles Lamb's whimsical remark that his children were to be brought up in their father's religion, if they could discover what it was. It is not difficult to discover a man's formal, conventional, traditional religion. That can be put into theological speech. But how difficult it sometimes is to discover about a so-called Christian what his genuine, inner, if you will, psychological religion is, his real reliance and his real allegiance.

Mr. Julian Arnold, long attached to the United States government service in China, tells the story of a Chinese bandit who was wounded in an encounter with some soldiers and taken to a Methodist missionary hospital. There after some weeks his broken leg mended and he was restored to normal condition. He was so grateful that he vowed that never again would he hold up a Methodist. Word of that vow spread through the countryside, so that whenever he did hold up anyone the victim protested that he was a Methodist. So the bandit went back to the hospital to find out how he could distinguish a Methodist when he met one. They told him that a Methodist would always know the Lord's Prayer and the Ten Commandments. The bandit, therefore, memorized them in Chinese, and at the next encounter he exclaimed to the victim: "You recite the Ten Commandments and the Lord's Prayer or Heaven help the spirits of your ancestors!" Such external tests of Christianity are really translatable into Western life. We know them well. And over against these superficial conformities, these traditional signs and symbols of our faith, how profound an experience it is when a man in some significant hour comes into personal confrontation with the God who made him!

One remembers Hugh Latimer's preparing a sermon for the next Sunday to be preached at the Royal Court, and hearing a voice that said: "Be careful what you preach today, because today you are going to preach before the King of England." But listening further he heard a voice that said: "Be careful what you preach today, since you are going to preach before the King of kings." That is a real experience, where one rises from facing the god we have made to face the God who made us.

It is impossible that a company like this should come together without some being in a moral and practical crisis involving that kind of choice. So midway in his experience came the turning point of Tolstoi's life. He had believed in the theological God, but now he faced something deep and interior. As he put it: "Five years ago, a strange state of mind-torpor began at times to grow upon me. I had moments of perplexity, of a stoppage, as it were, of life, as if I did not know how I was to live, what I was to do." Who does not know that kind of experience—as though life stopped you in midcourse and confronted you with the inquiry, What now are you going to do with me? There came the turning point in Tolstoi's life when, from the gods he had made, he faced the God that made and could remake him.

Do not, I beg of you, say that I have said that all the gods we make are evil. They are not. The love of home and friends, great music, great books, great art, the loveliness we find in nature, many a deep satisfaction in the human spirit, many a fine loyalty in human life—they are good. But to the Christian the God who made us includes them all, is the fountain of them all, overarches them all. Every lovely thing is a pathway to him; every lovely thing is a revelation of him. We did not make him. He made us—he "inhabiteth eternity"; his "name is Holy"—that is magnificent theology, but, continues the Scripture—and this is the psychology of it—"I dwell . . . with him also that is of contrite and humble spirit."

19

God Talks to a Dictator[1]

THIS IS NOT THE first time in history that the world has faced the military conquests of dictators. Long ago a Hebrew prophet lived through an era like ours, when his people were assailed by the Assyrians, but unlike most of us he achieved a standpoint from which to view the scene, that was distinctive of his religious prophethood—he heard God talking to the dictator.

Granted that in an absolute and literal sense no man can know what God would say to anyone! Yet this is one of man's distinctive attributes, that he can erect himself higher than himself and see the situations that confront him, not simply from a level stance but from above, as they might look to God. That is what a prophet is for—to help people see their contemporary world in wide perspective from a height, as God might see it. So Isaiah heard God talking to the dictator. "The Assyrians came down like the wolf on the fold," so that Judea lay under the thralldom of a conqueror, and in distress and confusion, as among us now, everyone was talking about him and to him. But history has thought it worth-while to record only what the prophet heard God say to him: "Ho Assyrian, the rod of mine anger, the staff in whose hand is mine indignation!"

The Jews hated that conqueror. He seemed altogether wild and law-less; he threatened their temple and their culture; his victory meant to them the downfall of their choicest values; he was to them anti-God, as though some volcanic evil, some demonic force, had escaped from God's control and was running amuck in the world. They felt about him as we feel about Hitler. Then Isaiah heard God talking to him, calling him, as Dr. Moffatt translates it, "my club in anger, the rod I wield in wrath." So that

1. From *Living Under Tension* by Harry Emerson Fosdick. Copyright 1941 by Harper & Brothers. Copyright renewed © 1968 by Harry Emerson Fosdick. Reprinted by permission of HarperCollins Publishers.

dictator was not merely wild and lawless; he had not escaped the sovereignty of God; he was a rod in God's hands; God had picked him up; God was using him; God could lay him down again. The dictator himself did not know this. Says Isaiah, "other plans has he, and other aims!" But even amid his devastations God talked to him as though to say, You are my instrument; I am using you; I took you up, and I can throw you down.

Like all typical religious language this is picturesque metaphor and simile. We may not interpret it to mean that God uses evil means to good ends. In two ways we deal with evil, sometimes choosing it as a method, as Jesus' enemies chose his crucifixion to secure a result they wanted, sometimes confronting it, as Jesus himself confronted the cross, not choosing it but forced to face it, and turning it to the purposes of man's salvation. The choice of evil for good ends is always wrong; the use of evil, when it is thrust upon us, to high purposes is one of the noblest forms of moral victory. It is in the second category, not the first, that we should place Isaiah's vision of God as he says to the Assyrian conqueror, You are my rod.

In the first place, Isaiah saw God using that conqueror as a just punishment on Judea for its sins. "Ho Assyrian, the rod of mine anger." That was a dreadful thing for the prophet to have to say to his own people, but he said it. He was like a faithful psychiatrist dealing with one of us when we blaze out with indignation against someone who, we think, is wronging us. For the psychiatrist says, Wait a moment; that was your own fault; you brought that on yourself. So Isaiah spoke to the people. They suffered their tragedy, he said, because they deserved it.

Unless we can see that truth about ourselves today, I am sure we have missed one of the major meanings of our catastrophe. We brought this disaster upon ourselves.

As a matter of historic fact, it was only by giving that interpretation to the conquerors that the Jewish prophets achieved the monotheism they have bequeathed to us. For in those days the theory was that there were many gods, each nation having its own deities, and the theological question then was which nation's gods were most real and powerful. The answer to that polytheistic question was naturally made evident in war. If one nation conquered another, clearly the gods of the conquerors were real and strong, and the gods of the conquered weak. So when Assyria triumphed over Judea, the popular conclusion was swift and clear—the gods of Assyria must be real; the gods of Israel must be futile. Monotheism never could have come from that interpretation of the conqueror.

The great prophets gave us monotheism because they saw the conqueror from another point of view. They said not that he disproved the one true God, but that he represented the inevitable punishment of the one true God on his people's sin. The victory of Assyria was to the prophets not evidence of God's weakness or abdication, but of God's terrific reality as the impartial administrator of ethical cause and consequence. The one God of Israel, they cried, is still the God of all the world, but he is a God of moral law; not even a chosen people can escape his punishments! When, then, the Assyrian conquered Judea, and all the people were tempted to cry, That proves the gods of Assyria to be real! the prophet said, Rather that proves that we have sinned, and that the Eternal God of righteousness plays no favorites in this world, but brings down his judgment even on Judea when she rebels.

As a matter of historic fact that is the way we got monotheism—from prophets penitent enough to acknowledge that their catastrophe was the one God's just punishment on their own people's sin. And that is not ancient history. Some today say that Hitler and Mussolini prove that the gods of naziism and fascism are the true gods. Others say that these conquerors with their cruel devastations prove that there is no God at all. The prophetic vision is needed afresh to see that what the dictators really prove is that we all have sinned, that this is a morally law-abiding world, that cause does bring consequence, that God cannot be mocked, that what we sow we reap, that our present tragedy is the inevitable result of our joint guilt.

There are many things in these troubled days that the church cannot do to help, but some things are the church's special business, and none, I think, more crucial and important than to keep penitence alive in this situation. Said a wise friend to me recently: "If all of us could go to the council table after this war is over in the spirit of penitence, there might be some hope." Well, without that there can be no hope at all.

Moreover, we of the democracies should be especially penitent. We won the last war. With utter and crushing completeness we won it. Never forget that. Endure, if you can, the reading of one paragraph from President Wilson's announcement of the Armistice to Congress in 1918: "We know that the object of the war is attained; the object upon which all free men had set their hearts; and attained with a sweeping completeness which even now we do not realize. Armed imperialism such as the men conceived who were but yesterday the masters of Germany is at an end, its illicit ambitions engulfed in black disaster. Who will now seek to revive it? The arbitrary power of the military caste of Germany which once could secretly and of its own single choice disturb the peace of the world is discredited and destroyed. And more than that—much more than that—has been accomplished." So completely did we, the democracies, win the war. We were in charge of the world. We could do what we would. As to what we did and did not do, the bill of particulars has been written again and again, and I know no judgment more unanimous than this—that we of the democracies are more responsible for the rise of the dictators than the plain people of the dictatorships themselves. Penitence becomes us well.

There are many angles from which one can look at Hitler and Mussolini today. I am not denying the truth in any of them, but they are partial and incomplete unless we humbly and penitently recognize that the dictators have come as an inevitable consequence of our joint sin, unless we hear, as it were, the moral order of this universe talking to them, saying: "Ho Assyrian, the rod of mine anger."

Now such penitence is not at home in wartime. In wartime pride is at home. Today pride rules our wills. In picking out sin and distributing blame we practice selective attention. We can easily see the iniquities of everyone except ourselves and our friends. We Christians should do better than that, as Lincoln did during the Civil War. I commend his spirit to you. "If God wills that . . . all the wealth piled by the bondman's two hundred and fifty years of unrequited toil shall be sunk, and . . . every drop of blood drawn with the lash shall be paid by another drawn with the sword; as was said three thousand years ago, so still it must be said, 'The judgments of the Lord are true and righteous altogether.'"

In the second place, however, this address of God to the dictator implies another meaning, namely, that God is employing the dictator to some good purpose of his own. When the populace upon the common levels saw the conqueror's victory, they cried, All is lost! But the prophets did not. God had picked up that rod of Assyria, they said; he would do something with it before he laid it down. They found, that is, not only humility and penitence, but courage and hope in the sovereignty of God.

There is a strange verse in one of the Psalms addressed to the Lord which says, "the wrath of men shall praise thee." How can that be true? It says that God can take man's evil and use it, that in his hands even man's wrath and iniquity are not a total loss. It says that God can use downright sin, as though a piece of grit that did not belong there, getting into an oyster shell, the oyster could make into a pearl after all. How can that be true about sin? Yet, where would we be in personal life if that were not true? When a man sins, need that be a total loss? No, not necessarily a total loss. It may seem dangerous for a preacher to give that answer, but it is the true one. Even downright wickedness need not be a total loss.

Did that Prodigal Son, for example, learn nothing in the far country that God could put to use afterwards? He learned a lot that boys who stay at home never know. It was dreadful. Only a fool would go through what he went through for the sake of learning it. But when in after days some boy was tempted to seek the far country, who was it in that Jewish town that best could help him? That Prodigal. He knew. He could put his very sin to use for the sake of God and of that other boy now tempted. We are often told that we ought to capitalize our troubles, and transform them into sympathy, understanding, and increased usefulness. That is true also about our sin. Here it is, a great mistake, a wrong committed. It is a loss, but thank God it need not be a total loss. Capitalize it. There are some people we especially can help because of it. God can use it. He can make even the wrath of men praise him.

Even unredeemed sinners God uses. We constantly and rightly exalt the ways in which God has used Christ, his perfect instrument. Yes, but he has used Judas Iscariot too. Someone, I suppose, had to try that experiment of betraying Christ, and stand there, an example of the way such betrayal looks when seen in the retrospect of history. How many of us, then, in some pinch in our lives when we have been tempted to betray Christ, have thought of Judas, and have said, No! not that! I'll not do that! God can use even Judas.

I am pleading for what our fathers called an overruling Providence, as though man's wickedness, like a stream, could indeed go wild, break its banks, and let loose a torrential flood, but lo! there is a lie of the land that gets control in the end, a limit beyond which no stream's wildness can go, a contour to the landscape, a shape to the eternal hills, a declivity in the valleys, that at last bring even the wildest streams to terms and force them into channels that they did not choose. That fact about the world the great prophets saw. "Ho Assyrian!"

As a matter of history, this has been true in man's public affairs. The Roman Empire was a vast imperialism, cruel, selfish, bloody. Was it a total loss? Far from it! God used Rome for an overriding of racial and national boundaries, a unifying of the known world, a creative building of law and order, to which we still are incalculably indebted. The French Revolution was terrible, with tumbrils rolling down Parisian streets, and heads falling daily beneath the guillotine. Was it a total loss? Far from it! In the retrospect of history it left gains that cannot be measured. Hitler and Mussolini represent everything that most we fear and hate in public life. Will they be a total loss? Not unless history reverses itself. My friends, a radical change in the world order has been long overdue. Our military and economic imperialisms, our subjugation of native peoples, our insane tariff barriers, our unjust division of the world's resources, have long cried out for change. We the democracies might have done it peacefully, but alas! we failed. Now the dictators come. They are to me as terrible as they are to you, but be sure of this, in the retrospect of history they will not be a total loss. God is saying to them today: Ho Assyrian, my rod!

Indeed, has it not occurred to us that Hitler may turn out to be a powerful, even though unintentional, friend of democracy? For consider! We in the democracies were slipping. Indeed, we were! We were taking democracy for granted. Was it not a lovely way of living that our fathers had bequeathed to us? What we could get out of it, not what we should dedicate to it, was foremost in our thoughts. Our life in this country had become undisciplined, soft, indulgent, careless, and what we took so easily for granted we had forgotten deeply and sacrificially to value. But now democracy is in danger, and there has been born in the United States more care about it, more study of what it means, more concern over its foundations, more sense of its value in the last year than in many a year before. Alas! we never value anything as we should until we face the peril of losing it. That is true even in the family, where some loved person who for years has been safely at our side, who has been assumed as part of the scenery of our life, falls ill, and we wake up to see how carelessly we have been taking for granted one whom we so easily might lose. So today we feel about democracy. It has become to us a dear thing. We have faced the possibility of seeing democracy crushed, and we have said that democracy should not die as long as free spirits were left in the world. Who has wrought this change? Hitler. What then? Am I saying, Thank God for Hitler? Far from it, but thank God for God, who towers over Hitler, who can use him, despite himself, for causes that he has no mind to serve. Thank God for that lie of the land that no overflowing flood can ultimately escape, but that will turn the wildest currents to channels that not they but God chooses!

See what I am pleading for—faith in the God of history. Throughout my ministry two aspects of God have been dominant in my thought and preaching—the God of nature, and the God of inner personal experience. But in these days another aspect of deity grows imperative—the God of history. Not to be identified with any national policy, not even with our own, the God of history sitteth above the circle of the earth, and the nations are accounted as a drop in the bucket. And there he is today, and his word to the dictators has not lost its power: Ho Assyrian, my rod!

This leaves us a brief moment for the final truth involved in the prophet's insight. When God picks up a rod, he can throw it down again. He always has. These rods of his, these conquerors that seem so strong, one by one have been thrown down. God picked them up. Well, then, "Shall the axe boast itself against him that heweth therewith? shall the saw magnify itself against him that wieldeth it?"

One of the great passages in Victor Hugo's *Les Misérables* is his description of the Battle of Waterloo. Recall how it ends: "Was it possible for Napoleon to win the battle? We answer in the negative. Why? On account of Wellington, on account of Blücher? No; on account of God . . . When the earth is suffering from an excessive burden, there are mysterious groans from the shadow, which the abyss hears. Napoleon had been denounced in infinitude, and his fall was decided. He had angered God." Napoleon himself had an intimation of this fact, for he said once: "As long as I am necessary, no power in the world will be able to brush me aside. But the moment I become unnecessary, an atom will be enough to smash me."

I am not saying that in this grim crisis that confronts the world we can shoulder off on God all the responsibility of getting rid of the conquerors, as though he would settle everything. We have our tasks, many and imperative, to make these dictators unnecessary and impossible. But if we are to have strength for them, we need to see and hear more than the daily news brings to our eyes and ears. Not we humans alone, but God also is talking to the dictators, and in the broad perspective of history it is not too difficult to discover what he is saying: Ho Assyrian! the rod of mine indignation, the punishment of the world's sins—he is saying that. I am using you, and, far beyond your will, you will serve my purposes and not be a total loss—he is saying that. But he is saying also, When I am through with you, you are done! No wild stream, however madly it grows turbulent, can in the end escape the lie of my land.

Ah Christ! How utterly different you are from the dictators! How weak today you often seem in comparison with them! Yet the long perspectives of history suggest another judgment.

> I saw the conquerors riding by
> > With cruel lips and faces wan:
> Musing on kingdoms sacked and burned
> > There rode the Mongol Genghis Khan;
>
> And Alexander, like a god,
> > Who sought to weld the world in one;
> And Caesar with his laurel wreath;
> > And like a thing from Hell the Hun;
>
> And, leading like a star, the van,
> > Heedless of upstretched arm and groan,
> Inscrutable Napoleon went,
> > Dreaming of empire, and alone ...
>
> Then all they perished from the earth,
> > As fleeting shadows from a glass,
> And, conquering down the centuries,
> > Came Christ the Swordless on an ass.

20

The Return to Discipline[1]

OUR WORLD TODAY FACES us with at least one elemental necessity—the need of discipline. Mankind can stand all sorts of evils, but it cannot long endure chaos, disorder, anarchy. When that reaches a certain point reaction sets in and some force rises to bring confusion under control and whip things into shape. The major movements of our time—communism, naziism, fascism, militarism, the growing elements of dictatorship in the democracies—are all endeavors to get some kind of order out of chaos, to put a bridle on this wild horse, to bring our nations and our world under disciplined control. Give the devil his due! The totalitarianism we fear today at home and abroad is an endeavor to get some social order out of the anarchic confusion of the world.

Willy nilly, therefore, we face a choice on which our personal lives and our social fortunes depend. Either we are going to have enough people who discipline themselves from within, or else we are going to have discipline imposed on us from without. From that dilemma there is no escape. In any population, large or small, let chaotic disorder reach too great proportions and the demand will rise, at all costs, for order. Though it take a dictator, that will seem a small price to pay for social order. The worst thing that mankind can face is anarchy.

Now there are two ways in which men achieve ordered societies: either they discipline themselves within or else they have discipline imposed on them from without. The first gives leeway for liberty, and makes democracy possible; the second is the nucleus of dictatorship. This morning, then, we try to measure the importance of self-discipline, not only as one secret in great personal living but as one of the most towering social

1. From *Living Under Tension* by Harry Emerson Fosdick. Copyright 1941 by Harper & Brothers. Copyright renewed © 1968 by Harry Emerson Fosdick. Reprinted by permission of HarperCollins Publishers.

necessities of our time. For look at the world, and see! In so far as we do not discipline ourselves, someone else will impose discipline on us.

Self-control has not been characteristic of our generation. Have we in this country been a disciplined people? In our personal morals, in our respect for law, in our family life, in our subjugation of self-interest to the common welfare, in any regard that you can think of have we been a self-controlled people? We have had splendid virtues—energy, vigor, pioneering venturesomeness—explosive and aggressive virtues that could blast new roads through high mountains, and win for us what we call success. But winning that, how often has liberty turned to license, self-restraint been thrown to the winds, laxness rather than self-control characterized us! How often has our use of power, like a wayward stream at flood, burst its banks, and our personal lives been undedicated and uncontrolled! Well, America faces now one of the most fateful hours in its history, and no saying of Jesus, I think, is more pertinent to our need than this: "Wide is the gate, and broad is the way, that leadeth to destruction, and many are they that enter in thereby. For narrow is the gate, and straitened is the way, that leadeth unto life, and few are they that find it." So! The loose life means ruin; only the disciplined life can be great.

Nevertheless, deep in human nature are moods and attitudes that resist this truth, so that we may well organize our thought this morning by listening as, one by one, these moods rise up in protest against it.

First of all, who does not feel within himself the mood that cries, I want a rich, free life; I resent restraint and control—that is not the end of existence; copious, plenteous, bountiful living is what I want? Confronting that mood is the fact that abundant life and how to get it was what Jesus was talking about. He said that a loose, sprawling, meandering course never reaches it, only the narrow gate and the straitened way of a disciplined and dedicated life.

The other day I heard Kreisler and the Philharmonic Orchestra play Beethoven's *Concerto in D Major*. It was glorious. He never arrived at that fullness of artistic power and life by traveling a broad, meandering course. He began playing the violin when he was a small boy, not too promising. When he was fourteen he toured the United States, only moderately successful, so that, returning to Vienna he could not get a position as a second violinist in the Philharmonic there. He dropped the violin, therefore, thinking he was a failure at it; tried medicine, did not like it; tried painting, was not contented with it; went into the army, was dissatisfied with it, and so came back to his first love again, the violin, and went to it. When he first made up his mind to that, he retired to solitude for eight solid weeks and did nothing except practice finger exercises, and from then till now he has daily gone through a narrow gate and down a straitened way of discipline. But it has been worth it.

What are the prerequisites of greatness in any realm? All of them, in Jesus' sense of the word, are narrow. *Attention* is narrow. When Gladstone was asked the secret of his success he replied in one word, "Concentration." The worthwhile mind can focus, but the inattentive mind sprawls every which way. *Decisiveness* is narrow. We cannot decide vaguely and in general; we must decide in particular. The decisive mind defines, excludes, wills this and not that, but the indecisive mind is a vagabond on a broad road. *Loyalty* is narrow. It binds me to a definite devotion. When I love my friend I am not loosely free; I do not wish to be loosely free; my limitation is my glory; I love my friend. But the unloyal man travels a broad road; he has no attachments; he is devoted to no friend; he is a man without a country - broad is the gate and wide is the way.

Here, as so often, Jesus is not so much a painter of beautiful ideals as a proclaimer of universal laws. Nothing left loose ever does anything creative. No horse gets anywhere until it is harnessed. No steam or gas ever drives anything until it is confined. No Niagara is ever turned into light and power until it is tunneled. No life ever grows great until it is focused, dedicated, disciplined.

One of the widest gaps in human experience is the gap between what we say we want to be and our willingness to discipline ourselves to get there. From the homeliest aspects of life—people who say they want to reduce ten pounds, but who will not discipline themselves to do it—to the greatest aspects of life—people who say they want to be Christians, but who will not leave their meandering course of inattentive, indecisive, undevoted living to achieve it—how wide the chasm is between our professed ideals and our willingness to pay the cost! And the cost in every realm is always self-discipline.

Today we confront a world that presses this matter home. One nation has shaken the earth to its foundations, and at the source of its power to do that one hears that nation's leaders commanding the people, Give up butter for guns. We all pray that such discipline may not be necessary here, but it is preposterous to suppose that we in American can preserve our democracy by living in a fool's paradise, with loose morals, disintegrated family life, self-interest taking precedence over public welfare, and a general attitude of loose and easy-going living. Broad is that gate and wide is that way, but it leadeth to destruction. And the very pith and marrow of the matter are here: Nothing worth having in this world, least of all democracy, can be achieved save as the cost of it is paid in self-discipline.

Nevertheless, a second mood within us rises in protest against this truth: I resent restraint and repression, it says; I want to do what I please, follow my whims, fancies, and passions; I want to let myself go. To which the answer seems plain to anyone who knows modern psychology at all. Which self do you want to let go? Do not tell us that you have only one self! You have a lot of selves. No one escapes the elemental problem that James M. Barrie's character, Sentimental Tommy, so well describes when he struggles to make up his mind: "It's easy to you that has just one mind, but if you had as many minds as I have—!" Self-discipline, therefore, begins of necessity at home within our own lives. Not all our selves can have gangway, or if we try to give it to them our inner life will be a mess that even the psychiatrists cannot put to rights. Some chosen self, out of all these many selves, must assume the regency within, must arrange the hierarchy of our loves and interests, establishing some government in the soul so that what we wish on top shall be on top and what we wish subdued shall be obedient. Self-dedication is a basic psychological necessity.

In the chapel at Harvard University is a tablet in memory of old Dr. Peabody, and the end of the inscription runs thus:

> His Precept was Glorified by His Example
> While for Thirty-Three Years
> He moved among the Teachers and Students of Harvard College
> And Wist not that His Face Shone.

Facing that kind of life, what does one mean by letting oneself go? Such a man as that inscription celebrates, among all the selves that thronged his life, chose which self should lead, and which should follow after. Unless one's life within is to be a mere mob, it must, one way or another, be organized, integrated, made into hierarchy with supreme values ascendant. All modern psychology at its best underlines the ancient saying: "He that ruleth his spirit is better than he that taketh a city."

It is a strange thing that so many people should talk of doing what they please in a world where modern science has come. No scientist in his special realm thinks he can do what he pleases. Tackle any new problem in the laboratory, strive after any new discovery, and there are countless ways of missing the mark, finding nothing, coming out nowhere. Broad is the gate and wide the way that leads to no discovery. But only one way leads to that particular truth you seek; there is only one way of so fulfilling the law-abiding conditions that you will get what you are after. Narrow is that gate.

I do not know why God so made the world that the wrong way is broad and the right way is narrow, but this is the way he made it, and in view of that I stand in fear of a sentimental kind of religion which forgets that. It was when Ophelia went crazy that she began distributing flowers indiscriminately to everybody. Some persons want a religion like that, and come to church, I fear, hoping that the preacher will imitate Ophelia and promiscuously distribute sweet messages—"Pansies, that's for thoughts." Jesus was not at all like that. Go through his teaching and his life from beginning to end and see if you can find anything sentimental; lovely, yes! beautiful, yes! but through it all a realistic facing of the facts and a realistic statement of universal spiritual laws. There are as many ways of messing life up as there are ways of missing truth in a scientific laboratory, but if we wish a life not messed up, then there is only one way and the gate is narrow—dedication, interior organization, integration, discipline, self-control.

Recall that great phrase of Ignatius Loyola about the man who puts on spurs, but no bridle, to ride a fiery horse. Too many of us have been doing that with ourselves in this country—spurs, but no bridle, to ride a fiery horse—and now we face a world where a dilemma confronts us. Either we are going to discipline ourselves for our own sake, the nation's sake, and the world's, or else discipline will be imposed on us from without.

Nevertheless, still another mood, native to us all, rises in protest against this truth. I hate coercion, it says; I resent repression; I want to be my own master and not the slave of codes and prescriptions of society; I want to be free.

That is what Jesus wanted. "Ye shall know the truth, and the truth shall make you free." Throughout the New Testament the note of freedom everywhere resounds: "Where the Spirit of the Lord is, there is liberty." Moreover, at the center of Jesus' ministry and of Paul's Epistles is a revolt against the small, enslaving scrupulosities of the ancient legal codes. Ask the Pharisees about Jesus, and they would have said that he himself was a rebel, refusing obedience to the prescriptions of the law, and traveling a dangerously broad road in a perilously loose and undisciplined manner. A friend of mine on a train trip sat behind a mother and her small son. She began saying "Don't" as soon as she came in, and my friend counted. Fifty-nine times in one hour and a half she said "Don't" to that boy. No one wants to live under such restriction, and least of all is Jesus' ethic like that.

At the start, therefore, we may expect his sympathy when we protest against repression and want freedom. Not all our so-called American looseness has been bad. Many trivial scrupulosities have masqueraded under the disguise of discipline. A woman of my generation can remember the Dean of Vassar College saying to the students: "Young ladies, I hope that I may never see the day when you will so far forget your dignity and delicacy as to appear upon the campus without gloves." All the way from that to endless rules and regulations in the moral realm, caricatures of discipline have cluttered up the field. No man is worth his salt who does not sometimes rise in rebellion, smash through some nonsensical repression, and claim his freedom.

When, however, we are through with that, we will face an inescapable fact—there are some things we can never be free from. Free thinking is not freedom from the laws of thought. Free living is not freedom from the laws of life. All scientific creativity goes back to obedience to scientific law. All artistic creativeness depends upon obedience to the laws of beauty. No one is free until he is mastered.

> Make me a captive, Lord,
> And then I shall be free;
> Force me to render up my sword,
> And I shall conq'ror be.

That is not poetry alone, but basic psychological fact.

Mark Twain, for example, lost his fortune. The accumulations of his brilliant life work tumbled into an abyss of debt. According to the public law he could have escaped all responsibility in bankruptcy. Why did he not travel that broad and easy way? Why did he voluntarily assume the burden of those debts, circumnavigating the globe, even, although on the threshold of old age, tirelessly speaking and writing until he paid the last penny? He told us why in one brief sentence: "Honor is a harder master than the law." Something inside himself he had to live up to. In Tennyson's phrase, he was "loyal to the royal" in himself. Narrow was that gate, and straitened that way, but it led to life. That kind of disciplined character is not a matter of small scrupulosities.

Today we may well celebrate the men and women in high or humble places who thus have within themselves something fine that they must live up to. They are the prerequisite of democracy. The storms of life beat on them, as they beat on all of us today, but they have a compass, something within them that they are true to and steer by. Over against that kind of life put the loose, lax, immoralism of our generation, where many voices have cried, like the witches in *Macbeth*, "Fair is foul, and foul is fair." We preachers are tempted to think of such loose living solely in ethical terms. We call it sin. But it is more than that. It is psychological and emotional disintegration. Such a life never gets itself together around any center, never is dedicated and disciplined to any end. Such a man has to say, like a character in one of H. G. Wells' novels, "I'm not a man but a mob." Only one who has been mastered by something worth being mastered by ever can be a real person.

Wherever you find a real person in any realm, Toscanini in music, for example, one thing is present—a devotion that it is his pride, joy, and freedom to live up to and discipline himself for. That is different from letting yourself go. That is not the same thing as subservience to conventional codes. That is having something within you, stimulating, empowering, controlling, around which your life grows integral and unified, so that your joy and liberation are in living up to it and out from it.

Until religion means that to a man it is an ineffective conventionality. When in Shakespeare's drama the Earl of Kent went out to King Lear in his exile to offer his allegiance, he gave this as his explanation: "You have that in your countenance which I would fain call master." When a man says that to Christ in earnest, until within himself Christ's spirit and way of life become an organizing center, an inner criterion, then he his a Christian.

America today desperately needs people who thus within themselves have something that they must live up to. See how we sit in comfort here! Destitution will not mark our dinner tables when we go home; fear will not haunt our night with sirens warning us that the bombing planes are coming. What right have we to this ease? I am not saying, Give up butter for guns. May that kind of coercion be spared us! But in a day when all the world on both sides of the battle line—often with a courage and a self-sacrifice that make us salute the grandeur of human nature even while we are appalled at what human nature does—is displaying magnificent self-dedication and self-control, by what exemption have we a right to live a lax, loose, unbuttoned life?

If America should ever fail, if after the promise of its start, and the unexampled marvel of its opportunity, it should come from a fair spring-time to a barren autumn, what would be the reason? Not lack of laws, not lack of outward regulation, not lack of dictatorship even, for we would try that before we fell, but lack of people who so discipline themselves from within that they were self-propelled, having liberty because they deserved it, keeping democracy because they helped create it, running themselves so well from the inside that they did not need to be run from the outside. And that profound and inner matter is, at its deepest, a great religion's gift. For the roots of a self-disciplined character are profoundly spiritual—faith that there are values worth being dedicated to, faith that there are ends worth being self-disciplined for, faith that beyond the torture of these years, by God's grace, there is a possible world, decent, fraternal, peaceable, that self-disciplined men and nations can build. When such faith is lost, it is all up with democracy. And the place for this kind of living to begin is within each of us. Whatever else we can or cannot do for the world, at least we can give it one more life that proves Tennyson's words true:

> Self-reverence, self-knowledge, self-control,
> These three alone lead life to sovereign power.

21

The Decisive Babies of the World[1, 2]

FROM OUR YOUTH UP we have heard about the decisive battles of history. One of the earliest books some of us remember is Creasy's famous volume on *The Fifteen Decisive Battles of the World*. But now Christmas comes again, engaging the thought and warming the heart of multitudes around the globe, and it concerns not a decisive battle but a decisive baby. "Unto us a child is born, unto us a son is given."

Even today, when all the world is obsessed with the clash of arms, Christmas suggests how much more decisive a baby can be than a battle. We moderns have lost faith in miracles, and if by miracles we mean occurrences involving the breaking of nature's laws, we are right, for nature's laws are God's and are never broken. But even so, the world "miracle" does not drop from our vocabulary, for some things are so unforeseeable, in advance of their happening so incredible, that they are to us miraculous. When Jesus was born in Bethlehem, what were the decisive elements in the world's life? Surely Cæsar Augustus upon his throne, the Roman Empire's vast extent and power, and legions tramping every road—any realistic mind would have pointed to such potent factors as the determining elements in mankind's life. As for a baby, born of a lowly mother in obscure Bethlehem upon the far fringes of the Empire, it would have been madness then to have supposed that two millennia afterwards millions of us would be singing of that event:

---

1. From *Living Under Tension* by Harry Emerson Fosdick. Copyright 1941 by Harper & Brothers. Copyright renewed © 1968 by Harry Emerson Fosdick. Reprinted by permission of HarperCollins Publishers.

2. A Christmas Sermon.

166

Yet in thy dark streets shineth
    The everlasting Light;
The hopes and fears of all the years
    Are met in thee tonight.

This is the miracle of Christmas—that a baby can be so decisive.

Babies are decisive. Long ago in Egypt a slave girl held in her arms a newborn infant for whom there seemed no hope, so that she framed for him a floating cradle, and pushed him out upon the waters of the Nile to survive or perish. But now, in retrospect, see what immense issues in the world's life went floating down the river in that slender craft! For Moses was one of the decisive babies of the world.

In our own country the forces of disunion were threatening; already the premonitions of disruptive strife were ominous, when out of a camp meeting in Kentucky a young frontiersman and his bride went to build a rough cabin on Nolan's Creek, and there a babe was born. Who can imagine what America's history would have been without Lincoln? He was one of the decisive babies of the world.

Today in the midst of war, pressed upon as we are by huge, impersonal forces that often seem irresistible, let us look at some of those deep needs in our lives to which this special message of Christ's birthday is pertinent!

In the first place, when we center our attention on the decisive babies of the world, a mood of expectancy and hope arises. If babies are among the main determinants of history, then we never can tell what may happen. Around the corner in a crib may be the tiny hand that will yet push open the door of a new era.

We habitually think of babies as small and weak, for whom we must care. True! But look at history in the large and see how often, when the world seemed hopeless, when the limits of man's achievements seemed reached, when the forces ranged against man's progress seemed irresistible, a babe was born who became the pioneer of a new era. Who, in the fifteenth century, thought that anything important had happened when in Genoa that child was born, unadvertised, unheralded, who was to open the door of the most amazing geographical expansion in history? Always when the world least expects it some Columbus is being born to introduce a new era. So long as there are babies, you never can tell!

The year 1809, for example, was one of the most discouraging in Europe's history. Napoleon was dominant, as Hitler is now. His battles and victories were the absorbing news, and, evil as our times are, I suspect that to those who lived then, 1809 seemed as bad or worse. But think of what was going on in 1809 that was not in the news at all. In that year Charles Darwin was born. In that year Lincoln was born. In that year Gladstone was born, and Tennyson, and Edgar Allan Poe, and Oliver Wendell Holmes, and Cyrus McCormick, the inventor of the harvester, and Mendelssohn. At the very least, one must say that the world was not as helpless as it looked.

Indeed, how transient for the most part are the effects of the decisive battles, and how permanent, often, are the effects of the decisive babies! Concerning the wars of 1809, history in the main writes, "futility," but concerning the babies of 1809, history will be thinking seriously for ages yet. In 1814, when Napoleon had been defeated, Russian and Austrian armies invaded Italy and took their vengeance by massacring many of the inhabitants of Piacenza. In one village the women fled to the church for safety, but the soldiers followed them even there, and slew them before the altar. One mother, however, with an infant at her breast, hid in the belfry and saved her child. That infant was Verdi, the composer. And now most of us could not tell a single thing about those decisive battles—not one—but we are still listening to *Rigoletto, Aïda, La Traviata, Il Trovatore.*

So Cæsar Augustus perishes—overpassed, futile, and damned in history—and the Roman Empire itself crumbles and falls, but 2000 years afterwards multitudes still sing, as though of a contemporary event:

> O holy Child of Bethlehem,
>> Descend to us, we pray;
> Cast out our sin, and enter in;
>> Be born in us today.

Indeed, take this truth not only literally but figuratively. All great ideas are born small, like babies. Why cannot great ideas come into the world full armored, like Minerva from the head of Jove? They never do. All saving ideas are born small. As Jesus said, they are like leaven, a little thing in the beginning, or like mustard seed, the smallest of all the seeds in the ground. In every generation, therefore, if we are to believe in the creative forces to which the future belongs, we must believe in something inconspicuous, newborn, just growing. Who of us does not need to see that truth today? If we believe in the noisy and ostentatious violence of the world, as though that alone were the real and determining factor in our time, what hope is there? But the wise men believed in a baby. That is the essence of the Christmas message to me this year—the wise men believed in a baby. Wise men? we are tempted to say; rather, fools and sentimentalists to do that, to follow a Star to a young child's manger, and worship where a newborn life was at its small beginning! But what the wise men did is a parable of mankind's best wisdom in every realm. They did not believe in Augustus, in Herod, in Cæsar's legions, in the imperial power that loomed so large and seemed so permanent. They did not believe in the noisy, the obvious, the ostentatious. They believed in a newborn thing.

Always, in every realm, that is the mark of wise men. The idea that the earth goes around the sun was once a newborn thought in the mind of Pythagorus, a tiny intimation long neglected that like a stray waif was picked up centuries afterward, tended, nursed, and cared for by Copernicus. Once more it was the wise men who believed in a baby. So William James of Harvard put it: "As for me, my bed is made: I am against bigness and greatness in all their forms, and with the invisible molecular moral forces that work from individual to individual, stealing in through the crannies of the world like so many soft rootlets, or like the capillary oozing of water, and yet rending the hardest monuments of man's pride, if you give them time."

If today we are to believe in anything worth-while at all, the possibilities of peace, for example, in a decent and fraternal world, organized at last for brotherhood and not for war, we must believe in it so. Peace is not a large and ostentatious matter now. But the idea of it, the hope of it, faith in it, the first tentative plans for it have been born. Such ideas are decisive in the end, and the hope of the world is in wise men who, even while Cæsar Augustus reigns in Rome, believe in them. The vulgar mob always follows the obvious, the blatant, the ostentatious, but all the wise men of the world, in every realm, have followed a star until it stood over a place where something newborn lay.

Let us go further now to see that this message speaks not only to our need of hope in days of discouragement, but to our sense of personal helplessness in the face of the world's catastrophe. Who does not feel at times this sense of helplessness, as though, in this wild disaster that has broken on the world, he were facing some titanic eruption of nature's forces, a hurricane or earthquake? What can he do to stop it? But listen to the Christmas gospel. Personality counts, it says. Again and again the world seems to have reached an impasse; it is stymied; it lands in a dead end street, and, lo! a child is born, and a new way opens to unsuspected hopes. Personality counts. Who can watch what the decisive babies have meant in history and not see that?

Today one fears not so much that someone here will deny the abstract truth of this as that someone will deny its application to himself. This sermon, someone may be thinking, is not about me at all. I was not a decisive baby. I am no messiah for whose birth the world was waiting. I am plain, ordinary, everyday, commonplace, John Smith. If the hope of the world lies in some messiah to be born who will open the door to a new era, that lets me out.

To such a one, I answer, My friend, consider what it is that makes a baby decisive. It is not the baby alone. What made Charles Darwin decisive? Countless people puzzling over the problem of how all these different species of animals came to be. For generations people had puzzled over that, and more than once the query had arisen: Did these species suddenly appear, or was it by a long process of developmental change? The air was full of guesses, wonderings, intimations, prophetic insights. Read even Tennyson's *In Memoriam*, written before Darwin had published anything at all, and you will find evolution foreshadowed there. Then, and only then, that unsuspecting babe was born who was to draw all this together and focus it. That is what a decisive life does—he focuses into a burning flame what had been there already, everywhere dispersed and unco-ordinated. Darwin could not have been Darwin without all that preparation. Multitudes of people helped to make his life decisive.

Of all decisive lives this is true—they are concentration points where multitudes of hopes, thoughts, faiths, and aspirations of common men and women are drawn together and focused. This is the meaning of Paul's saying about our Lord in his Letter to the Galatians: "When the fulness of the time came, God sent forth his Son." So even Christ could be born, and be Christ only when the fulness of the time had come. If he had come a few centuries before, he could not have been himself. Multitudes of plain people had to come first to prepare the way of the Lord, and make straight in the desert a highway for our God. Prophetic spirits, catching glimpses of his coming truth, hungry souls wanting it, intimations and foreshadowings of a gospel greater than the world had known, hopes of a new birth of spiritual life, faith in a new era of God's power—all these were in the air when Jesus came in the "fulness of the time," and he precipitated them. Multitudes of people helped to make him decisive.

Indeed, this truth has its dreadful as well as its inspiring side. What has made Hitler decisive? Hitler is more than Hitler. He is a burning glass that has gathered into a consuming flame the humiliations, the bitterness, the sense of gross injustice, the desire for vengeance, the compensatory dream of a master race, that the last war and its aftermath left everywhere among his people. For good or ill, it is we, the plain folk, who always make the messiahs possible. It is we who supply the heat that they focus into flame.

So everyday, ordinary, commonplace people do count. Indeed, I venture a prediction, buttressed I think by history. Some day, I predict, a man will rise by whose hands a federation of the world will be so effected, and wars so stopped thereby, that his name will go down across the centuries associated with that great achievement, as Copernicus' name is with the new astronomy, or Lincoln's with the preservation of our union. That man will come. Some day he will arise. For all we know he may be lying this morning in some unknown village in his crib. But when he comes, what will it take to make him decisive? Multitudes of us who have gone before, who have believed in peace when belief was difficult, prophetic spirits undaunted by man's brutality, hungry souls with faith in brotherhood's possibility—a multitude of plain people must prepare the way before the decisive messiah can come with peace in his hands. All of us do matter; personality even in us does count.

So far we have said that this truth about the decisive babies of the world brings us a two-fold encouragement—hope in our hopelessness, and a sense of importance and responsibility in our seeming weakness. But it does more than that. It brings rebuke as well, a stern and chastening rebuke, for what we in this brutal world do to newborn children. Even in the Christmas story, despite our popular sentimentalizing of it, there are brutal elements. Herod nearly killed the infant Jesus. He tried his hardest. He slew all the little ones of Bethlehem, so runs the story, to stop if he could this decisive babe from growing up. What if he had succeeded? How incalculable the difference to the world! Well, that is what war does all the time, and poverty, and slums, and all our social cruelties. They kill decisive babies.

In 1805 Napoleon bombarded Vienna. The bombardment was terrific for those days. The shells burst everywhere, and one of them struck the

Jesuit Grammar School, falling in the stone-flagged corridor, and blasting walls and windows. One of the students, an eight-year-old boy, was in his room practicing on the piano, and in terror he fell to the floor and hid his face. Then in a moment came the voice of one of the schoolmasters, calling through the ruined corridor: "Schubert, Franz Schubert, are you all right?" So nearly did war take its toll of a decisive child.

Has someone here been tempted to think that this talk about decisive babies is sentimental? No, in the light of the scientific doctrine of evolution it is not. What is one of the most decisive factors in the whole story of evolution? Ask the scientists and they will tell you that it is the development of the human child. For the human child has a prolonged infancy; he cannot take care of himself; he must be taken care of. So, say the scientists, the whole ethical life of man grew up around the child. The first human altruism was for him. The first self-sacrifice was for him. The first co-operative loyalty was for the family's united support and sustenance of him. The child in the evolutionary process was the creator of every impulse of unselfishness and goodwill that mankind knows. When Jesus put a child in the midst of his disciples, he did in his way what the scientists have done in theirs. And now, in this so-called modern world, we have reversed the process, turned back the course of evolution, and we decide our national disputes and settle the issues of our so-called statesmanship by starving children, bombing children, murdering children. How many a father or mother, do you suppose, after the havoc of some fearful raid, has called out for some boy or girl who might have been decisive to the world: "Schubert, Franz Schubert, are you all right?" only to receive no answer?

I say this not to play upon your feelings, but for an ethical reason. We are all tempted in these days to become hard, callous, so used to brutal things that we do not care much any more. I plead with myself and with you against this hardening of our hearts. Never get used to the idea of war—never! And when tempted to that, remember what war does to children, all children that it touches, decisive children that could have been the hope of the world. Listen to this—I will give you two guesses who said it: "War is one of the first necessities of civilization. War in a righteous cause lifts men above the sordid and selfish things of life, and discloses in them those Divine attributes which the Maker gave when He created man in His own image." Who said that? Hitler or one of his minions? No! Mussolini, or one of his minions? No! That was said by one of our own American Major Generals. That way of thinking is here in America today, growing in power, casting its spell upon millions of our people. Surely it is right that on the festival of Christ's birthday the church should cry out against that dreadful blasphemy, that ultimate profanation of the name of God, that blots from the skies of human faith and hope the song of peace and exalts the way of war, applauds Herod, slayer of the children, as the revelation of the Divine nature. Never get used to the idea of war! Never think of it without hearing the cry that every war has caused innumerable times: "Schubert, Franz Schubert, are you all right?"

One step further, however, we must go, to reach the personal conclusion of this matter. We have spoken of Jesus as though he were one of the decisive babies of the world, but to us, as Christians, he is more than that. He is *the* decisive baby of the world. So Christendom acclaims him this Christmas-tide. But, I ask you, how decisive has he been in your life and mine? That is not a general question, but a particular and individual inquiry that each one for himself must answer.

Say, as we will, that in the realm of music Johann Sebastian Bach was decisive, yet there are many people of whom it is true that so far as they are concerned Johann Sebastian Bach might just as well never have been born. Whether or not anybody is decisive for us depends on us. So when one thinks of all the outward show of Christmas, its endless pageantry and singing, even its lovely commemoration in our homes and churches, the question still rises about many of us carried along in this stream of public festivity: How decisive now, is Christ in your life and mine?

> Though Christ a thousand times
>   In Bethlehem be born,
> If He's not born in thee
>   Thy soul is still forlorn.

The Christmas story represents the very angels in heaven as knowing how conclusive his coming was, but to how many he was not important in the least! To those people at the inn who crowded him out, so that he was laid in a manger, he did not mean a thing. And one knows well that here today we cannot take it for granted that Christ has been in any serious sense a decisive influence in our lives. Rather, our affirmation that he is decisive changes now to a question and a challenge. Is he really that to us? How differently do we live because he came? How deeply are our attitudes toward life, toward war, toward human need and personal character affected by his coming?

This is no year to be content with the frills of Christmas. This is no year for its sweetness alone to fill our thoughts. For the world is dark, and out of its black background come such cries of suffering and need as human ears have not often heard before. Far from being less significant because of this, Christ seems to me amid this darkness to hold in the substance of his teaching and the quality of his spirit, that guidance for men and nations to which in the long run we must come back again if there is to be any hope. It is true: They that sat in darkness have seen a great light. His coming was decisive. He has it in him to be decisive. He waits for the hour when his determining influence can be made decisive. But all that comes back to each individual's doorsill. When Christ has become decisive for enough people, one by one, he will become indeed the most decisive baby in the world.

22

A Great Time to Be Alive[1]

THIS CERTAINLY IS A ghastly time to be alive. Behind the stirring head-lines that narrate the clash of armies and the march of victory, an unheralded mass of human misery exists, the like of which our earth has seldom, if ever, seen before. Because of the last war, says Dr. Hambro, late president of the League of Nations, thirty-five million human beings died of starvation and epidemics, but that is only a drop in the bucket compared with this war's disaster. Whether one thinks of what our enemies have done to us—of Warsaw, Lidice, Rotterdam, Coventry—or of what we have done to them—"We drop liquid fire on these cities," says one expert in air warfare, "and literally roast the populations to death"—we are living in a grim and hideous time.

If only we could hope that war would solve the problems it has set out to solve, *that* would redeem, in part at least, our estimation of our era, but war never does that. When this conflict is over and its immeasurable sacrifices have been poured out, Hitler, to be sure, will be gone, but the basic problems that confronted us before, even the fear of totalitarian dictatorship, will confront us still, and endless new problems as well that the war itself has caused. As one of our social research scientists pitilessly puts it: "The war will have solved no basic problems. As a matter of fact, it will have made a good many of them more complicated. . . . To expect otherwise is like expecting that pneumonia will have cured the physical debility that brought it on. You're lucky to be as well off after the siege is over."

Moreover, this is an especially hideous generation for Christians. Ralph Waldo Emerson, when a young minister, attended an important

1. From *A Great Time to Be Alive* by Harry Emerson Fosdick. Copyright 1935 by Harper & Brothers. Copyright renewed © 1963 by Harry Emerson Fosdick. Reprinted by permission of HarperCollins Publishers.

Bible society's convention in a southern state, and by chance the meetings were held in a room whose windows opened on a slave market where Negroes were being auctioned off. So Emerson describes the scene: "One ear therefore heard the glad tidings of great joy, whilst the other was regaled with 'Going, gentlemen, going.' And almost without changing our position we might aid in sending the Scriptures to Africa, or bid for 'four children without the mother' who had been kidnapped therefrom." Such an intolerable contradiction we face now in a generation where one listens with one ear to the faiths, hopes, and ideals of the Christian gospel, and with the other to this war's unbridled violence and brutality.

Recently a woman said, "I adore my children, but lately I have caught myself almost wishing I had never brought them into the world," and a man said, "I am discouraged. All the ideals and values for which I have worked during recent years appear to be losing out." Such moods are natural, for we confront a generation such as faced the writer of the fourth Psalm: "Many there are that say, Who will show us any good?"

Nevertheless, this is also a great time to be alive, and alike the personal and the public issues of it depend on whether we see that.

For one thing, ours is a day when we cannot seek for ease but must seek for adequacy. Life's restful days we love, but other days come too— great days—that require of us not ease but adequacy. Some eras are like a lullaby; some are like a spur. Which of the two is likely in the end to be greater?

Recently we celebrated the two-hundredth anniversary of Thomas Jefferson's birth. What kind of era did he live in? He thought it appalling. The gains of civilization thrown away, he saw in the early nineteenth century a dismaying renaissance of primitive barbarism: "Those moral principles and conventional usages," he wrote, "which have heretofore been the bond of civilized nations, . . . have given way to force, the law of Barbarians, and the nineteenth century dawns with the Vandals of the fifth." Yet, looked at now in retrospect, what kind of generation was it in which Thomas Jefferson, George Washington, Alexander Hamilton, John Marshall, and their colleagues, lived? We glory in it! It offered them no ease; it demanded of them adequacy, and, rising to meet it, they made of it a great time.

Surely this thing we are trying to say is true to life both public and personal. Victor Hugo, for example, during his early years enjoyed a happy and resounding success seldom equaled in France—he was the pet of the populace, the pride of the theater, the glory of Paris. Then Napoleon III rose to power, and with superb courage Hugo withstood his growing tyranny. For him ease vanished and tragedy began, until the edict of banishment made him for nearly nineteen years an exile. Of course he hated that deplorable experience, yet out of those years came his greatest work. His biographer calls that fateful period "miraculously inspired," and during it, he says, "books that were far stronger than everything that had gone before, . . . came from his hand," and "he became twice the size of the man he had been." Even Hugo himself exclaimed, "Why was I not exiled before!" What if instead of making such creative response to a tragic time he had settled back, saying, "Who will show us any good?"

Whether or not I am talking to your need, I am talking to my own. I dreaded the coming of this war as one might dread perdition, hating it as the summation of all villainy. War is essentially the denial of everything Christ stood for. For youth it is bad enough, but for an older man too it is a ghastly time to live. Yet that is not the whole story. One who knows history knows that in just such times as these, turbulent and revolutionary, whole generations have been brought to their senses; strong souls called on for adequacy have proved adequate; creative gains have come as from travail, and long afterwards flags have been flown by rejoicing nations because of what was done in them. To such a generation it is shameful to make no better response than to cry, "Who will show us any good?"

Our Lord, too, had his hours of serenity and ease when he looked with joy upon the flowers of Galilee and said that "Solomon in all his glory was not arrayed like one of these." But he came at last to another kind of place, where no ease was his but fearful crisis, demanding adequacy, as in Gethsemane he prayed for insight to see, and strength to do, the will of God. That too was a great day.

Not only is this a generation which, if we will, can call out personal adequacy, it is an era also when we cannot remain static, when change is forced upon us, when willy nilly we must make momentous decisions that will affect for good or ill the whole world's future.

Human nature instinctively dislikes change. We love to play safe by staying put. We settle down in a familiar place, clinging even to its faults rather than risking the unknown that alteration brings. There is in humankind a natural timidity that

… makes us rather bear those ills we have
Than fly to others that we know not of.

In church we pray that the world may be saved, but commonly when we leave the church we still try to save the world without changing it. Many Americans today would love to save the world if only they could save it without changing their isolationism, without changing their ideas of absolute national sovereignty, without changing their racial prejudices and their economic ideas to fit the new interdependent world. Then history, tired and impatient of our lethargy and our reluctance to alter anything, hurls us out of our peaceful decades into a maelstrom like this, crying, Now you have got to change! And when that kind of era comes, like it or not, it is a great time to be alive.

The three major forces of our time are fascism, communism, and democracy, and our main emphasis is on the difference between them. They stand in contrast, their unlikeness stressed and evident. But on one point these three predominant elements in our contemporary world agree: They are at one in demanding radical change. Fascism insists on political change, seeing that we cannot go on in this new interdependent world with the old national disunities, but that we must have some kind of new world order. Communism insists on economic change, seeing that the new technology forces on us new co-ordination in production and distribution. Democracy insists that we cannot continue plunging from one war into another, with conscriptions and regimentations multiplied until democracy itself will become impossible unless a co-operative world order stops these recurrent conflicts. These three—fascism, communism, and democracy—do radically differ, but one suspects that history, looking back, will say that the major fact in our time was that these three most powerful forces of our day were agreed on the necessity of radical change if a civilized world was to be possible. Well, when the three most powerful forces in the world call for change, we are going to get it. So intelligent minds are saying now that this is not simply another war—this is a revolution.

Who of us has not dreamed what it would be like to live in one of the world's stormy and tumultuous eras—the Reformation, the French Revolution, or what you will? They were fearful times but they were great times, too. Today no one need dream about that any more. We are now in the midst of the most revolutionary era in human history, with such momentous choices facing us as seldom have faced mankind before.

What makes any era seem great or little to a man is the man's own eyes, his capacity of insight and vision. Put some people in a great generation and they will only cry, "Who will show us any good?" But from Moses in the desert at the burning bush, seeing in an enslaved Israel in Egypt the hope of the future, to our own founding fathers, seeing in thirteen disunited colonies the possibility of a great venture in free living, men with eyes to see possibilities in times of travail and change have created the most hopeful advances in man's history. That is what we need to pray for now—eyes to see—for if we have them this will be for us a great time for great living.

We are not saying that the outcome of this war will necessarily be a constructive peace with a new and better era following. Upon the contrary, war is the most uncertain, the least precise instrument man handles. He picks it up to do something with it, and lo, when he is through he finds he as done something else altogether!

We fought the last war with two clear objectives in mind: First, to end the military threat of Germany. That end, however, we certainly did not achieve. We created Soviet Russia; we broke up the Hapsburg and Ottoman empires, trebled the size of Serbia, doubled the size of Rumania, created Iraq, Estonia, Lithuania, and Czechoslovakia. Such things, that we never intended to do, we did, but what we started out to do, conclusively to end Germany's military might, we did not do at all. Second, we fought the last war to make the world safe for democracy. Instead, we opened the door to one dictatorship after another—Kemal Ataturk in Turkey, Mussolini in Italy, Pilsudski in Poland, Salazar in Portugal, Franco in Spain, Hitler in Germany, but the one thing we started out to do, to make the world safe for democracy, we never did at all.

Always, world-changing conditions that we have not the slightest intention of producing come from war, while the aims and objectives we say we are fighting for are the very things it is least likely to achieve. Such is the essential nature of war. War is a blunderbuss with which one shoots at a bird and commonly hits everything in the vicinity except the bird.

Nevertheless, that is no excuse for us to cry, "Who will show us any good?" It still remains true that the eras of enforced change present supreme opportunities. They challenge us with a sober and stimulating fact:

We are living, we are dwelling
>In a grand and awful time,
In an age on ages telling;
>To be living is sublime.

This is true not only because ours is an era calling for personal adequacy and forcing on us the necessity of momentous change, but an era also that reveals with unmistakable clarity the false reliances we have been trusting in.

We have trusted in inventive science, and it is magnificent, but in the lurid light of this generation it is clear that what inventive science does is to furnish mankind with power, and that, far from solving the human problem, complicates it. The real question still rises: What moral quality shall exercise that power and to what end? There is no more scientifically competent nation on earth than Germany.

We have trusted in education, and its achievements have been splendid. Charlemagne towers as a great figure in history, but Charlemagne could neither read nor write. The spread of literacy, the invention of printing, the dispersion of books, the privilege of schools—all this is a thrilling story but it does not solve the problem. Education too is power, and still the question rises: What moral quality will use it and to what end? There is no more literate and educated nation on earth than Germany.

In such realms as these—inventive science and education—we commonly picture man's progress in terms of society's growing up from infancy to maturity. See, we say, our race has grown out of its primitive childhood! That is a true picture. We of the modern world have grown up and are not in our infancy any more. But is it not the grown-up people who cause all the trouble? It is not that little child who toddles about our home we are afraid of. We do not have to put him in prison or lock him up in an insane asylum. It is grown-up people for whom jails and asylums are built; it is maturity that suffers the appalling collapses. So society, when it is scientifically and educationally mature, can go berserk and insane, suffering such breakdowns as no primitive society ever knew. That is our problem—a society, growing scientifically and educationally mature, falling from one collapse into another.

This is a great time to be alive if only because it drives us back to the fundamentals: What shall it profit a man or a nation to gain the whole world and lose the soul? Many moderns have supposed that science and education were displacing the gospel and making it needless. Upon the contrary, the more mature society becomes, scientifically and educationally, the more critical is man's need of the principles of life, the sustaining faiths, the goals of endeavor, and the kind of character that Christ brought to the world. After the last war one of our popular artists drew a cartoon showing a group of men sitting down as a governmental cabinet to organize the new world. At the head of the table sat the President, and there too were the familiar portfolios, Secretary of War, Secretary of State, and all the rest, but a new figure was at that council table—there sat Christ with his portfolio, Secretary of Human Relationships. Until something like that happens I see no hope for the world. My fellow-Christians, for us especially this is a great time for great living now.

Finally, the greatness of our time lies in the fact that it not only calls thus for Christianity but challenges Christianity, too. We have said that scientific inventiveness and education cannot solve our problem. Yes, but there is plenty of Christianity that cannot solve our problem either—little, petty, hide-bound Christianity, an escape from life, utterly irrelevant to the vast issues that confront mankind.

In days like these one recalls that great Christianity commonly emerged in troubled eras. We still go back to Saint Augustine, that towering figure, across the centuries standing like a lighthouse on a stormy sea. When, then, did Augustine live and write his masterly *City of God* that is still one of the major events in Christian history? In the days when the Roman Empire fell and the whole earth was shaken. A great time calls for a great religion.

If I were preaching today to fundamentalists, I would lay this heavily upon their consciences. All this Biblical literalism, this insistence on the peccadilloes of tradition, this sectarian provincialism in the church, this belated theology, is a travesty of what Christ's gospel ought to mean in such a day as this. I am speaking, however, not so much to fundamentalists as to liberals, and we too have sinned. For a long generation we have been engaged in simplifying the gospel, in saying to the intellectually perplexed, You need not believe this to be a Christian and you need not believe that. We have pared down the gospel, shrunk and reduced it until in our churches preachers have sometimes seemed to be playing a game to see how little a man can believe and still be a Christian.

Under no circumstances is that an adequate approach to religion. Science too has had to slough off old ideas and discard ancient superstitions. But science has not done it by shrinking the universe and making it simpler. It has enlarged the universe and made it more profound and vast than it ever was before. It has said not, See how little you have to think, but See how great a cosmos you live in and what immense vistas are open to your gaze!

So let Christianity speak in an era like this! Our problem is not to see how little we can believe but what great things we can see in the Christian message and make real to the world that desperately needs them. This is a great time for great convictions.

A prevalent mood, like a fog, settles down around us, in which we say, "Who will show us any good?" I have hoped that for some souls here we might bring in a northwest wind that would blow that fog away and give us a day of clearer seeing. This is a ghastly time to be alive—that is true, but not the whole truth. This is a great time also for spiritual adequacy, for wisdom and courage to face and create momentous change, for realistic appraisal of our false reliances, and for profound convictions about God and man and the kingdom of righteousness on earth. We are living

> In an age on ages telling;
> To be living is sublime.

23

On Being Fit To Live With[1]

"A YEAR OF DISENCHANTMENT . . . remarkable for the number and magnitude of illusions which have perished in it"—that fairly well describes this twelvemonth following World War II. Yes, but those words were written in 1867 after the war between the states. We are not the first generation to live through post-war disillusionment, with its confusion and dismay. The futility of war, the transiency of its victories, its fecundity in producing problems worse and more numerous than any that it solves, this is an ancient experience. What distinguishes our generation in dealing with it is the global scale on which it confronts us. Never before has the whole human race been involved together in such a general and inclusive catastrophe as ours.

Many, therefore, stand looking at the world's calamity as at a gigantic spectacle, its problems so staggering that we, as individuals, feel unrelated to it, our ability irrelevant to its solutions. I do not see how we can stay there, however, if we perceive what the gist of the world's problem really is: being fit to live with. Our one world calls desperately for that. Wives and husbands, parents and children, Russia and the United States, Britain and India, Orientals and Occidentals, whites and Negroes, Roman Catholics, Jews and Protestants—the world, with catastrophe awaiting failure, is crying for those qualities of life and character that make men and nations fit to live with.

If this seems oversimplification I agree that it is a minimum statement, but it has this advantage: it presents a responsibility none can deny, each of us knowing that he is under obligation at least to be decent to live with, and each of us also day by day either adding to or subtracting from

1. From *On Being Fit To Live With* by Harry Emerson Fosdick. Copyright 1946 by Harper & Brothers. Copyright renewed © 1974 by Elinor F. Downs and Dorothy Fosdick. Reprinted by permission of HarperCollins Publishers.

that basic quality—fitness to live together—without which no problem in the world can ever be solved.

Paul was dealing with this matter when he wrote his twelfth chapter of First Corinthians: "Many members, but one body. And the eye cannot say to the hand, I have no need of thee: or again the head to the feet, I have no need of you . . . whether one member suffereth, all the members suffer with it; or one member is honored, all the members rejoice with it." Applied to our world's estate now, that simile represents a momentous fact: races and nations forced to live together, before we are fit to live with. Facing that kind of situation, Paul swung out into his thirteenth chapter on love, driven to it by the logic of the situation, seeing that only love can meet the issue. That is not simple, but penetrating, far-reaching and profound.

Of course, being fit to live with is the secret of a good home. Many associate broken homes primarily with outright infidelity, but any personal counselor sees homes where even adultery has been forgiven but where some other things can no longer be endured, and other homes too he sees where infidelity did not come first, but last, after a long, long series of other troubles had paved the way. It is what many people call little things that commonly break up homes—sullenness, moodiness, hypersensitiveness, irritability, petty jealousy, quarreling, nagging, bad temper—that is to say, the things that make folk unfit to live with. As one wife said about her husband who was an actor, "He was a comedian on stage, but he was a tragedian at home."

Some of us came from homes lovely to live in, and considering what made them such we see why Paul moved out from his twelfth chapter into his thirteenth. That is what it takes to be fit to live with in a home: "Love suffereth long, and is kind; love envieth not; love vaunteth not itself, is not puffed up, doth not behave itself unseemly, seeketh not its own, is not provoked, taketh not account of evil . . . beareth all things, believeth all things, hopeth all things, endureth all things." Our theme is not oversimplification. It fathoms the depths of our lives; it is about the loveliest thing that can be true of us, that we are really fit to live with.

On a large scale, this is the world's problem. Today we all are thinking of the vast political overhead the United Nations is trying to build up—absolutely indispensable. But here in the church of Christ, consider the foundations of it all, the spiritual basis on which alone a peaceful world can stand. Races and nations decent to live with—that alone will do it, and one by one we individually are in the thick of that. Every unfair discrimination a white man practices against a Negro, every nasty slur voiced by a Gentile against a Jew, or by a Jew against Gentiles, every expression of contempt against a whole race or nation, every outburst of meanness, discourtesy, prejudice and bad temper, makes less possible the solution of mankind's gigantic problem. Our theme brings the whole world's deepest need within the scope of every man's responsibility.

We have always talked about world brotherhood. It was a beautiful ideal, but now the entire aspect of the matter has altered, world brotherhood no longer an ideal but the absolute condition of civilization's survival. It is world brotherhood now, or else!

To be sure, for decades the realistic facts of world-wide interdependence have been creeping up on us, but still we have clung to old nationalistic ideas, picturing the world's peoples, to use another's metaphor, "as strung together without continuity, like wash on a line." But for a long time now the world's races and nations have been growing less and less like "wash on a line," their economic interdependence, for example, becoming more obvious every year. Where do our telephone instruments come from? Japanese silk, Indian mica, Malay rubber, Irish flax, Russian platinum, Egyptian cotton, South African gold—these are a few items in an ordinary telephone.

This kind of thing, after a fashion, we have known, but now, the dramatic conquest of the air, the shrinking of the planet in travel time, and the release of atomic power, have suddenly confronted us with history's most momentous crisis, long building up but unmistakably here at last—races and nations forced to live together before we are fit to live with. The most serious aspect of this situation is that being fit to live with is a spiritual matter; it can be politically expressed, but it cannot be politically manufactured; it must start in the intelligence, conscience and good will of people. Can we meet that test of survival now? And it takes us all in!

We should be able to do this much: stop talking about international peace, world brotherhood and all that, as beautiful ideals. They are no longer ideals, but hardheaded, desperately necessary endeavors to catch up with the realistic facts. It is the facts, not the ideals, that have gone far, far ahead of us—facts of conquered distance, compulsory interdependence, enforced propinquity, inescapable relationships as members of one body—the facts have outdistanced us, and every endeavor after world brotherhood is simply the spirit of man trying to catch up with the facts before it is too late. As Prime Minister Attlee said, "We cannot make a heaven in our own country and leave a hell outside." No! The day has passed for that.

The phrase, "bring up to date," is commonly used in trivial ways, but think what it means to be up to date now! At the very least, it means being citizens of one world. Josiah Quincy was one of the early legislators of this nation, but in 1811, when the admittance of Louisiana to the Union was proposed, and was violently resisted by the Federalists, Josiah Quincy said in Congress: "If this bill passes, the bonds of this Union are virtually dissolved . . . as it will be the right of all, so it will be the duty of some, to prepare definitely for a separation—amicably if they can, violently if they must." So lightly to propose secession from the Federal Union! How could he? He said once, "The first public love of my heart is the Commonwealth of Massachusetts. There is my fireside; there are the tombs of my ancestors." See, we should like to say to him now, you were far behind the times when you talked like that; the welfare of Massachusetts was involved in the Union; it could never be well with Massachusetts without the Union, intelligently to care for Massachusetts meant putting the Union first; only with national loyalty and unity paramount could any state be safe.

It would be easy for us so to talk to Josiah Quincy, but we ourselves are in a similar case. Now for us to put the nation first is to be disloyal to the nation. The world comes first. It can never be well with the nation unless it is well with the world. If the world goes to hell the nation will go with it. To see that, to act on the basis of that, in personal and public attitudes to become citizens of the world—that is just catching up with the facts. More than that, it is catching up at last with the New Testament: "The field is the world."

We Americans had better watch our step now! We naturally take it for granted that we are fit to live with. Granted, we are doing some good work, but we are close to being the most powerful single nation on earth, and we had better not flourish that power around, as we are tempted to. What if some other nation—Russia, for example—were the most powerful on earth? What if she alone possessed the secret of the atomic bomb's manufacture? What if she in the Pacific blew up millions of dollars worth of ships with her bombs, and what if she frankly said what our American admiral in charge of the experiment has said is the purpose of it: first, to translate the result "into terms of U.S. sea power"; and second, to train

"Army Air Forces personnel in attack with atomic bombs against ships." Suppose Russia were doing that, how would we feel?

Alas, all the great powers, Russia not least of all, now are trying to move in two directions at once: on one side supporting the United Nations to abolish war, and on the other beginning what may prove to be the most fatal competitive armament race in history to prepare for war—in this country proposing to establish, for the first time in our history, universal military conscription in peacetime. The nations cannot pursue both those purposes at once—not for long! May God bring all of us up to date before the bell tolls! As our own Secretary of State put it: "There must be one world for all of us or there will be no world for any of us." So, whether in a home or the world this is man's critical need—to be fit to live with—and it takes us all in.

Consider now that if we are to meet this momentous issue anywhere, in a home or a neighborhood or a world, we must follow Paul out from his twelfth chapter into his thirteenth. A Biblical scholar once whimsically said that one of the strongest arguments he knew for the inspiration of the Scriptures was that they had survived their division into chapters and verses. Nowhere has that division been more disadvantageous than in First Corinthians. Sometimes we read the twelfth chapter by itself, and forget what comes after; often we read the thirteenth chapter by itself, and forget what went before. But when Paul wrote this letter, what we call the twelfth chapter poured out like a river into the thirteenth; the moving current of his thought demanded it. If we are many members in one body, then hate will not do; vengeance, ill will, selfishness—not by them can the problems of such interdependence be solved; only love can solve them.

Love in the New Testament is not a sentimental and affectionate emotion as we so commonly interpret it. There are three words in Greek for love, three words that we have to translate by our one word, love. *Eros*—"erotic" comes from it—that is one. In vulgar use it meant sensual lust; in Platonic philosophy it meant the yearning of the soul for the realm of the gods. The New Testament never employs that word; both in vulgar and in philosophic usage it had connotations that would not do. *Philia*—that is another Greek word. It meant intimate personal affectionateness and friendship. The New Testament does use that, twenty-five times, when intimate affectionateness is meant. But the great Christian word for love is something else: *agape*. Over two hundred and fifty times the New Testament uses it, and *agape* means nothing sentimental or primarily emotional at all; it means understanding, redeeming, creative good will.

The New Testament commands us to love, for example, but no one can command us to feel intimate affection for another; that is not within our volition's power. What the Christian God can and does command us to do, however, is to practice always and everywhere, with friend and enemy, with neighbors close at hand and with strangers we have never seen, an understanding and creative good will. "Whatsoever ye would that men should do unto you, even so do ye also unto them"—that is the expression of *agape*. "Love your neighbor as yourself"—that is *agape*. "Love your enemies"—it is nonsense to command that, if it means feeling affection for our foes; but if it means, as it does, extending even to them an understanding, saving, creative good will so that, by God's grace, enemies may at last be turned into friends, that makes sense. Love the Russians, millions of them, love the Chinese, the Italians, the South Sea Islanders, and all the rest—no wonder men think that idea silly when they interpret it to mean emotional affectionateness. But to extend to the Russians, the Chinese, and all the world, understanding and creative good will—that is not silly, but the *sine quo non* of civilization's survival now.

A little child in a family I know heard the phrase, "human beings," and asked its meaning. "It means all of us," was the answer, "father, mother, brother, sister, our neighbors. Everyone we know is a human being." "But," said the child, "all the people we do *not* know—are they human beings too?" That is the towering question now, and *agape* answers it. To see all men near and far as sons of God, to practice understanding and creative good will to all men as human beings—that is the Christian ethic.

Just now this is critically important because so many of us are relying on a lower range of motive. Fear, for example—will not the atomic bomb frighten mankind into brotherhood and peace? Well, the atomic bomb presents an ominous alternative, and there can be a constructive use of fear, but no man or nation was ever yet frightened into real brotherhood and peace.

Along with fear, we are relying on selfish calculation to save us. We can have nothing, we say, that we do not share. Freedom from deadly epidemics is a world-wide matter now; we must share health with all men if we are securely to possess it ourselves. So we argue about one good after another, from economic welfare to freedom from the tragedy of war. That is all true! No major good can be possessed in this new world unless it is shared—we had better say that! But such selfish calculation by itself alone can never bring real brotherhood and peace.

When American missionaries went to the South Sea Islands did they argue it all out that some day there might be a world war, and American boys might come there, and so, on the basis of selfish calculation, Christ had better be preached and practiced there first? They did not! They never thought of it! It was the Christian gospel that took them there, stronger than fear, nobler than self-interest, all men children of God, all men the object of Christ's redeeming sacrifice, love the law of life, mankind one family with every soul priceless in the sight of God—that, and that alone, took them to the South Sea Islands, that alone transformed cannibals into folk finely fit to live with.

This recognition of the New Testament's meaning of *agape* dissolves the too strict lines of distinction, now currently drawn, between love and justice. To be sure, these two are not identical. All of love is not included in justice, but the deepest meanings of justice are included in love, and without love and the insight and understanding it confers justice inevitably degenerates into injustice. The Golden Rule, the essence of justice, is not outside, but within the boundaries of Christian love, and today it is the political implementation of the Golden Rule in some effective form of world government that most concerns us. Only so can we be fit to live together.

The political difficulties in the way everyone sees, but behind them are the emotional difficulties inside the hearts of men. Were there ever such sweeping mass emotions of distrust and suspicion, vindictiveness and hatred on earth before? In George Bernard Shaw's play *Major Barbara* is a character, whose conscience, so the quotation runs, is clear and her duty done, when she has called everybody names. Such people bedevil the world, and mankind's hope lies in those who resist such regimentation by vindictive mass emotions, rising above them to an altitude more far-sighted, constructive and redeeming.

How did Abraham Lincoln ever do that, as he did, during the Civil War? "With malice toward none, with charity for all," he said. He was not soft. He was the wisest man of his generation, and his wisdom consisted, how much! in his ability to rise above the popular passions of vindictiveness. "I have not suffered *by* the South," he said to a friend, "I have suffered *with* the South. Their pain has been my pain. Their loss has been my loss." In retrospect how high his character towers, how constructive his wise statesmanship! In our world now there are vicious evils to be ended, their resurgence made impossible, their guilty perpetrators punished. But God help us, for our children's sake, to rise into *agape* and in a redeeming peace, that at last will take all nations in, to do for the world what so-called justice, without *agape*, can never do!

Ah Christ, you are the answer still! We want world brotherhood; all that we and our children most desire depends on that, but neither fear nor calculating self-interest alone can achieve it. We must have faith—that is basic; we must have hope—that, certainly; and we must have love. And if we are to be really fit to live with, in families, neighborhoods, nations and one world, "the greatest of these is love."

24

Standing by the Best in an Evil Time[1]

THIS IS WORLD COMMUNION Sunday and countless Christians around the planet will meet at the Lord's Table today to express their gratitude to Christ.

> "Love so amazing, so divine,
> Demands my soul, my life, my all"—

the Lord's Supper is centered in such gratitude. It is rightly called the Eucharist, for "Eucharist" is simply the Greek word for "Thank you."

Nevertheless, there was another aspect to that last meal Jesus ate with his disciples—not alone their gratitude toward him, but his gratitude toward them. One of the most moving scenes in the Gospels, so it seems to me, is that moment in the upper room when, as Luke tells us, Jesus looked round on his disciples and said: "It is you who have stood by me through my trials." That was rather fine of him. Those first disciples had not done so well. They had continually failed to understand him and had let him down. Peter was there, soon to deny him thrice. Even at the table, Luke tells us, a contention arouse among them as to who was the greatest. They were not much to be grateful for.

To be sure, this much can be said for them—they had not altogether quit. The brief years of Jesus' ministry had been difficult, opposition mounting, foes dangerously massed against him, many and powerful, and yet despite weakness and failure those few men in the upper room were still at his side. At least they had not quit, and for that much Jesus was grateful: "You who have stood by me."

---

1. From *On Being Fit To Live With* by Harry Emerson Fosdick. Copyright 1946 by Harper & Brothers. Copyright renewed © 1974 by Elinor F. Downs and Dorothy Fosdick. Reprinted by permission of HarperCollins Publishers.

This morning we try to lift that scene out of its ancient setting and reproduce it among ourselves. Of how much history is that scene the summary! Once, they say, George Washington, in the desperate days of the Revolutionary War, reviewed a fresh contingent of raw recruits from Connecticut, and, looking at their thin and tattered ranks, said, "I have great confidence in you men of Connecticut." And one of those recruits has left the record how he wept at that and clasping his musket in his arms vowed to himself that he would do his best. So often in history has a great personality with a great cause in his heart been compelled to trust such frail backers and to be grateful for their support. Long indoctrinated in the Christian gospel, we are used to the idea that we should be grateful to Christ. But that Christ is grateful to us, that he says to us, as it were, I have great confidence in you—that idea I, for one, looking at this war-blasted world, with its shocking evidence of our Christian failure, find very disturbing. To be sure, as of those first disciples this much is true of us—we have not altogether quit. Here we are in his sanctuary, wistfully, sometimes desperately, believing in him, bound to him still by faith that will not altogether let go. In a sense, we have not quit. But were Christ to thank us—"You who have stood by me through my trials"—every one of us would feel we did not deserve that.

Certainly Christ is having trials enough. That first crucifixion was hard, but these successive crucifixions—everything he stands for denied and outraged—must be worse yet. And we, his disciples, have not prevented this ghastly horror of war and its consequence. Nothing has prevented it—not all our education, our science, our statesmanship, our jurisprudence, not all the ennobling effect of our best literature, or the civilizing influence of our art and music—nothing has prevented it. But worst of all, we Christians have not prevented it. Some six hundred millions of us on earth today—we have failed to stave off this catastrophe. Were Christ to condemn us as unworthy of him, we should feel the justice of that. But to be grateful to us!

Nevertheless, let us picture him today thanking us as he did his first disciples. What would it do to us to hear him out of the unseen saying to us what he said to them?

For one thing, it would surely be humbling. To those first disciples it must have been that. One can imagine what unhappy memories flashed through their minds when Jesus thanked them—James and John recalling his well deserved rebuke to them: "Ye know not what manner of spirit ye are of"; Peter recalling his Lord's stern censure—"Get thee behind me, Satan"; all of them remembering deplorable scenes, as when they tried to keep little children from coming near him, or when, slow of understanding, they faced his question: "Are you totally ignorant?" Such humiliating memories, I suspect, poured into their minds when Jesus said, "You have all stood by me."

Here is a strange fact about us all. When we have scathing condemnation from outsiders, self-defense is at once aroused, and we vigorously justify ourselves against accusation; but when, from the inside, someone whom we love gratefully praises us and assures us of all we have meant to him, we at once feel humble and begin to accuse ourselves. Were a stranger to criticize my relationships with my father, accusing me of having been a poor son to him, I should resentfully rise in self-defense. But if today out of the unseen I should hear my father himself saying, You were a good son to me, a loyal son, I would of course be melted into humility. Oh no, I would say, not half good enough, not half! and memories would rise of all the things I might have been to him and was not.

We are a queer lot. One minute, reacting to attack from outside, we defend ourselves; the next minute, responding to gratitude from the inside, we accuse ourselves.

Just that is happening among Christians today. When bitter assaults are made, as they are made, on Christianity, the Christian church, and on us as Christians, we resent the attack and defend ourselves. When in a recent book I read this sentence: "The wholesale murder, torture, persecution and oppression we are witnessing in the middle of the twentieth century proves the complete bankruptcy of Christianity as a civilizing force," my dander rises. Hold on! I say, what do you mean, "complete bankruptcy"? The best we still have left in our western heritage came from Christianity, and mad as the world is, think what it would be if Christianity had not been here at all. And when that same writer, having utterly damned Christianity, says that only one thing can save the world, namely the law, I am indignant. If anything has broken down, I retort, the law has. The failure of the law to cover our international relationships is the very gist of our catastrophe. Thus today Christianity is being passionately attacked from the outside, and passionately defended from the inside, and that gets us nowhere.

Today I prescribe another kind of medicine. Suppose that from the unseen we should hear Christ saying to us, "You who have stood by me through my trials." Is there any Christian here who would not feel the answer rising in his heart? Oh no, Lord, we would say, we have not stood by you. We have badly failed you. Look at us with the world going to hell, all obsessed as we have been with our miserable sectarianisms, creedalisms, ritualisms, still tithing mint, anise and cummin, and neglecting the weightier matters of the law. We have not stood by you. We Christians and the whole Christian church profoundly need to be converted. Antichrist has whipped us, because we have put so many lesser, trivial things in place of genuine loyalty to you. In the very heart of Europe, where Christianity has had its long chance, some six million of your own people brutally slain in cold blood! Do not thank us for standing by you!

Friends, that mood—not defensive self-justification, but humility—is the healthy one for us Christians to be in. We call on the wicked world to repent, but we Christians ourselves had better repent. And such penitence does not come from vehement self-defense against outside attack. It comes from the thought of Christ himself, after all our failures still trying to be grateful to us, if only because we have not altogether quit. Let us take that to ourselves today, one by one! I find it disturbing. If I could, I would run away from it—that picture of Christ trying to say to me, "It is you who have stood by me through my trials." Alas! what failures—personal failures, world failures—that conjures up.

Nevertheless, to say that is not the whole story. This word of Jesus awakens another response; not humbling only, it is dignifying too. Those first disciples must have felt that. Unworthy to have it said of them—yes—but still, if only it were a little true, it was the finest thing that could be said of them. I wonder if those words of Jesus did not become a slogan oft repeated in their thinking in the after years, when the Christian cause was hard bestead, the going difficult, on days when life sagged down and gloom closed in—"It is you who have stood by me through my trials."

What is it that gives dignity to life, lifts it out of mediocrity, saves it from futility and insignificance and makes it in the long run worth living? To get one's eye on the best, even in a bad time, and to stand by that! We are not much as individuals; we can terribly despise ourselves; but there is something that can give even our small lives dignity and significance. To have seen the best in our time, and to have stood by it—that does elevate even the humblest life to dignity and worth.

Let no one push this off as though it were an ideal, visionary matter of being spiritually noble and all that. It is a matter of being fundamentally a worth-while human being, healthy and strong, with a life that is at all worth living. Dr. Jung, the pioneer psychiatrist, quotes one of his patients as saying: "If only I knew that my life had some meaning and purpose, then there would be no silly story about my nerves!" Just so! That sums up countless cases, all knocked to pieces because life has been futile, with no meaning and dignity in it. And the secret of dignity in life is the consciousness that with all our failures there is some best, some Christ, by whom and for whom we have stood in our time.

Say if we will that as individuals we are futile and insignificant, we do not need to be that. Sir Alfred Zimmern, one of our leading experts in international affairs at Oxford University, was one day walking in the gardens there with Basil Mathews when Mathews asked him, "What, in your opinion, is the greatest obstacle between us and the building of enduring world peace?" And Sir Alfred's unhesitating answer was, "The small-scale individual." So that's the ultimate trouble—the small-scale individual who in an era terrific in its chaos, ominous in its perils, immense in its opportunities, gets no vision of the great matters, of the Christ in our time, and does not stand by *that*. This is the trouble! And this trouble is not only the curse of the world, but the curse of the individual too. For think what could happen to that small-scale individual, if, like those first fishermen from Galilee, who were small-scale individuals to start with, if ever there were any, he should rise to the place where Christ could say, even though it took divine mercy to see it, "You who have stood by me."

This plea to the small-scale individual is critically urgent now. Multitudes, finding themselves in this mess of a world, respond to it by being a mess themselves. But others, often fishermen from Galilee, men and women, that is, who might easily be small-scale individuals, make another response. They see the necessity of the best because the worst is so bad; they catch a fresh vision of the Christ because Antichrist is so intolerable. It is such who across the centuries when times were evil have preserved and furthered, in every realm, the faiths and hopes that still sustain mankind. It was their glory that some saving excellence could say to them, "You who have stood by me."

As one grows older one feels the meaning of this more and more. So many things one has cared about and worked for pass away. But if in the end some best hope, some princely excellence of his era, hard bestead but to which the future belongs, could say to him, though he deserved it but a little, "You who have stood by me,"—that would make everything worth while.

So Bono Overstreet put it:

"You say the little efforts that I make
will do no good:
they never will prevail
to tip the hovering scale
where justice hangs in balance.
    I don't think
I ever thought they would.
But I am prejudiced beyond debate
in favor of my right to choose which side
shall feel the stubborn ounces of my weight."

World Communion Sunday ought to mean this to us as Christians. If some one says that he is fed up with contemporary Christianity, its divisions, its theological hair-splitting, its dry-as-dust conventionality, and all the rest—I am too, disgusted with it and ashamed. What difference do most of the things Christians split up about matter in a world like this, with Christ and Antichrist at loggerheads and the fate of all mankind in the balance? You are right to be disgusted with it, but not with Christ—not with his master faiths and principles of life. To be a Christian is to stand by Christ. Get that basic, cental matter clear, for Christ towers up today more relevant to our need, more certainly the hope of the future, than I for one have ever seen him. I want some young man or woman here today to make a decision, so that thirty, forty years from now he too can hear the Christ, humbling him, yet dignifying him, too: "You who have stood by me."

Humbling and dignifying this word of Jesus is, but it is challenging too. Let us face that before we stop. In days like these, someone has got to stand by the great spiritual heritage that has come down to us in Christ. None of us really wants that lost out of the world. We all of us are pensioners on it. The best in our lives, our homes, our societies has come from it.

We say that Christianity has been here two thousand years, as though that were a long time, but it isn't. When one thinks what kind of world this is, when beneath the thin veneer of civilization one sees the unredeemed brutality in human nature, and when one considers the contrasting heights of life and character, personal and social, to which Christ calls us, two thousand years are not long. We are still, as it were, in the infancy of Christianity, its message still appearing to most of the world incredibly too good to be true, too difficult to be tried.

We are not the first generation to be discouraged by the contemporary scene. Victor Hugo reminds us that we now think of the sixteenth century as one of history's main turning points, with the Protestant Reformation and all the rest, but that Erasmus, who lived then, called it "the excrement of the ages"; that we see in the seventeenth century thrilling discovery and adventure, opening up the whole new world, but that Bossuet, in the thick of it, called it "a wicked and paltry age"; that to us the eighteenth century presents a stirring scene of political liberation, with the French and American Revolutions and the like, but that even Rousseau in a disheartened hour described it as "This great rottenness amidst which we live." So in the sixteenth, seventeenth and eighteenth centuries the people who really fooled themselves were the skeptics, the cynics, while those who saw the possibilities and with a faith that moved mountains believed in them were realistically right. Surely, in this regard, history can repeat itself in our century, if only we stand by the best.

In that upper room it was a gamble when those first disciples stood by Christ. How little they had to go on, with the whole world against him! But we know now that they were right, Caesar and the whole Roman Empire were as ephemeral as a skyrocket compared with him. And if in our day, in personal character, in faith and loyalty, we join those first disciples, we shall be right. Whether or not you actually sit at any church's communion table this Sunday, may the day have this meaning in your experience—that you do join them, that you bet your life as they did theirs that when all the Romes have fallen Christ will still be here.

It is not generals alone, but privates, who get the Victoria Cross and the Congressional Medal, and this is the Victoria Cross, the Congressional Medal of Christian life—to deserve even a little: "It is you who have stood by me through my trials."

25

Finding God in Unlikely Places[1]

As we think about finding God in unlikely places we may well begin with the familiar hymn, "Nearer, my God, to Thee." Despite its popularity, many of us do not live up to it.

> Though like the wanderer,
> The sun gone down,
> Darkness be over me
> My rest a stone—

that is not a likely place to feel nearer to God.

> So by my woes to be
> Nearer, my God, to Thee—

that is not easy. We naturally find God in life's lovely experiences. "Praise God from whom all blessings flow"—that is where we find him, in our blessings. But when darkness and disaster come we commonly cry, Where is God?

One Englishman recently said this: "I don't know what I believe, but I don't believe all this God is love stuff. I have been in two world wars. I have been unemployed eighteen months on end. I have seen the Missus die of cancer. Now I am waiting for the atom bombs to fall. All that stuff about Jesus is no help." Well, did you never feel like that?

This morning we study the kind of person who, in such difficult situations, does not lose God, but finds him. We will be back in New York in a moment, but we start far from here, out in the wilderness of Sinai some thirty-two centuries ago, where Moses, facing a desperate situation, heard

---

1. From *What Is Vital In Religion* by Harry Emerson Fosdick. Copyright 1955 by Harper & Brothers. Copyright renewed © 1983 by Elinor F. Downs and Dorothy Fosdick. Reprinted by permission of HarperCollins Publishers.

the divine voice say: "The place whereon thou standest is holy ground." Into that wilderness Moses had fled, a refugee from Egypt. In anger he had killed an Egyptian taskmaster who was beating as Israelite and, compelled to flee, had escaped into the desert to lose himself in the Bad Lands. Whether one thinks of the public evils of his time under Pharaoh's tyranny, or of the slavery of his people in Egypt, or of his own personal fall from being the son of Pharaoh's daughter to facing the niggardly life of the sheep range, he was in an unpromising place, and it was news to him when amid the sagebrush and the sand, the arresting message came that that was holy ground.

Far from being merely thirty-two centuries old, that scene is here in this congregation now. We find God in life's lovely things. Yes! God is in life's lovely things, but sooner or later all of us come to the place where, if we are to find God at all, we must find him in a wilderness. How we admire people who do that! When Helen Keller says about her blindness and deafness, "I thank God for my handicaps for through them I have found myself, my work and my God," that is something! I can find the divine in the Ninth Symphony or in sunsets when the sun, supine, lies "rocking on the ocean like a god," but to find God where Helen Keller found him, or Moses, that calls for insight.

Today we all need that insight. Not only does life land each of us in an unpromising situation, but our whole era is tragic, desperately tragic. How does one find God here? Yet some of the most momentous discoveries of God in history have been made in just such situations. A verse in the Book of Exodus has fascinated me for years, but I never have dared to preach on it. Here it is: "And Moses drew near unto the thick darkness where God was." What a place to find God! Nevertheless, that kind of experience has made history.

In 1754 George Washington in his early twenties was on a tough spot. He had been defeated at Fort Necessity. He was accused of taking hasty action before reinforcements came so as to get all the glory for himself. His officers were called "drunken debauchees." His report on French plans was denounced as a crooked scheme to advance the interests of a private land company. It looked like the end of George Washington. But now Douglas Freeman, his biographer, looking back writes this: "Just when one is about to exclaim about some mistreatment, 'What an outrage!' one reflects and says instead, 'What a preparation!'" So from Moses to Washington holy ground has been found in a wilderness. What a preparation!

What went on inside Moses that made possible his discovery of holy ground in the wilderness? First, he found something to be angry at. He had been brought up as the son of Pharaoh's daughter, living a soft life, a playboy, it may be, at the royal court, but as maturity came on he began to be angry. How he must have fought against it, this disturbing indignation against something intolerably wrong, the slavery of his people! The more he grew up, however, the angrier it made him, until one day, seeing a Hebrew slave beaten by an Egyptian taskmaster, he was so incensed that he slew the taskmaster.

That was foolish. That did no good, but at least this is to be said for Moses, he was no longer a playboy. He was angry at something unbearably wrong. That was the beginning of the real Moses. His anger needed harnessing but it was basic to all that followed.

Said Martin Luther centuries afterward, "When I am angry I preach well and pray better." Said William Ellery Channing, the great New England Unitarian minister, "Ordinarily I weigh one hundred and twenty pounds, but when I am mad I weigh a ton." Anger is not ordinarily presented as a Christian virtue, but remember our Lord, of whom our earliest gospel says that when he saw a deed of mercy being held up by a ceremonial triviality, he "looked round about on them with anger"; and when he saw little children being roughly brushed aside, he was "moved with indignation." Paul did write the thirteenth chapter of First Corinthians on love, but he also said, "Be ye angry and sin not." That is to say, control it, harness it for good, but still in the face of some evil you are not a Christian if you are not angry. Great character is not soft; at its very core is indignation at some things intolerably wrong.

So in his grim generation Moses began his discovery of holy ground, and when he came down from Sinai he carried with him ethical convictions that have shaken the centuries: "Thou shalt not kill." "Thou shalt not commit adultery." "Thou shalt not steal." "Thou shalt not bear false witness against thy neighbor." "Thou shalt not covet." His indignation against evil got him somewhere.

Need I expand the application of this to ourselves? Look at our world! It is hard to find God here, we say. Well, we can start. We can see the evil here that ought to arouse our indignation. We can see the everlasting right here calling for our backing and support. We can at least quit our moral apathy and wake up to the momentous issues of right and wrong in our community, our city, our nation. That is where Moses started when he found holy ground in the wilderness.

This start, however, led him to a second stage: Moses in the wilderness confronted Moses. He had never had such a searching look at himself before. Outward wrongs were there demanding that someone set them right but, if Moses was to help, he had to tackle Moses. We had better get this austere aspect of our theme into the picture, because the whole idea of seeing divine meanings in life is so commonly sentimentalized.

> The poem hangs on the berry bush,
> When comes the poet's eye;
> The street begins to masquerade
> When Shakespeare passes by.

That is true. Life is just as rich as we have the capacity to see. But that lovely aspect of the truth is not the whole of it. To confront oneself in the wilderness, to be told that there is divine opportunity, is a soul-searching experience. Tackle yourself, God said to Moses.

Of course, Moses at first backed off from that. Who was he to do anything about the Egyptian situation? "Meek as Moses" is a cliché now. Moses was far from being meek in any soft sense but he was humble. All great character is humble. William Carey, one of the supreme figures in Christian history, a major pioneer opening India to the gospel, in his elder reminiscent years said, "If God could use me, he can use anyone." Moses was like that, and when at last on Nebo's top he surveyed the Promised Land and recalled the long, long years in the wilderness, I can imagine him saying: "If God could use me, he can use anyone." So, of course, he shrank from God's formidable call at first, but not finally. He *confronted* himself until he *dedicated* himself. He found his vocation in the wilderness. That is the gist of it. By God's help, he would be Moses.

How often scenes like that have been the turning points in history! Once a man named Wilfred Grenfell landed in Labrador on a gala vacation cruise, visiting for fun a strange coast. Landing on that bleak, inhospitable shore, however, he wrote afterward, "I attended nine hundred persons who never would have seen a doctor if I had not been there." That got him! He had to come back. He had to identify himself with Labrador. A divine voice had said to him in a wilderness, "The place whereon thou standest is holy ground."

God is saying that to someone here today about some situation—personal, domestic, social, national. It is dreadful, we may be thinking. Yes, but if a situation is dreadful, then there is need. Tragedy is simply need spelled with different letters, and so opportunity to help is there. You can do something for somebody, not despite the fact that it is Labrador, but because it is Labrador. "The poem hangs on the berry bush, when comes the poet's eye." Yes, but the real miracle arrives when the poem does not hang on the berry bush, but is deep hidden in a wilderness, or in Labrador, or in some forbidding personal tragedy, and then comes the poet's eye. So the great souls have found holy ground in unlikely places; they have found their vocation there.

We come to grips with our central theme, however, when we follow Moses' experience to a deeper level. In this encounter with right against wrong, in this self-dedication for his people's sake, he came face to face with God. Whatsoever may have been his idea of God, it is clear from the record that he had not in the least expected to meet his God there. What kind of situation was that in which to encounter God?

Many of us are precisely in that state of mind. We habitually talk of God in terms of love, beauty, goodness so that when we face a situation in our personal experience or in the world at large where love, beauty, goodness are singularly absent we lose all sense of God. Where is he? we ask. Our modern liberalism has contributed to this state of mind. Sings James Russell Lowell,

> God is in all that liberates and lifts,
> In all that humbles, sweetens and consoles.

That is true. Wordsworth sings of God as

> A presence . . .
> Whose dwelling is the light of setting suns,
> And the round ocean and the living air,
> And the blue sky, and in the mind of man.

That is true. But if the only God a man has is a God who thus is seen in the lovely things of life—its beauty and graciousness, the light of its setting sun, its liberating and consoling hours, then when he finds himself in some tough, dismaying experience in a desert where beauty, goodness and loveliness are absent, where has his God gone? In days like these I need the God who encountered Moses in the wilderness; who challenged Grenfell in Labrador, the God who confronts man in unlikely places.

As a matter of historic fact, some of the most memorable encounters with God in history have been of that type. Moses in the desert; the great Isaiah in Babylon with his exiled people; Job, out of his tragic calamity saying, "I have heard of Thee by the hearing of the ear, but now mine eye seeth Thee"—the Old Testament is full of such experiences. As for the New Testament, there is Calvary. My soul! Crucifixion is not lovely. Who, casually looking on, would have thought God there? But countless millions since, with hushed and grateful hearts, have seen that Calvary was holy ground. It is no accident, I tell you, that man thus finds in tragic situations some of his profoundest insights into the divine. Soft occasions do not bring out the deepest in a man - never! Rather in formidable hours when loyalty to the right means the risk of everything, perhaps life itself; in dismaying generations when right is on the scaffold and wrong is on the throne; in personal calamities when God is no mere frosting on life's cake but the soul's desperate necessity, then have come man's profoundest religious insights and assurances. Where did Jesus say, "Not my will but Thine be done"? In Gethsemane. When did Luther write, "A mighty fortress is our God"? When he was risking his life. When did Sir Thomas More say, "I die, the king's good servant, but God's first"? On the scaffold.

I do not know where this truth hits you but for myself, now in my elder years, I bear my witness. My deepest faith in God springs not so much from my Galilees, where God clothed the lilies so that "Solomon in all his glory was not arrayed like one of these," but from times when the rain descended and the floods came and the winds blew and beat, and God was there so that the house fell not. You know the familiar argument that the world is such a mess, its evil so senseless and brutal, that we cannot believe in God. Well, the world's evil is a great mystery. It raises questions which none of us can answer, but over against the souls who because of the wilderness surrender faith in God I give you today the souls who found him in the wilderness. They are a great company. Let us look at some of them.

Can you think of anything much worse than being a hopeless alcoholic? That's a wilderness for you. Well, here is my friend, Mrs. Mary Mann. She was there. Fifteen years ago she was in that hell. Listen to her story of what happened then. "In the depths of my suffering," she writes, "I came to believe that there was a power greater than myself that could help me, to believe that because of that power, God, there was hope and help for me." So in the wilderness she found God, and like Moses she is today leading many from the desert to the promised land.

Or, can you think of any much tougher situation a nation could go through than Britain experienced in the last war? I quoted one Englishman who lost God then, but Edward R. Murrow tells us, "In the autumn of 1940 when Britain stood alone, when the bombers came at dusk each evening and went away at dawn, I observed a sign on a church just off the East India Dock Road; it was crudely lettered and it read, 'If your knees knock, kneel on them.'" Thank heaven! the power to find holy ground in the wilderness did not die out in England and with it came, what Edward Murrow calls, "steadiness, confidence, determination."

Or, let me be autobiographical, as I trust some of you are being now. In my young manhood I had a critical nervous breakdown. It was the most terrifying wilderness I ever traveled through. I dreadfully wanted to commit suicide but instead I made some of the most vital discoveries of my life. My little book, *The Meaning of Prayer*, would never have been written without that breakdown. I found God in a desert. Why is that some of life's most revealing insights come to us not from life's loveliness but from life's difficulties. As a small boy said, "Why are all the vitamins in spinach and not in ice cream, where they ought to be?" I don't know. You will have to ask God that, but vitamins *are* in spinach and God is in every wilderness.

> Out of my stony griefs
> Bethel I'll raise;
> So by my woes to be
> Nearer, my God, to thee.

Indeed consider not only personal situations but our world situation now. Think of the calamitous era of the American Revolution, so terrific that many then could perceive nothing but chaos and tragedy. Yet beneath the surface see what was going on. The thirteen colonies had been for years at bitter odds, sometimes at swords' points with one another. Then in 1774 at the first Colonial Congress, Patrick Henry made a speech in which he said this, "Throughout the continent government is dissolved. Landmarks are dissolved. Where are now your boundaries? The distinctions between Virginians, Pennsylvanians, New Yorkers, New Englanders are no more. I am not a Virginian, I am an American." See what was going on for those with eyes to perceive! A nation was being born. One of our contemporary historians describing that scene exclaims, "Forty-three delegates sat spellbound, hypnotized altogether. It was crazy what they had just heard; they knew it was crazy; an *American*, in God's name what was that?" But Patrick Henry was right and he would be right again if he could be here with us and beneath all our seething turmoil could see the emergence of new germinative ideas of world unity and world citizenship. This era too is holy ground. Play your part in it, large or small, against the little-mindedness, the prejudices, the hatreds that divide individuals and neighbors, races and nations. When Rip van Winkle went to sleep the sign over his favorite inn was George III; when he woke up the sign was George Washington. He had slept through a momentous revolution. Don't do that now! This is holy ground and God is here.

Now a brief final word. When any man thus finds God in unlikely places one may be fairly sure that he first found God in some likely places. Some beauty touched his life, some love blessed him, some goodness made him aware of God. If you have that chance now to discover the divine don't miss it! It's not easy to find God in unlikely places. Start now by finding him in a likely place. Beauty, goodness, loveliness are here, nobility of character, unselfish sacrifice, moral courage, and lives through which a divine light shines like the sun through eastern windows, and Christ is here too, full of grace and truth, in whom we see the light of the knowledge of the glory of God. Find God in these likely places that you may find him in the unlikely places too.

26

Conservative and Liberal Temperaments in Religion[1]

L ET US SET OVER against each other this morning two passages of
Scripture which convey an antithetical message about what used to
be a live problem in religion. Both passages concern the sacred ark which
Moses made of shittim wood, which contained the tables of the Law and
which the ancient Hebrews called "the ark of God." How venerable it was
in their sight one feels when, for example, one reads Joshua 7:6: "Joshua
rent his clothes, and fell to the earth upon his face before the ark of the
Lord until the evening." There was the appropriate place for Joshua to
pray. There God, so he thought, particularly dwelt. And one has only to
read the subsequent history of that ark, when David carried it up to Zion,
and Solomon put it into the Holy of Holies as Israel's most precious talis-
man, to see how indissolubly those early Hebrews associated their faith in
God with that sacred chest.

Let nearly six hundred years pass by, however, and we are opening
the Bible at the prophecies of Jeremiah. In his third chapter and sixteenth
verse he is talking about this same ark but in a tone of voice how different! "In those days, says the Lord, they shall no more say, The ark of the
covenant of the Lord. It shall not come to mind, or be remembered, or
missed, it shall not be made again."

Here, obviously, is a clear contrast. On the one side, Joshua has his
faith in God identified with that sacred ark. Where the ark goes he thinks
God goes. But here, on the other side, is Jeremiah, ardent prophet of the
living God, for whom that ark is meaningless. He is glad that it is gone. He
wishes it no more to be remembered or rebuilt.

---

1. From *What Is Vital In Religion* by Harry Emerson Fosdick. Copyright 1955 by
Harper & Brothers. Copyright renewed © 1983 by Elinor F. Downs and Dorothy Fosdick.
Reprinted by permission of HarperCollins Publishers.

We call our generation a time of religious transition. We say that everything is in flux, but in a sense every generation has been a time of religious transition and here in the Bible itself we see so typical an example of changing faith that it may have a worth-while message to bring to us. For here too the people associated their religion with one of its particular historic exhibitions: a holy ark. Around that ark their faith gathered, about it their enthusiasms burned. When they thought religion they thought ark. Here, however, is a prophet of the living God who towers higher than all the generations that venerated the ark, a man who became a forerunner of the Christ and a sharer of his spirit. He has no use for the ark at all. He is thanking God that it is gone forever.

Nobody who knows anything about human nature can suppose that such a change took place easily. There must have been the same distress of mind, doubt, lost faith, and hurt bewilderment of spiritual life that comes in every time of religious transition. May it not be that we have here a typical instance of changing faith so far removed from our passions and prejudices that we may look at it coolly and objectively and find light upon the problems that concern us?

One comment immediately suggests itself as we ponder the significance of this ancient incident. The idea that the Bible is a unanimous book upon one level is quite incredible to anybody who knows the Bible at all. Open the Book of Psalms and you will find David, who in his time was accounted a man after God's own heart, represented as roundly cursing his enemies:

> Grant that his children be fatherless,
> And that his wife be a widow.
> Up and down may his children go begging,
> Expelled from their desolate home.
> May all that he owneth be seized by the creditor,
> May strangers plunder the fruits of his toil.
> May none extend to him kindness,
> Or pity his fatherless children.

So cursed the Psalmist. But when one turns the pages and comes to the place where the Master speaks, how different is the tone! "Ye have heard that it was said, Thou shalt love thy neighbor, and hate thine enemy: but I say unto you, Love your enemies, and pray for them that persecute you." You cannot iron those two passages out to one level. The Bible throughout is the record of religious movement, in constant process of transition, and our morning's incident is only one illustration of a universal fact about Scripture: wherever you get an ark, organize your religion about it, try to settle down with it, a growing faith says, Move on! and prophets of the living God cry out that the ark should no longer be remembered or remade.

A second comment grows out of this incident: religion, on the one side, and, on the other, particular exhibitions of it like an ark, are not the same thing. Arks pass away but religion remains. Should we go down to Joshua in the flat marl plain at Gilgal where he lies before the ark and try to explain to him that some day folk will come devoutly loving God, deeply believing in him, who will have no care for that ark at all, how difficult it would be for Joshua to understand! Real religion without that ark? How can he imagine that?

It is easy for us in retrospect to see that Joshua would be mistaken, but, nevertheless, we commonly make the same mistake. We identify Christian faith with some particular expression of it until we find it difficult to think that anyone can have genuine Christian life who does not share our veneration for that special custom, ritual or belief.

My grandmother said to me once that if she could not believe that the whale swallowed Jonah she would lose her Christianity. Hers was a beautiful spiritual life whose secret sources were deep hid with Christ in God, and yet she thought that spiritual life was indissolubly associated with a special whale swallowing a special man. Of course it was not. Of course that was an artificial adhesion. All of us who knew her knew that her radiant and luminous Christian spirit was not necessarily related with any whale.

What your whale is you probably know. We all have them: those points of view in theology, those special expressions of religion, that have been precious in our spiritual experience so that we are tempted to identify real religion with them until it is difficult to think that anyone can have real religion without them. It is a great day, therefore, in a man's life when he sees that religion is greater than and is separable from these special exhibitions of it, as living water can be carried in many a receptacle to which we ourselves have not been accustomed.

In this regard religion is much like courtesy. Courtesy is an inward spirit, as religion is, easy to recognize, difficult to define, that expresses itself in many forms. The courteous American and the courteous Japanese have the same spirit but they express it differently, as any traveler in Japan must see. Who would insist that a Jew going into a synagogue and keeping his hat on is less courteous than a Christian going into church and taking off his hat, when through two different customs the same reverence is expressed? He who deals with many groups of people must learn to discern courtesy below many forms.

Such discernment, however, which is not difficult in the matter of courtesy, comes very hard in the matter of religion. When, for example, all Western Christendom was Roman Catholic and Protestantism began, how hard it was to think that you could have a genuine Christian life without the old embodiments in which it had been expressed! Real religion without the mass, without the veneration of the blessed Virgin and the saints? Yet when Protestantism, like Catholicism, began to produce its own great souls, its prophets and apostles, its martyrs, saints and mystics, then it became plain that real spiritual life is separable from those ancient arks. When, then, Protestantism began building its own arks, as religion always does—its creeds and liturgies, its rituals and sacraments—the Quakers came. They did not like creeds. Especially, they did not like rituals and sacraments. Could there be genuine Christian life on such a basis? You know how hard that was for the old-time Protestants to see. But when souls like Whittier had begun to live as well as sing,

> O Sabbath rest by Galilee!
> O calm of hills above!
> Where Jesus knelt to share with thee
> The silence of eternity,
> Interpreted by love,

there was no denying that that was bona fide Christianity, deeply rooted in Christ.

It is a great hour for a man, then, when he perceives that religion is like the sea, that it flows into many different bays, taking a different shape in each and getting a different name. That does not mean, to be sure, that one must think one bay is as good as another. One bay may be very broad and deep, where the navies of the world could ride; another bay may be small and shallow, choked with marsh and mud and blockaded by sandbars. But the wise man will discern the same sea in all of them and a wise man will never identify the sea with any of them. For the bay may grow or dwindle, may flourish or be deserted, but the sea remains.

That is the central message of the morning: from Joshua to Jeremiah what a change! how many alterations! Joshua's ark had gone! But religion had not. Religion had thrived and grown.

Obviously, this morning's truth has practical bearing on a very lively modern problem—the way in which our two temperaments, the conservative and the liberal, behave themselves in matters of religion. Some of us are temperamentally conservative and some of us are temperamentally liberal. You who still love Gilbert and Sullivan operas remember the song:

> That every boy and every gal
>> That's born into the world alive
> Is either a little Liberal
>> Or else a little Conservative!

That is true, not simply in politics; it is true in religion also and, moreover, it is a good thing that it is true. We need both those temperaments.

It takes two hands on a clock to make it tell time. One goes fast and the other goes slow, but it takes both of them to make a good clock. So it takes the liberal and the conservative temperaments to make a good country and a good church, and the most balanced and wise leader is the man who has both elements in him. It may be that this morning's message has something to say to both these temperaments by way of wise warning and good counsel.

First, let us address ourselves to the conservatives. Consider what it means to the conservative temperament that Joshua's ark was overpassed but that in Jeremiah spiritual life flowed out into forms much nobler and more beautiful than Joshua knew. It is always difficult for a conservative Joshua, with his ark, to believe that a man like Jeremiah may come without his ark and, not missing it, may yet fly higher and plunge deeper into real religion. That is the tragedy of the conservative temperament when it goes wrong.

Remember what the conservative Athenians, for example, called Socrates. They said he was an atheist. Yet read Plato's *Phaedo* and see how much of an atheist he was—one of the great believers in God and immortality, one of the high spirits in the history of religion. Only, he did play Jeremiah to their Joshua and say, The ark is gone. And so they made him drink the hemlock.

So Jesus laid his hands upon the Sabbath laws of his time. They were very sacred. Religion had hallowed them. And the ardent partisans of conservative Judaism said that he had a devil, that he was a blasphemer of God, and in the name of religion cried "Crucify him" against the one who was religion's transcendent expositor. That is the tragedy of the conservative temperament when it goes wrong. It finds difficulty in recognizing the reality and beauty and power of a real religion when it turns up in new forms with fresh methods of expression.

Some time ago I ordered a book from a bookstore. I was familiar with it. I had seen it before. When, therefore, I undid the package I was vexed. See, I said, this is not the book I ordered; they have made a mistake and wasted time. Then I looked again and saw that I was wrong. It was the same book but it was in a new binding. And as I turned its pages I recognized that, for all its unfamiliar appearance, the old delight was waiting for me still. That is perhaps the deepest thing that the conservative temperament needs to cultivate: insight to perceive old truth in new bindings.

Of course, the psychological fact that causes this difficulty with the conservative temperament is obvious. Religion makes sacred everything it touches. Religion, for example, associates itself with a world view, like the flatness of the earth or fiat creation. Religion twines its tendrils around that world view, hallows it, makes it sacred, so that, when science utterly shifts the scene, religion only reluctantly gives up its hold on the sacredness of the old view or, it may be, does not give it up at all. Within my recollection Voliva of Zion City was using the radio to tell the world that the earth is flat.

Or religion may associate itself with a language like Latin, in which the Roman rituals used to be performed. Then times change, new vernacular tongues come in, all the business of the world is done in living languages. Still the ancient church worships in Latin, as many religions worship in old and sometimes dead tongues.

Very powerful is this preservative spirit of religion that hallows everything it touches, so that in Jerusalem today you can find Jews who would not for the world set foot upon the sacred platform where their ancient temple stood, because they think that underneath it somewhere is this very ark that Moses made and Joshua prayed before is waiting, and they would not profane the spot where it rests.

What your ark is I do not know. We all have one. It may be some special doctrine, some denominational peculiarity, some bit of ritual, some miracle in history; it may be fiat creation or the Virgin Birth or baptism by immersion or a special theory of the Atonement. Such things may have been very precious in your experience. Your religion has twined itself around them. No considerate man, no matter how clearly he disagreed with your opinions, would speak a disrespectful word about them. Let us practice the fine art of reverencing each other's reverences. But what one would say is this: beware of your judgments on people who do not venerate your ark. Beware how you suspect that they cannot have genuine Christian life without your ark. You say you want to keep the faith. Aye, but keeping the faith is one thing and keeping the ark is another. Jeremiah kept the faith; he carried it out into a new day; he lifted it higher than it ever had been lifted before; he became a forerunner of the Christ. He kept the faith but he did not keep the ark. Keeping the ark would not have helped; it would have hindered. Whatever may be your ark, and in this regard we all have our conservatisms—that is the message of the morning to the conservative temperament.

Perhaps the morning's message to the liberal temperament is even more important. Think what it means to the liberal that it took a man like Jeremiah, the finest exhibition, I think, of personal religion in our history before Jesus, successfully and helpfully to overpass that ark.

This business of reforming religion and getting rid of old symbols and old ideas that impede the progress of religion is a good deal more serious matter than many liberals seem to think, and this is the gist of the matter: nothing can reform religion except religion—finer, deeper, more devout, more spiritual, more creative religion. Nothing else can reform religion but that. If the world is to be any better because Joshua is overpassed, it will take a Jeremiah to do it.

You see, there are two ways of getting rid of an ark. One is to smash it, to say: That ark is nothing but superstition, away with it! But it is not true that that ark is nothing but superstition. It is more than that. It at least is a trellis around which some very lovely things have twined themselves. It is to many a symbol of the best spiritual life they know up to date. If liberalism can do nothing else but smash arks, it may succeed merely in leaving the spiritual life of a whole generation bereft, without trellises to twine around, without symbols to express itself through. If helpfully the ark is to be overpassed, that must be done by men and women who possess in themselves religion deep, find, devout, creative.

Some time since, a housewife, wanting to clean stains from her tablecloth, tried to do it with nitric acid. The experiment worked but there was a serious drawback to it. For the nitric acid not only took away the stains; it took away the tablecloth. Some of our theological liberalism has been doing that. Contemporary religion, it says, is soiled; it is stained; it needs to be reformed. I do not see how any man with half an eye can doubt it. But nitric acid will not get us anywhere. That not only takes away the evils of religion; alas, too often it takes away religion too.

Here in our morning's incident, therefore, we have a clear indication of the right method. Go down to the Gilgal plain and watch Joshua as he bows before that ark. What an odd way to pray to God, as though he inhabited a sacred chest! Away with that kind of prayer! one would say. But when you come to Jeremiah he is not spending much time in saying, Away with that, or any other, kind of prayer. He is most positively praying. He is praying with a depth and a height that Joshua never could have imagined: "O Lord, my strength, and my stronghold, and my refuge in the day of affliction." He is reforming religion with religion.

Or come down to the plain of Gilgal again and think how Joshua conceived God housed in a sacred ark, so that where the ark went God went. How pathetic a theology! Away with that superstition! But when you come to Jeremiah you see that he is not wasting much time saying, Away with any theology! He is lifting up positively a new conception of God so much higher, so much deeper, so much finer than Joshua could have dreamed, that anyone with spiritual discernment must see it. Listen to Jeremiah's God: "Can any hide himself in secret places that I shall not see him? saith the Lord. Do not I fill heaven and earth?" That is reforming religion with religion.

Or go back once more to that Gilgal plain and watch Joshua pray. What is he praying for? He is praying because he is angry, because yesterday his warriors went up to Ai to sack the town and were defeated. He wants to know what is the matter. He wants tomorrow to send those warriors back and massacre, as he did at last, man and woman and child without mercy. Away with such superstition! one would cry. But when you come to Jeremiah you see how it must be done. Listen to him positively talking about war: "I cannot hold my peace; because thou has heard, O my soul, the sound of the trumpet, the alarm of war."

Nothing can reform religion except religion. In every realm that principle runs true. What a marvelous renaissance in art came from Cimabue and Giotto, through Raphael. They broke away from the stiff unreality of Byzantine painting and created an art of unsurpassed beauty. But they did it by the positive production of loveliness. They reformed art with more art, finer, more resplendent, more true to life.

We liberals should not miss this lesson. Nothing but religion can reform religion. Intellectual dilettantes cannot do it. Undedicated Athenians, spending their time "in nothing else, but either to tell or to hear some new thing," cannot do it. Only men and women who really know what vital religion is can do it. You say, Religion ought to be reformed. So say I. But when we say it, let us look humbly into our own souls. How much better do you think the world would really be if it had no other quality of spiritual life than that which we possess?

This is the upshot of the discussion, then, that we people of conservative and liberal temperaments would better make up our minds to work together. We need each other and at our deepest and our best we both want the same thing: vital, personal religion of the kind that produces character and sends out unselfish servants to build the kingdom of righteousness in this world.

Consider the significance of this simple fact, that we Christians are separated by our creeds and rituals but are united by our prayers and hymns. Go into a church and listen to the creed and how often you will say, I cannot repeat that creed; that church is not for me. Go into a church and observe the ritual and say, I cannot feel the significance of that liturgy; that church is not for me. We are divided by our creeds and rituals. But because they come from nethersprings of life we are united by our prayers and hymns. Pick up any great compilation of Christian prayers. Where do they come from? They come from everywhere, from Paul and St. Augustine, from Thomas à Kempis and George Matheson. They come from all ages of the church and all kinds of Christians. There are the deeps of religion that underlie division.

It is because of that, I presume, that our hymnal is the most catholic element in Christianity. There we sing with a Fundamentalist,

> Rock of Ages, cleft for me,
> Let me hide myself in Thee,

and with a Unitarian,

> Nearer, my God, to thee,
> Nearer to thee.

There we sing with a Roman Catholic,

> Lead, kindly Light, amid the encircling gloom,

and with a Quaker,

> Dear Lord and Father of mankind,
> Forgive our feverish ways.

Then we go far back across the centuries and paraphrase the ancient Psalms,

> The king of love my shepherd is,
> Whose goodness faileth never,

and we come down to sing with contemporary saints,

> Spirit of God, descend upon my heart.

If, then, you ask what a true liberalism is, I should say that it is one that pays little attention to the arks that divide, but cares with all its heart about the religion that unites us. Such religion has issued in many arks in the past and will issue in many more; out of it have come our theologies and rituals and were they to be wiped off the earth today many more would spring from the same source. Such religion is the blue sky behind the passing clouds, it is the deep sea beneath the transient waves. For here, too, what is seen, the outward embodiment, is temporal, but what is unseen, the life that is hid with Christ in God, is eternal.

27

A Religion to Support Democracy[1,2]

IN THE GENERATION IN which some of us were reared, we assumed that as knowledge increased and progress continued mankind would, of course, accept ever more universally the democratic faith and practice. Instead, democracy stands now in critical peril and we are celebrating Lincoln's birthday under circumstances that lend peculiar poignancy to his desire that "a government of the people, by the people, for the people" should not perish from the earth.

With this situation we, as Christians, are vitally concerned. There is an essential relationship between the individual Christian conscience before God, on one side, and, on the other, civil liberties, the Bill of Rights, and the freedom of minorities under democratic rule. Say as we will that Christians can manage to be Christian under any kind of government, still they are having a desperate time of it in Russia. Democracy has done for us as Christians an incalculable service, and now in her hour of need democracy asks us what we can do for her. What kind of religion ought ours to be if it is to support the democratic faith and practice?

As we face this theme, one fact towers high. Democracy cannot be merely inherited. It must be reborn with every generation. Dictatorship can, in a way, be inherited; it rests upon coercion, and a tyrant, if he be skillful and powerful enough, can hand on to his successor the regime he has by force established, as has been done in many a dynasty. But democracy is spiritually engendered in the hearts of its individual citizens. It depends on qualities of personal character, the responsible use of freedom, the willingness to hear and weigh contrary opinions debated in the state,

1. From *What Is Vital In Religion* by Harry Emerson Fosdick. Copyright 1955 by Harper & Brothers. Copyright renewed © 1983 by Elinor F. Downs and Dorothy Fosdick. Reprinted by permission of HarperCollins Publishers.

2. A Lincoln's Birthday sermon.

inner devotion to the public good that makes outer coercion needless, voluntary performance of the duties democracy entails. So the democratic faith and spirit, depending on qualities that cannot be coerced, must be reborn in each generation. Unless the inner spiritual factors that created democracy in the first place can thus be constantly renewed, its outward forms fall into decay.

Here have been our fault and our apostasy. We have taken democracy for granted. We have thought our fathers created it and handed it down to us and that we accepted it. Now, however, it is clear that if we are to preserve democracy we must ourselves recover the creative spiritual factors that originally produced it. The first line of democratic defense is not against an external foe but against an internal loss of those ideas and qualities that must in every generation reproduce democracy.

Today I share with you a strong conviction that these ideas and qualities are impregnated with a religious character, that they are in their source and sustenance spiritual, and that few questions are as important as this: What kind of religion ought ours to be if it is to support a government of, by and for the people?

In the first place, obviously it must be a religion that dignifies personality. Democracy springs from a high estimate of persons. At the heart of democracy is not so much a political process as a spiritual faith that values and trusts persons. Said Thomas Jefferson: "The care of human life and happiness, and not their destruction, is the first and only legitimate object of good government." We take that for granted but at first it was new, like the discovery of Copernicus that reoriented the solar system. Democracy lifted a revolutionary idea that persons are central in importance, that they do not exist for the sake of the state but that the state exists for the sake of them.

Moreover, democracy not only values but trusts persons with an amazing faith whose validity has yet to be proved, trusts people with freedom to think, to say what they think, to hear all sides of public questions discussed, to balance opposing arguments and to decide. That is an astonishing confidence in people. The dictators would say that it is an insane confidence. There are few articles of the Nicene Creed which require more downright faith than that. The founding fathers themselves were not unanimous about it. Said Alexander Hamilton, "The people is a great beast." Yet faith in people is the soul of democracy.

Nowhere is the contrast between democracy and dictatorship more evident than here. Dictatorship says that persons exist primarily for the sake of the state; democracy says that the state exists primarily for the sake of persons. Dictatorship herds persons like sheep, hypnotizes them by mass propaganda, coerces them by mass pressure; democracy trusts persons as the ultimate sources of decision in the commonwealth. As between these two estimates of personality, the one democratic and the other dictatorial, there is no question, is there, where the genius and spirit of Christ's teachings stand? When Jesus said, "It is not the will of your Father . . . that one of these little ones should perish," when he pled for the one lost sheep, lost coin, lost son, when he said about even the most sacred institutions of his people, "The sabbath was made for man, and not man for the sabbath," when from every angle of approach he moved up to personality as supremely valuable, loved of God and capable of being God's child, he was not simply laying the foundations of a new religion, he was laying the foundations of Western democracy. For our democracy has sprung from two main sources: early Greek experiments with popular government and Christ's emphasis on the worth of persons. That is where democracy came from in the first place. There its strength must forever be renewed.

Materialistic irreligion denies this estimate. It reduces the human being to an accidental collocation of physical atoms. Carried to its logical conclusion, it makes people what another calls "impotent nobodies hurtling toward nothingness." We cannot build a successful democracy on that idea. Some of us can recall when first this doctrine of material irreligion came up over our horizon. How roused and shocked we were as Christians! This idea, we said, will destroy the church. But today we see a further truth. I wish it could be shouted from the housetops: this devaluation of persons will destroy democracy.

This last week I stepped into the office of one of the leading exponents of scientific medicine in this city. "What do you think of the world?" he said. "It is in a sorry state," I answered. "Yes," he replied, and then, as though he were the preacher and I the layman, he added, "It will be in a sorry state as long as we think there is nothing more to the human mind and spirit than two physical cells that accidentally got together."

If there is no more in persons than materialism sees, why should we trust them to think, to hear all sides of great questions and to decide? Why should we commit to such creatures' collective judgment the destiny of nations? What right have such physical automata to the sacred privileges of intellectual and spiritual freedom? In the name of democracy I plead on Lincoln's birthday for a return to a Christian philosophy of life and a Christian estimate of the worth of persons—not accidents of the coagulated dust, but sons and daughters of God with possibilities that only the eternal ages can reveal, not, therefore, merely existing for the sake of the state, but the state and every other human institution existing for them. Never can we achieve a successful democracy on a slighter faith than that.

In the second place, the kind of religion that will support government of, by and for the people is one that recognizes a higher loyalty than the state. Let a man stand back from the democratic process and look at it as though he saw it for the first time and how easy it is to understand why dictators deride it! For we set up a government to rule a nation and then deliberately introduce opposition parties and minorities to hector the government, criticize it and obstruct its policies. That seems to a dictator a weird idea. Yet behind it is an essential democratic faith that there is something higher than any government, to which our primary allegiance belongs. You are not the slaves of government, says democracy; think for yourselves, if need be differ from the government and oppose it; there is a higher loyalty than the government to which you must be true. It is as though democracy, with its doctrine of minorities, essentially were saying, We must obey God rather than man.

All too common is the idea that the essence of democracy is the rule of the majority. That is not true. Dictatorship also can be and often is the rule of the majority. Would not even a free election in Russia bring a majority for the dictator? Russia too may claim to be under the rule of the majority. But the unique distinction of democracy Russia utterly lacks—not the rule of the majority, but the rights of the minorities. There lies the peculiar quality of the democratic idea.

That idea is not to be taken easily for granted. The possibility and validity of the idea have yet to be proved, and if we here in America cannot make a success of it, then I suspect it is doomed. See how crazy it can be made to appear! We set up a government and then actually pay salaries to opposition party members in the legislatures to criticize and obstruct the government. Looked at in cold logicality, that is an insane idea! Yes, but it is magnificent too, one of the greatest political faiths ever ventured on in all history. The British have a phrase that in these days moves me deeply: "His Majesty's Most Loyal Opposition." That is democracy and it is magnificent.

It takes real faith, even in this country, to support this democratic idea in our time. For communists play a clever game, working temporarily within the democratic system, praising democracy, using democratic slogans, whereas everybody knows that, were they to win, they would kick out from under them the ladder of freedom by which they climbed and destroy the very Bill of Rights they temporarily made use of. Moreover, in opposition, fascist minds arise, impatient with this turmoil of minority opinions. We cannot sail the ship of state, they cry, by a weather vane, and this democratic clash of opinion is like a medley of winds blowing from all directions; give us somebody's strong and settled will from whose arbitrament there is no appeal.

Even in this country it is not easy to hold hard by the democratic idea. Yet though the rights of minorities be abused and though the impatience of dictatorial minds be understandable, still the democratic faith remains the best hope of mankind, and without it—I measure my words—Christianity may not survive. For to the Christian no human government can ever be the highest loyalty. The rights of minorities were, as a matter of history, created in the first place by the religious conscience obeying God rather than men. There, in a religious idea, this element of democracy was first produced and there it must find its perennial renewal. Here, too, the church can help to kindle the faith that supports the democratic system and, what it claims for itself, can contend for on behalf of others, whether agreeing with them or not—a loyalty that surpasses the state, the right to be, "His Majesty's Most Loyal Opposition." For the Christian conscience and civil liberties are done up in one bundle of life.

In the third place, the kind of religion that will support the democratic faith and practice must genuinely care not only for the liberty but for the equality and fraternity of the people. Our attention in these days is concentrated on the external enemies of democracy, the dictatorships that threaten war. It would be insane to minimize that peril. But the deeper danger to democracy is still within. It lies in the inequalities among our own people that spoil fraternity, destroy loyalty, divide us into economic classes, and make real democracy impossible.

Let no one try an easy escape from this by laughing off the phrase in the Declaration of Independence about all men being created equal. The founding fathers did not think that all men have the same I. Q. They did

mean, however, that equality of right, of opportunity, and of general economic condition underlay the hope of a free nation. When De Toqueville
visited this country in its early days, he said, "Amongst the novel objects
that attracted my attention during my stay in the United States, nothing
struck me more forcibly than the general equality of condition among the
people." So political democracy was born out of economic democracy,
when there was a general equality of condition among the people. Recall
how Daniel Webster put it in 1820: "With property divided, as we have it,
no other government than that of a republic could be maintained, even
were we foolish enough to desire it." So, it was a general economic equality
that made political democracy inevitable.

Then, only a little more than a century after Webster's remark, one
listens to the Brookings Institution reporting on incomes of American
families: "Thus it appears that one-tenth of one per cent of the families at
the top received practically as much as forty-two per cent of the families
at the bottom of the scale." That bodes ill to the republic.

This does not mean that the people in the one-tenth of one per cent
at the economic top are the enemies of democracy and the people in the
forty-two per cent are its friends. Upon the contrary, one finds among the
one-tenth of one per cent some of the most intelligent friends of democracy and among the forty-two per cent one sometimes finds crazy movements that make straight for the totalitarian state. This is not a matter
for personal blame; it is far too serious for class recriminations; it is the
situation itself, in which both sides are caught, that is perilous.

Would not Jesus say that? For here, too, one runs headlong into the
essential kinship between democracy and Christ. The dignifying of personality—there they are at one. A higher loyalty for conscience than the
state—there they are at one. The peril to mankind of the rich over against
the poor, Dives on the one side, Lazarus lying at the gate upon the other—
there they are at one. With what constant emphasis Jesus bore down on
that—the peril of economic privilege to the soul of the possessor, the peril
of economic inequality to the brotherhood of man.

In our time, the danger in this situation, so far as democracy is concerned, has become acute because it is on this that communism feeds;
it is the alleviation and cure of this that communism promises; it is because of this that communism spreads. The way in which communism
proposes to solve the problem, however, runs all against the democratic
grain. Communism proposes the state ownership and conduct of eco-

nomic processes. That means that the two most powerful coercive forces in the world, the political and economic, would be concentrated in the same hands. Now, when the political and economic powers are thus concentrated, in the same hands, no nation can stop there. The nation must go on, as communism has gone on in Russia, to destroy opposing parties and minorities, deny the dangerous liberty of speech and press that might impede the smooth running of the regimented system on which now the people's subsistence hangs, must go on to solidify under mass control the thinking and action of the people. When we centralize in the same hands these two most powerful coercive forces in the world, be sure that our civil liberties will soon be gone. The price is too high for what is promised. Recall the saying of Chateaubriand about his temptation to easygoing solutions, "agreeing," he said, "to a century of bondage to avoid an hour's fuss." Well, we must decline communism's century of bondage to save ourselves from an hour's fuss.

All the more, however, as Christians and as believers in democracy, we must face the fact that ultimately there is no possibility of a successful political democracy without economic democracy. If we cannot achieve that end by communism's way, then we must find a democratic way of achieving it. Let any Christianity that would sustain democracy see and say this in the name of Christ, at the very heart of whose teaching lies the principle on which the fact rests. So long ago it was said in England, "That which makes a few rich and many poor suits not the commonwealth."

Finally, the kind of religion that will support government of, by and for the people must create responsible personal character in the individual citizens. Our American scene lamentably displays the lack of this. We commonly praise freedom as the essence of democracy. Our fathers won liberty for us and this gift we have inherited—so runs popular thinking—and all the time the solemn, yes tragic, aspect of the matter goes forgotten, that freedom is a curse when not accompanied and balanced by intelligent, responsible personal character. What do we mean by so centering all attention on freedom? There are some people we dare not set free. It is worse than throwing dynamite about. It is dangerous to set criminals free. It is dangerous to set morons and imbeciles free. It is dangerous to set free too many irresponsible egoists, motived by greed, who think all of themselves and nothing of the common good. That spells ruin. Too many people in our republic, high and low, clamor for freedom with no sense of responsibility for its public-spirited use. A chastened stress on liberty and more stress on responsibility befits us well. For freedom has an indispensable correlative: namely, responsible, public-spirited personal character.

Put it this way. A great population must be controlled. No sentimentality should blind our eyes to that realistic fact. If there is to be order and not chaos, discipline not anarchy, people must be controlled. And there are only two ways of controlling them. Coercion from without—that is one. Voluntary, responsible, public-spirited character spiritually engendered within—that is the other. A dictatorship stakes its very existence on the method of coercion, while a democracy remains a democracy only in so far as voluntary, responsible, public-spirited character takes coercion's place. In any nation, the more we have of one, the less we have of the other. If we have a growing ascendancy of coercion, as, alas! is true in this country now, be sure it is because the responsible initiative of personal character is failing. If we have less and less necessity of coercion, be sure it is because the responsible initiative of personal character is growing. Is not this the very crux of the matter in America? We cannot go on forever in the republic neglecting those character-building faiths and incentives from which personal quality and moral integrity spring.

Here, too, Christ and democracy are at one. Whatever else Christianity at its best has done, it has produced self-starting, self-motivating, self-driving character. Church of Christ, this day of crisis and alarm is also the day of your opportunity if democracy is to be saved. A republic must be built, not on coercion but on voluntary, inwardly right, responsible, personal character, to produce which should be your specialty. And you who have been careless of religion, negligent of the church, thoughtless of Christ, in general separate from the character-building faiths of mankind, but who do care about government of, by and for the people, have we not a right to appeal to you to rethink your attitude?

Some tell us that the devotion of Russian youth to the Kremlin is thrilling and that we in America have nothing to match it. I wish we could feel an equal thrill born of an equal devotion to democracy and to the kind of religion that sustains it. The dignifying of personality, the giving of conscience to God above all human institutions, the achievement not of popular liberty alone but of popular equality and fraternity, the erection of human society on transformed, inwardly regenerate, responsible personal character—that is the cause on which the highest hopes of mankind depend. There is the cause that on Lincoln's birthday should stir the imagination and elicit the loyalty of us all.